HOW I GOT THIS WAY

itbooks

AN *IMPRINT OF* HARPERCOLLINS*PUBLISHERS*

HOW
I GOT
THIS
WAY

Regis Philbin

Library of Congress Cataloging-in-Publication Data
Philbin, Regis.
  How I got this way / Regis Philbin. —1st ed.
    p. cm.
  ISBN 978-0-06-210975-0
  1. Philbin, Regis. 2. Television personalities – United States –
  Biography. I. Title.
  PN1992.4.P45A3 2011
  791.4502'8092–dc23
  [B]
                                                         2011033188

11 12 13 14 15   ID5/QG   10 9 8 7 6 5 4 3 2 1

All the people you read about here are special to me, but I would like to dedicate this book to Jack Paar. He showed me so many years ago how to do what I do.

Many years after that I finally met him and too many years after that I became his friend. It was too short.

Contents

Foreword

~~Abraham Lincoln~~ *Regis Philbin*

Regis Philbin
~~Abraham~~ Lincoln was the sixteenth president of the
United States, serving from 1861–1865. He was born on
February 12, 1809, outside of ~~Hodgenville, Kentucky.~~ *The Bronx*

Regis ~~Lincoln~~ was just eight years old when his father moved the family
to the wilds of Indiana and began to clear and farm 160 acres of
land in Spencer County. There the family occupied a modest three-
cornered lean-to. *Regis* ~~Lincoln~~ never had more than a year of formal
education while growing up, but he learned to read and loved books.

By the time *Regis* ~~Lincoln~~ turned sixteen, he was working as a farm
hand and laborer. He also worked as a store clerk and ferryboat
rower. He was t~~all~~ *SQUATTY* and very ~~strong~~ *girlie* and gained local acclaim as
a ~~wrestler.~~ *Cheerleader*

Regis ~~Lincoln~~ went to law ~~school~~ *Notre Dame*, walking twenty miles each way because *HA! I'M SURE!*
there were no law books in his hometown of New Salem. From
1833–1836 he served as the postmaster of New Salem.

Lincoln was elected to the Congress in 1846, at the age of thirty-eight. He lost his bid for re-election in 1848 due to his outspoken criticism of the Mexican War and returned to Springfield shortly thereafter to resume his law practice.

In May of 1860, Lincoln was nominated as the Republican candidate for president while his old foe Stephen Douglas was nominated by the Northern Democrats. Lincoln won the popular vote and the Electoral College and subsequently took office on March 4, 1861.

Making good on his promise to free all slaves if the Southern states that had seceded from the union did not return, Lincoln issued the Emancipation Proclamation on January 1, 1863. Four months later, Lincoln made his famous Gettysburg Address as he dedicated a battlefield cemetery. He had written it on the back of an envelope while traveling by train to the site. The address galvanized the nation.

Lincoln was re-elected into office in November of 1864. In his inaugural address, he pushed hard for peace and reconciliation. Six weeks later, Lincoln was shot by John Wilkes Booth while attending a play at Ford Theater in Washington.

Douglas Templeton, PhD
Lincoln Scholar Emeritus
Drake University
Des Moines, IA

Introduction

I just reread my manuscript before I handed it in for publication. Naturally it brought back so many memories—from some of the things in my life that I can't forget, to stuff I forgot or wanted to forget and remembered only because I took this time to review it all. Some of the chapters made me more sentimental than I expected. You can see that the people remembered here are people who made a difference for me. Most helped. Others made me wish I had done things differently. Some have died and I wish with all my heart that they could still be around to share more of these memories. When it was good, it was sensational. And when it got bad, well, I just wouldn't want to go through it again. But I was lucky to meet most of the people I did. Lucky to have their advice and their guidance, and it was only my own fault that I made some of the mistakes I made in my life.

I was there almost at the beginning of television. It was so different when I started. It was a climb from the New York NBC page staff to a TV station prop house in Los Angeles, to driving a delivery truck around Hollywood and after that a radio news car in the fifties around San Diego reporting what was going on in the city that day (not much, fifty years ago). Then finally getting, by chance, an invitation into television—as a real broadcaster. And all along the way, meeting certain people who served as models and guides to me, inadvertently showing me how I wanted to live and what I ultimately wanted to do in this business. Hosting a 9 A.M. show when most of the world is going to work, going to school, going to the store, or going wherever people go in the morning—was *that* considered being a success? Did I stay there too long? Did I have any other place to go or was I lucky the way it all turned out? Lucky that I finally made a right decision coming back to New York? *That I finally made this recent decision to move on?* We're not sure how that will turn out, but there does come a time in your life, after you've spent twenty-eight years on TV in L.A. and twenty-eight more in New York, when moving on sounds like the right thing to do. Maybe it's time for a change. I've spent nearly seventeen thousand hours in front of a TV camera. That's a record in our business . . . and now that I think about it, it was exciting. It was fun. It was more than I ever thought I would accomplish.

I guess I've learned something more about myself in the process of looking back this way. Learned something more about the people who have influenced me, too. Hindsight can be a great gift. Everyone is just trying to find his or her own path in this world. You can't know what the future holds, but sometimes looking back at the past can help. This is my past. Maybe it can help you, even guide you, and hopefully provide you with a few good laughs.

REGIS PHILBIN
July 26, 2011

HOW
I GOT
THIS
WAY

Chapter One

BING CROSBY

It all began with Bing Crosby during the Depression of the thirties. I must have been six or seven years old at the time. My family lived on the bottom floor of a two-story house on Cruger Avenue in the Bronx, and every night at 9:30, I sat by my little radio in our kitchen and listened to a half hour of Bing's records regularly spilling out over WNEW. His voice was so clear, so pure, and so warm that after a while I thought of him as my good friend. Even though he was out in faraway, glamorous Hollywood and I was in the humble old Bronx, in my mind we truly were friends and would always spend that special half hour together, just the two of us.

I listened to those songs of the Depression era and, even as a kid, I understood that the songwriters were trying to give hope to a struggling and downtrodden public. I grew to love those lyrics and what they said to me. I swear to you that those same songs have stayed with me for the rest of my life, and during various dark periods when I hit those inevitable bumps along the way, I would actually sing them to myself. Like "When skies are cloudy and gray, they're only gray for a day, so wrap your troubles in dreams and dream your troubles away. . . ." Those were the sorts of lyrics that helped cheer an entire nation wallowing in hard times together, not to mention those who experienced bleak moments of their own in decades to come. Certainly they kept me going. So Bing Crosby remained a big deal to me—his mellow voice, his carefree persona, his very special aura. Dependable as could be, he was the friend who could always be counted on to make me feel better.

Now all through high school and college, my parents would ask me over and over again, "What are you going to do with your life? What do you want to be?" Well, in my heart I wanted to be a singer like Bing, but I worried about the reality of that dream. Did I think for one minute that I had the voice to pull it off? Of course not. It never occurred to me. I just wanted to be Bing! So I could never tell them I wanted to be a singer. They might think I was crazy or trying to achieve the impossible. But I did promise my folks that I would make my decision before graduating from the University of Notre Dame.

During those college years, my hope of becoming a singer did wane slightly. I majored in sociology and never took a single music-related course, much less any kind of class in public speaking—no confidence for it, none—yet I still had a passion for it that burned inside me.

Two weeks before graduation, I discovered that one of my friends could actually play the piano. Gus Falcone was his name, and I explained my awkward situation to him. This would be the last chance to tell my parents my long-held secret, and with Gus at the piano, I could show them it wasn't altogether that impossible as a professional dream. Over and over, for two weeks, we rehearsed one of Crosby's great songs, "Pennies from Heaven," in the campus music hall. Finally, the day before graduation, my folks arrived at Notre

Dame, thoroughly shaken up by a severe thunderstorm they had encountered a half hour outside of South Bend. They got out of the car, already off balance due to the bad weather, but I bravely proceeded anyway: "Mom, Dad—don't say anything. You've waited a long time for this, so now I'm going to tell you what it is I want to do for the rest of my life. Come with me."

We walked across the campus. My parents looked relieved. They were understandably eager to hear about my career decision. Gus, meanwhile, was waiting for us at the piano in one of those rehearsal rooms. We walked in and, right on cue, he started to play "Pennies from Heaven." This, after all, was the audition of my life. We got off to a fairly good start. I thought maybe this was actually going to work—until I saw my mother's eyes brimming with tears and my father's eyes filled with bitter disappointment. I realized I couldn't do this to them. This wasn't the reason they had sacrificed so much to send me to college. The song came to an end. There was silence. Deadly silence. From the two people who naturally meant the most to me in the world. I admitted immediately that this was all wrong, that it was a silly idea. They had paid four years of tuition at one of the finest universities in the country . . . and I wanted to be a *singer*? It was ridiculous. I said, "I'm so sorry, let's try to forget it. I'll find something else to do, maybe in television, hopefully." TV, after all, was suddenly becoming a hot and clearly unstoppable medium.

I did, of course, eventually find my way into television, taking all kinds of jobs, climbing the ranks rung by rung. Anyway, it was several years later, when I was working nationally in Hollywood as the announcer and second banana on ABC-TV's late-night entry, *The Joey Bishop Show*, that I had my big moment. To help Joey relax before every show, he and I had a private daily ritual of walking from our studio on Vine Street to Hollywood Boulevard and back again. During those strolls we talked about everything, until finally one afternoon we got around to that old topic "What did you want to be when you were a kid?" He told me that, at ten years of age, he would entertain people on the street corners of Philadelphia, telling jokes that left them rocking with laughter. He knew then that he wanted to be a comedian. And so I confessed my dream: I told him that, at the age of six, I decided I wanted to be Bing Crosby—that I knew every lyric of every song Bing had ever sung, that nothing had made me happier than singing along with Bing on the radio.

So it had to happen: three months later, Bing was booked to be a guest on our show. I remember spotting him backstage—this easygoing but towering legend wandering our hallways—and I truly couldn't take my eyes off him. Unfortunately, there were no plans for him to sing that night; he'd simply agreed to come on the show as a panel guest, along with his beautiful wife, Kathy, and share some of his great old stories, then leave. But it was all still terribly exciting. Especially for me. Especially when he walked out and sat right next to me. My whole life flashed before me—thirty years prior to all this I was just a dream-filled kid, freezing on those cold Bronx winter nights, listening to Bing sing on my little radio. How did all this happen? Who could have imagined that now, so many years later, I would be sitting next to Bing Crosby on a big network TV show in Hollywood?! It's one of those times when you have to pinch yourself in order to believe it.

The show's producers, of course, would have loved for Bing to sing anything that night, but they were afraid to ask him. Then, as the interview progressed, Joey had an idea. He would try to talk him into it by using me as his pawn, right on the air! "Bing, see this kid," Joey said, nodding toward me. "He's the biggest fan you ever had. It would be the biggest thrill of his life if you would sing a song for him. How about 'Too Ra Loo Ra Loo Ral'?" I was getting nervous. How would Bing react? Well, he turned, looked directly at me, and

simply sang the song a cappella. He sounded great. It was so exciting, my head was spinning. How could I tell him what he had meant
to me all these years? I should have, but I couldn't.

After the applause, Joey continued. He hadn't had enough. He
said, "Bing, this kid knew all your songs when he was a little boy." I
couldn't believe he was going to tell that whole embarrassing story,
but thank God he didn't. Instead he said, "Regis would now love
to sing one of your songs to you!" *Is he nuts?* I thought. *Is he looking for a few laughs at my expense? How do I get out of here?* Bing
turned and gave me a pleasant enough look—but straight at me. I can
still see those steely blue eyes. He didn't know what to expect either.
It had been nearly fifteen years since I had sung "Pennies from
Heaven" with my pal Gus at Notre Dame for my bewildered parents.
I was nervous, but when was I ever going to get a chance to sing to
Bing Crosby again? So I went for that song with all I had, even including the little-known opening verse. I looked right at Bing, singing every word of it directly to him. I could hear the band, Johnny
Mann and His Merrymen, struggling to find my key for support.
Two great musicians were the first to get into it, God bless them:
Herb Ellis on guitar and Ray Brown on bass. And Bing himself even
joined in with some notes here and there. It was a supreme moment
in my life. I'll never forget it. The next day, believe it or not, I actually received a recording contract from Mercury Records. Would I
want to do an album and include some of Crosby's songs? I said yes,
of course, but I was terribly self-conscious about the whole thing.
Nevertheless, the first track I recorded for them was (you guessed
it!) "Pennies from Heaven."

I never saw Bing Crosby again in person. Foolishly, I was too
intimidated to call him and say thanks for playing along with me
on that special night. Ten years later he died of a heart attack on a
golf course in Spain. It hit me hard, just like losing a lifelong friend.

To have that magnificent voice silenced forever—I couldn't believe it. I have never forgiven myself for not reaching out to tell him what a thrill it was to meet him and what he'd meant to me growing up.

About two years ago, however, I finally had the unexpected privilege of touring the very places where Bing had grown up. My concert booking agent from William Morris Endeavor, Kenny DiCamillo, brought me an offer from an Indian casino near Spokane, Washington. Because it's such a long haul from New York to Spokane, he wondered if I'd be interested in making that far-off trip. *"Spokane!"* I said. "Why, that was Bing Crosby's hometown!" I told him of course I'd love to go there to do a show, but more so to explore the actual home Crosby grew up in and Gonzaga University where Bing completed his college career. Before we even left New York, Kenny had made arrangements for me to visit the Crosby home, which during Bing's youth was located across the street from the university but now has been absorbed right onto the expanded campus grounds. Every morning Bing would pop out the kitchen door of that house and go whistling all the way to his classes.

Of course, Gonzaga remains one of the finest Jesuit universities anywhere—and the Jesuits, as you've probably heard, are known for their teaching prowess. Crosby was a terrific example of their schools' graduates. Not only was he a very good student, bright and well mannered, but it was at Gonzaga that he developed his wonderful vocabulary and elocution, which helped him deliver those songs so memorably. You can hear it in his always precise inflections, whether in song or in film or in later television appearances. He attributed all that smooth expression and eloquence to those exacting Jesuit teachers.

Anyway, Kenny and I rolled into Spokane after a long night's drive through the far Northwest. Then we checked into the historic Davenport Hotel in the heart of town. Looking out of the window of my room, right there across the street I saw the glittering marquee of the Bing Crosby Theater. This was the same theater I read about in Gary Giddins's fine Crosby biography, *A Pocketful of Dreams.* Back then it was called the Clemmer Theatre; Bing, in fact, worked there as a stagehand at the age of fourteen and witnessed the great Al Jolson giving one of his typically thrilling performances on that stage. The young Crosby was knocked out by the unmatchable way Jolson dominated that auditorium. Four years later, Bing happened to be working backstage again, picking up a few bucks, when Jolson returned to Spokane and was still pure dynamite in front of that Clemmer Theatre audience. More than ever, Jolson had at that moment inspired Bing to consider a career of his own in music. The two of them actually met that night (briefly, I'm sure), never knowing that in later years they would work together countless times, performing the most unforgettable duets on Bing's *Kraft Music Hall* radio shows. And they were a brilliant match, too: Jolson, dynamic, dramatic, over the top; and Crosby, laid-back and solid with that beautiful voice and ability to play perfect straight man for Al, while still getting his own share of laughs. I remember lying in bed listening to those shows when I was a kid. I loved them then and still do, thanks to remastered radio recordings of the two of them live together in action so long ago.

Anyway, on that first night in Spokane, I stared out my hotel window for a long time at this grand old theater, which had been renovated and renamed many times through the years until its present owner was persuaded, in 2006, by a citizen's group to at last christen it in Bing's name. I couldn't believe it; right there across the street was the place where Bing Crosby began his illustrious career, by doing the very same job that would decades later serve as my own beginnings in television. That is, we had both started out as stagehand prop house guys!

The next morning was spent wandering through the Crosby home—the one he left each day whistling as he made his way to campus nearly a hundred years ago. Now on that Gonzaga campus there's an enormous statue of Bing wearing his fedora hat, pipe in hand, presiding over everyone strolling by. But as years pass and memories fade, I wonder how many of today's young students really know just what a giant king of American culture he was. One Gonzaga building holds the Crosby archives, with its phenomenal collection of records, movies, photos, radio broadcasts, TV shows, books, magazine clippings, and articles of clothing worn by him—all of it fascinating and mind-boggling at once. He was the one who simply invented pop singing—the Voice who started it all—and everyone who followed him happily admitted as much, none more so than Frank Sinatra.

But let me add a special postscript for you here: Nearly forty years after the Bishop show went off the air, I happened to receive a package in the mail. Of course, I receive a lot of these—video or audio copies of things viewers thought I'd enjoy—and I'm certainly grateful to get them. This one was from someone in Wisconsin. It looked like another CD to me. So much material like this comes in that it's hard to keep up with it. But one day I finally got around to opening this package and, sure enough, it was a CD. I put it in my disc player . . . and I could not believe what I was hearing! It was a recording of that remarkable night when Bing Crosby and I sang to each other on Joey Bishop's show. Why I had never asked for a copy of that program after it aired, I'll never know. I've always regretted not having it. But now here was the audio version of that very special show, somehow dug up by an avid Crosby fan named Greg Van Beek of West Bend, Wisconsin, who's now an editor of the quarterly devotee magazine *Bing*. The copy had been handed off to him by another Crosby archivist, Martin McQuade, who lives in Brooklyn,

New York. Immediately, I called Greg to thank him. Because it was one of the nicest surprises of my life. To listen to that show again—and hear myself trying to sing along with this man whom I'd always dreamt of becoming when I was just a kid . . . I promise you, that young fella had no idea what this recording he'd sent would mean to me and will probably never know what beautiful memories and joy it brings to me even now.

(**NOTE TO READER:** *I think you'll see that those moments recovered from the Bishop show even play pretty entertainingly in transcribed form, an excerpt of which I've included on the next couple of pages. Welcome to a wild and wonderful sliver of my history, exactly the way it happened. . . .*)

WHEN REGIS SERENADED BING

ON *THE JOEY BISHOP SHOW—*
JUST THE WAY IT HAPPENED, CIRCA 1968

JOEY: (*to Bing*) I don't know whether you are aware of it or not, but Regis Francis Xavier Philbin is a Notre Dame graduate.

BING: What happened this year? Purdue . . . SC . . .

REGIS: Looks like a long season, Bing.

BING: It's going to be tough.

JOEY: "Bing," eh?

BING: Naturally.

JOEY: (*mocking Regis*) "Gonna have a long season, *Bing!*" I made a promise to him (*pointing to Regis*), although I've never even approached you on it. Now you can say yes or no.

BING: What is it?

JOEY: Because of his complete Irish background, I said I would try to persuade you to, facing him . . . to do "Too Ra Loo Ra Loo Ral."

BING: Yeah? Facing Regis? How much of it?

JOEY: Just enough to make Regis happy.

BING: (*begins singing intently to Regis*) "*Over in Killarney, / Many years ago—*" (starts laughing) I can't look at that kisser!

REGIS: Now wait a minute, Bing!

JOEY: Now you know what I go through—night after night after night!

BING: No, but he looks so receptive. (*resumes singing*) "*My mother sang a song to me, / A tune so soft and low. / Just a simple little ditty, / In her good old Irish way, / And I'd give the world if I could hear / That song of hers today. / Too ra loo ra loo ra li, / Too ra loo ra loo ral, / Hush now don't you cry. / Too ra loo ra loo ral / Too ra loo ra li, / Too ra loo ra loo ral, / That's an Irish Lullaby.*" (applause)

REGIS: Thank you, Bing.

JOEY: Are you happy now?

REGIS: Very happy.

JOEY: Okay, I'm going to make your dream come true. I'm now about to reveal Regis's dream. He would like to sing in front of Bing Crosby and Kathy Crosby "Pennies from Heaven."

BING: Oh really?!

JOEY: Wait till you hear this!

REGIS: Wait a minute. I don't even know what key.

JOEY: I know what key!

REGIS: Can I do it a cappella?

BING: You can rest assured that if they found my key, they can find yours, Regis.

REGIS: Hey, Bing . . . why don't we . . .

JOEY: *"Hey, Bing"* now?! *"Hey, BING?!"*

REGIS: You know, I'll probably never get to see him again and it's really a thrill to—

JOEY: When you sing this song, I'll GUARANTEE ya, you'll never get to see him again.

REGIS: You know, I don't want to sing the song, but may I sing the verse? The verse is very rarely heard.

BING: Good verse, too!

REGIS: It's a beautiful verse.

JOEY: But then segue into a little bit of the chorus.

REGIS: (*begins song*) *"A long time ago . . ."*

JOEY: Take your time now. I want you to be a hit.

(*Regis proceeds to sing the song "Pennies from Heaven" while Bing jazzily hums along. The final note is followed by applause from all.*)

REGIS: Ah! So embarrassing. Ah! Oh! Thank you.

JOEY: I'm so proud of you. Do you honestly think in your heart—now that you've done it—that you sing better than he does?

REGIS: You know I was kidding!

BING: Naww, you really do. You've got a greater range than I've got.

REGIS: (*instantly excited*) Would you like to hear another one? (*audience explodes laughing*) What's the matter? I've got a million of 'em, Bing! How about "On Behalf of the Visiting Fireman"?

BING and REGIS: (*singing*) "*On behalf of the visiting fireman from Kansas City, / Let's have a drink on me!*"

REGIS: See ya later, Joe.

JOEY: Go ahead. No, go ahead—finish it!

REGIS: Nah, Bing doesn't remember the words.

JOEY: I'll go to the audience in between commercials. Go ahead. "*Bing* doesn't know the words?"

BING: He's got me on that one.

REGIS: How about "Small Fry," Bing?

BING: Well, I remember that, yeah.

REGIS: Do ya? Can I get on your lap?

JOEY: I'll tell ya, boy, the bigger the star, the less humble he becomes!

WHAT I TOOK AWAY FROM IT ALL

The moment of your college graduation
is *not* the moment to surprise your parents
with the sudden declaration of a new
and offbeat career ambition.

Keep those favorite songs of your youth with
you for life and pay attention to the lyrics.
If you love them, use them as your
inspiration and guide.

Chapter Two

TWO MAJOR MARINES: MAJOR RANKIN AND MAJOR FLAKE, USMC

I guess I'd been pretty bold on the night long ago when I met and sang to my idol, Bing Crosby, on *The Joey Bishop Show*. It was a do-or-die situation, after all. But believe me, I wasn't always that way. It took some time for me to learn that every move you make as a young person sets you in a certain direction, and you never know where it will lead you until you get there.

In my particular case, there were two remarkable men who entered my early years and somehow helped put me on a path that brought me right here, to exactly where I find myself today. Back then, they had no idea where I'd end up, and I couldn't have guessed it either. But their strong influence set me on my course and filled me with a new kind of determination I'd never known before. Here is how it all got started. . . .

My father, a wise old former marine, had a hunch that another war would break out while I was off at college and thought that I ought to join the Naval Reserve Officer Training Corps (NROTC) program at Notre Dame. I did as he suggested, and sure enough, the Korean War soon erupted. So, after four great years in South Bend, I headed off for a two-year hitch in the United States Navy. First I attended the Navy Supply Corps School for a couple of months in Hoboken, New Jersey, and was then assigned to an LSM squadron based out of San Diego, California. There, I was to work on the commodore's staff, charged with inspecting inventory and advising the supply officers aboard the ships. Whenever those ships were in port, we would work out of a Quonset hut on the amphibious base in Coronado, across the bay from San Diego. This was also the base where the Navy SEALs would train: that tough bunch of men running hard and working out so brutally at all hours, day and night, along the Silver Strand beaches. Those intense drills of theirs were as intimidating to watch as they were fascinating. But you knew right away that you would never want to mess with any of those guys.

On our LSM squadron staff, there were five officers and maybe six sailors assigned to various duties; it was a close-knit group. It was also an entirely new life for me. Every day the California sun was shining and the palm trees were swaying gently in the breeze—nothing at all like what I'd ever known in New York or Indiana. The war had lasted for just under three years, so by the time I ended up where I had, the action and tensions were gradually easing all around us. When ashore, I lived in the base's Bachelor Officer Quarters (or BOQ), and had my meals at the Officers' Club. It was pretty sweet.

It was in the BOQ that I met a marine major named Bill Rankin, also a bachelor and a very impressive guy. He was about eleven years older than me, a professional military man who had a chest full of medals, walked with a swagger, was in the marines for life, and loved every minute of it. He drove a beautiful Cadillac, seemed to have girlfriends in every town up and down the California coast, and was the envy of most all the married naval officers on the base. His physical fitness was also a point of great pride: He kept in shape with a special, personal set of weights and had even turned a large vacant room on the base into his own gym. Most every afternoon we would work out there together with the weights, dumbbells, barbells, springs, you name it. Some time earlier, Rankin had been wounded in action during a flight mission over Korea; his leg and hip had been badly injured when enemy gunfire blew 123 holes through his plane, which he still managed to bring back to his aircraft carrier and land before blacking out. The carrier crew had to lift him out of the cockpit, but he always firmly believed that it was his superior physical condition that had saved his life.

Also on the same floor of our quarters was a storage room where guys could leave behind trunks full of their belongings whenever off serving overseas. Once, when Rankin and I happened to wander together into that storage room, he specifically brought to my attention a certain trunk. "You must *never* touch *that* trunk," he warned me. "Understand? In fact, don't even *look* at it! It belongs to the toughest marine in the corps." I thought he was kidding when he said that, but he wasn't.

Turned out that the trunk contained the property of another major, whose name was Keigler Flake. Keigler, who by reputation was as fearsome as they come, was temporarily off on some kind of mission. Rankin had known him for many years. Both had enlisted in the Marine Corps in the late thirties, during the Depression. There were no jobs to be had for them in those days and certainly no money for college. The Marine Corps was the next and only option for those two—Rankin from Pittsburgh and Flake from Ohio. When World War II broke out, they were ready and eager to serve. They both hit the beach at Guadalcanal—the first of many bloody battles across the Pacific Islands. By then they were sergeants. The fight for

Guadalcanal was fierce. The casualties were high. In many cases, young marine officers were killed in combat and their sergeants received battlefield commissions to continue directing the fight. Because of their great leadership instincts under those hellish circumstances, both Rankin and Flake became second lieutenants. By the time the fighting ended and that good war was over, they'd each been made captains, and it was clear they were now in the corps to stay. And they loved it. Both men worked hard to remain prepared for whatever war would next call for their courageous service—which would come soon enough in Korea.

But between those two engagements, Rankin chose to continue his career as a marine pilot, while Flake remained ready to direct troops from the trenches. Rankin, in fact, became quite the pilot and, years later, was given command of the first-ever marine supersonic jet squadron. But before all that, for various reasons, they'd both found themselves assigned to our amphibious base, where their formidable presence kept everyone around on their toes.

Anyway, as you may have already guessed, Bill Rankin and I developed a friendship, one that would last the rest of our lives, no less. We must have looked like a strange pair to all the rest of them—the great distinguished major and the green young Supply Corps ensign fresh from Notre Dame. Meanwhile, Coronado itself was a swinging, sweet little town, accessible to San Diego by way of a short ferryboat ride across the bay. It was home to the famed and still magnificent Hotel del Coronado, where so many great movie scenes were set. In fact, you've probably seen it in the classic Marilyn Monroe film *Some Like It Hot*. Also, its North Island Naval Air Station was bouncing every night with "happy hours" and packed with gung ho navy pilots letting loose. Terrific restaurants like the Mexican Village were always jammed with raucous crowds. And there we were—Bill Rankin and I—having our run of all the hot spots, sharing laughs wherever we went.

With the Korean War nearing its end, the little amphibious ships that came into port were gradually being replaced by larger, more efficient craft—which meant that my job was never too detailed or demanding. Each ship in the squadron had its own supply officer, so I would simply go aboard, check things out, write up a complete inventory, and that was about it. Eventually, I guess I started getting a little bored. Thank God the major was around to keep things lively. One day, he happened to show me a copy of *Saga Magazine*, a popular men's adventure monthly back in those days. In that issue, there was a story about the bombings of the bridges at Toko-Ri in Korea. Rankin's name was prominently mentioned in the article. Yes, he had been there—although he'd never said a word about it to me. That had been a historic and crucial bombing because those bridges were carefully defended by many enemy antiaircraft guns hidden all over the area. Since the bridges were built so low, the bombs would have to be delivered underneath them, delayed long enough to explode and break the bridges in half while still giving our planes enough time to fly off without being downed by the detonation blasts. Of course, *The Bridges at Toko-Ri* later became a best-selling book by James Michener and then a terrific movie starring William Holden. But at the time, only this dramatic article in *Saga Magazine* had described all the action in detail.

I took the magazine to my room and, the next day, to my office so I could finish reading it. Also in *Saga* that month was a story about Kid Gavilán, one of the great boxers of the period. Now there was one particular sailor in our hut, this sweet and happy Filipino kid named Ettie Gomez, who I always liked to joke around with. He spotted the magazine on my desk and begged me to let him take it to lunch so he could read about his favorite fighter. I warned him not to lose it because it belonged to my friend, the famous marine Major Rankin, who was known to strut around the base with all his medals gleaming—the Distinguished Flying Cross, the Purple Hearts, and so on—always with that no-nonsense look on his face. Gomez had been especially afraid of him, in fact.

Naturally, you know what happened: Gomez took that copy of *Saga* to lunch, read about Kid Gavilán, and inevitably left the magazine on the table. I was upset with him. After all my warnings, how could he do such a thing? He was very apologetic, but later that night I was embarrassed to have to tell Rankin about it. Rankin couldn't have cared less. He brushed it off. Wasn't important to him in the least. But the more I thought about it, the more a plan of mine came into focus. We could have a little fun with Gomez over this, I realized, maybe a bit devilishly.

Over the years, I had pulled some elaborately planned pranks on my friends—and now this one was forming pretty quickly in my head: Tomorrow I would confront Gomez in the hut and tell him that the major was very angry about that lost magazine. I would say that Rankin wanted to speak directly with him. I could already imagine the color draining from Gomez's face! Then I would tell Gomez it was time for him to water the flowers outside of our hut—and that's when I would call Rankin over to just kind of run into Gomez out there and pretend to give him hell for losing that magazine. I spelled it all out for Rankin, who shook his head and told me he didn't want to get involved. But in the end, he finally relented—just to keep me happy.

Next morning, I put the plan into action. I told Gomez that Rankin was upset about the lost magazine, then sent him outside to tend to the flowers while I made my call to cue Rankin that it was time to walk over and really lay into poor Gomez. I was already giggling to myself. *This*, I thought, *was going to be fun!* But there was one problem: Gomez had fallen into such a funk after I told him about the major that he didn't go outside right away. He was too stricken over what he'd done, too upset that he had angered this formidable marine. Plus, I didn't want to push too hard on the subject of the flower-watering chore, thinking it might somehow tip off the prank. So I didn't mention it again, figuring he'd step outside after another few minutes or so. But in the meantime, the major was already striding toward the hut, looking for his prey. When Rankin didn't see him anywhere outside, he entered our hut and bellowed: "I'm looking for a man named *Gomez!*" Gomez almost fainted.

Now there happens to be a rule in the military about how far you can go in reprimanding another company's soldier. But Rankin was now inside our hut and Gomez was trembling—and all those formalities had just gone right out the window. Rankin had literally crossed a serious line. And it was *all because of me*! Thank God the commodore was away for two weeks at sea with the squadron. Rankin, meanwhile, was imposing enough—this huge marine tightly gripping his swagger stick, with rows and rows of medals up and down his chest. Gomez had practically hit the ceiling, leaping to attention and snapping off a salute, while Rankin, I thought, was rather mild, yet firm, in telling Gomez that he wanted his magazine back. Gomez babbled in broken English, saying that he didn't know where it was. That someone had stolen it at lunch. But he would somehow return it, even if it took him the rest of his life. Rankin told him to make sure that he did. Then he left. Gomez sulked the rest of the day, speaking to no one. *And he never did water the damn flowers!* That night the major and I had some laughs about it, but in my heart, I wished he hadn't come into our hut like that. The next ten days were uneventful. And Gomez was strangely quiet the whole time. I wondered if I had gone too far, so I tried to console him and tell him the major had forgotten all about it. As it was, the magazine hadn't mattered to Rankin in the least.

Then, after his two weeks at sea, the commodore returned. It was late on a Friday afternoon and I'll never forget it. As he entered the hut, Gomez flew across the room and began sputtering about what happened: "Commodore, Commodore! The major come here and yell at me. *'The magazine, the magazine!'*"

Oh my God, I said to myself, this is *not* what I'd planned. *This is not good.* The commodore had no idea what Gomez was talking about. But I did. He looked at me for an explanation and I tried to soft sell it: It was just some magazine the major wanted back that Gomez had lost at lunch, and so he stopped by to talk about it. No big thing, really.

"Did he come inside our hut?" the commodore barked.

"Yes, sir," I answered. "But just a couple of steps."

"Who was the officer in charge here at the time?" he barked again, now looking at Gomez.

"Mr. Pillbin," Gomez replied. (He never did get my name right.)

Now you've got to understand, the commodore never liked me. Never liked Rankin either, for that matter. He used to say that there were four types of military people that he hated most: ensigns, reserves, college graduates, and supply officers. And then he'd glare at me and say: "Philbin, you're all four!" So he eyed me with special disgust that day, because I didn't have the guts to stand up for one of my men and protect him against this marine major who'd had no right to be on our property in the first place. As the commodore became hotter and hotter, his face went beet red. Meanwhile, I noticed Gomez smiling for the first time in two weeks.

The whole plan, stupid to begin with, had backfired into a catastrophe. If the commodore ever found out that I'd done all the plotting behind it—my idea of a harmless little joke—I could be court-martialed, I thought. Maybe even wind up in front of a firing squad! The commodore was appalled—not only upset with me, but now wanting a face-to-face meeting with the major to get to the bottom of this. He would call Rankin on Monday morning, he said, still red-hot. Then he left the hut.

I was staggered by how all this had turned out. How in the world could it have gone so wrong? Certainly I was 100 percent to blame, and now there would no doubt be a price to pay. I was scared stiff. That night I explained it all to Rankin: How the commodore came back. How Gomez threw himself across the room at him, almost crying about the major intimidating him and how Mr. Pillbin didn't protect him. Rankin roared with laughter. He thought this was the funniest story he had ever heard in all of his military career. "It's nothing," he reassured me. "The commodore will forget about it over the weekend. Don't worry about it."

Well, of course, all I did that weekend was worry about it. No sleep at night and a heavy, heavy heart by day. It was a nightmare. I completely dreaded Monday. And just as I expected, it was the first thing the commodore mentioned that morning. Still seething, he sat down at his desk directly opposite mine and dialed a number. His face was just a few feet away. Close enough for me to see that it was flushed and braced for a fight. My face, I'm sure, was pale and getting paler by the minute. I looked at some files, pretending that I couldn't have cared less, that this call had nothing to do with me. I then heard the commodore ask for Major Rankin—and I just held my breath.

"Well, where is he?" the commodore snapped into the phone receiver. "Up flying? I'll call back."

And that's the way it went for the next three days. Turned out that Rankin himself had been answering the phone and pretending he was another officer who just kept telling the commodore that the major was out doing his job. Finally I couldn't take the anxiety of it all anymore—I was now totally beside myself—so I pleaded with Rankin, "*You have to see the commodore. He won't stop call-*

ing! And every time he can't get you on the line, he gets worse. He said that tomorrow he's just going to come over to your hut to find you. . . ." Rankin saw how the panic was killing me, so he promised, "I'll call him first thing in the morning and then come over to see him."

And true to his word, early the next morning the commodore's phone rang and Rankin made a date to come to our hut an hour later for a meeting. I was a complete wreck. The commodore brought out his medals for the showdown, and he looked pretty good, too. He just wanted Rankin to know he was no kid, that he'd been through a couple of wars himself. We were all very tense, but the time had come for them to have this out. Promptly, the major arrived, his uniform glistening—and again, Gomez threw himself against a wall, appearing terrified. The commodore stood up, and these two military officers began a heated argument that kept escalating—all of it because of something a junior officer thought would be fun. There was yelling and some threats were exchanged as they planted themselves practically nose to nose. I stood there frozen at the sight of the two of them going at it. I was almost prepared to break down and confess my sin. It would have been so easy for Rankin to tell the commodore that I was the reason he had invaded our hut in the first place. But the major never gave me up. He skillfully handled his position, as did the commodore, yet there was no defending the fact that Rankin had disregarded official protocol when he walked, uninvited, into the hut that day. It just ended up in what I'd call a draw, and *God, was I relieved when it was over!* The commodore had had his say and would claim victory. And Rankin left with his head held high nevertheless. I vowed to myself: No more stupid jokes ever. And that afternoon, Gomez smiled again, feeling vindicated, while never having known even the half of it.

So anyway, only a few weeks later I was walking down the

hallway at the BOQ when I noticed that the door to the storage room was ajar. Since it was rarely left that way, I peeked inside. I didn't see anyone, but I did notice that the particular trunk Rankin had forbidden me to ever touch, much less even look at, was pulled out and its lid was wide open. I was tempted to go inside to close it when a face slowly rose up from behind it and stared straight at me. It was a tough-looking face, let me tell you, belonging to this imposing man with a crew cut and piercing eyes. Yes, here at last, in person, was Major Keigler Flake. He had returned from his mission. Giving me the up-and-down, he asked in a menacingly quiet voice, "Who are you?" I answered, "Ensign Philbin, sir! I just saw that the door was open and didn't know you were in here. Excuse me, sir." Then I quickly closed the door behind me and fled.

Major Flake, in fact, was a truly intimidating guy. His presence alone would set you on edge. One day, for instance, when he was going through the breakfast buffet line, I noticed that most of the sailors on duty in the galley knew to deliberately avoid his gaze. Except for one new guy who was clueless and looked Major Flake directly in the eyes before giving him a friendly, innocent smile. Instantly, Flake pushed his face close to this kid and said, "Don't you ever smile at me." The sailor froze in his tracks and probably never got over the experience. But that was Keigler Flake. You might have been afraid of him or offended by him, but in a war or a fight you wouldn't have wanted anyone else by your side.

It was just a matter of time before Flake moved his set of weights into Rankin's workout room, positioning his mat right across from us. Both of these men were fastidious in every way, each with his mat on his own separate side of the room, each side of the room personally swept clean every day. It was almost a contest—these two marine majors doing their individual housework, competing with each other as to whose side looked better. And do you know why they did it themselves? It was because, as they would tell you, nobody else could do it better.

I learned a lot from both officers. I thought they were exceptional men—in just the right place at just the right time for them and for this country, serving the United States Marine Corps. I was proud just to be near them.

Anyway, the months flew by. My time in the navy was almost up. I had confided to Bill Rankin all about my desire to try my hand at the television business, while also confessing that I had absolutely no idea what I would or could do in that business. Television was still in its infancy. In San Diego, there was a local newscast every night on KFMB-TV, a CBS affiliate, with Ray Wilson delivering the news and Harold Keene conducting interviews with people who were making the headlines. I thought they were great together—the whole show mesmerized me in some special way. At the time, there were just two TV stations in town, but I loved keeping track of them by reading the daily television column in the *San Diego Union-Tribune*, written by Don Freeman. He had a superb way of reviewing and covering TV shows and their stars, always seeming dead-on right about every topic he touched. I love good writing, and from the start, I thought Don Freeman was just exceptional. Once I spotted him on the street outside his newspaper's building and wanted so badly to introduce myself and ask him for advice on how to go about getting into TV as a profession. But I was too much in awe, so I didn't bother him. Now, though, with just a few weeks left to my tour of duty, I knew it was time for me to approach this great local television expert and ask all the questions that I've been asked by others over and over again for the last four decades: "How do I start? Where do I go? Who do I see? How in the world do you get into the television business?"

So one afternoon I left the base early, took the ferry to San Diego, and headed directly to the Union-Tribune Building. I was, of course, terribly nervous. What would this terrific writer who knew everyone in the business think of me coming to him—without even so much as an appointment—just to ask him all these crazy questions? The receptionist in the lobby told me on which floor I could find Freeman. My heart began pounding as the elevator rose. Finally it reached the level where I was headed. I stepped out into a large room filled with rows of men at desks, clacking out stories on their typewriters. Now my nerves were on fire. I spotted Freeman at his desk, which was next to the last one in that particular row. I started down the aisle. My heart was practically leaping out of my shirtfront. God, how I hated to bother him! I'd almost reached his desk when he looked up at me for just a moment, didn't recognize me (of course), and then returned to banging away at the keys of his typewriter.

I know I should have introduced myself . . . but I couldn't stop walking. There was just one more desk behind his, occupied by yet another writer, and then a wall. Suddenly I realized *I would have to stop. There wasn't any other place else to go! I didn't even know who the man at the last desk was!* Why was I stopping here to talk to him about television when it was *the guy in front of him* who had the answers I wanted? Too late now. I introduced myself to this gentleman and plowed right into it: *Television. How? Who? Where? Help me, please.* Turned out this fellow was the paper's movie critic. I wish I could remember his name. But he was the one who said that his newspaper, owned by the Copley Press, was also part owner of KCOP-TV in Hollywood, and that I should see a man named Al Flanagan, who was the station manager up there. Flanagan, he said, might be able to help me. I was so grateful just for that, just for a name of a place and a person who could possibly help me. In those few minutes with this nice movie critic, I'd now at least gotten myself a starting point. I thanked him profusely and left.

But still I had doubts. Everyone I saw on television was so talented. And all I could think of was *What's my talent?* I had no idea. And I had absolutely no confidence either. All my life I had dreamt about entertainment. But what could I really do in that business?

The night before I was officially discharged, I had dinner with Major Rankin. He, of course, was gung ho about my dreams. He told me I *must* pursue them. (Even though I had all but given up on them.) The next day we said good-bye, talked about how we would stay in touch and all the other things you say to a friend you make in the service. Then I continued my packing. I was almost done when I heard a knock on the door. I was surprised to see that it was Major Flake. He entered the room carrying his shoes in his hands. I had a feeling Rankin had stopped by Flake's room just to tip him off that I was leaving, and caught him in the middle of shining those shoes. He walked in—not smiling, of course—and said, "I hear you're leaving us today. What are you going to do with the rest of your life?"

I blurted out, "Well, I'd love to work in television, sir, but I don't know what I can do. I don't really have any special talent."

And Flake, who hated any kind of negativity, put that very stern face of his right up close to mine, almost forcing me to look directly at him. Then he growled, *"Don't you know you can have anything you want in this life! You've only got to want it bad enough. Now, do you want it?!"*

My answer came feebly: "Well, I'm not sure. . . . I don't know. . . . I really don't have any—"

And that's when Flake hit the ceiling. He slammed his shoes together and he shouted: *"I said, Do you want it?! So? DO YOU WANT IT?!"*

That's when I finally said to him and also, at last, especially to myself: "Yes, sir! I want it!"

"Well, get in your car and get up to Hollywood and make it happen! Now! Right now!"

And in that moment, I thought of that name I had gotten at the newspaper office two weeks earlier. Al Flanagan. Station manager. KCOP-TV. I got in my car, full of blind hope, drove off the amphibious base for the last time, and then straight on up to Hollywood, determined to start something, anything, in what I would now have to make my new career.

Because I *did* want it.

Oh, and by the way, the reason that the great, unforgettable marine Major Keigler Flake was shining his own shoes that day was because no one else could do it better, of course.

WHAT I TOOK AWAY FROM IT ALL

Fate will somehow throw certain (possibly unlikely) characters into your life— but usually for reasons much larger than you will know at the time. Be open to their influence.

Practical jokes can all too often backfire (especially in the military and in the workplace). So always carefully consider the consequences beforehand.

If you really want to conquer an
important quest in your life, go after it.
And don't look back.

Chapter Three

STEVE ALLEN

With navy life now behind me, and big dreams looming before me, I suddenly felt an actual sense of direction—a real path to follow. This, I must tell you, was something new for me. And pretty thrilling, too. I had, after all, just been ordered on *high command* to go make my dreams come true, to be absolutely *determined* to get what I wanted. No excuses allowed anymore. I would no longer be tentative, or wishy-washy, about pursuing a career in the television business. So that very afternoon, following my official discharge, I drove my old Hudson convertible up the Pacific Highway and into Hollywood, equipped with only this bolstered air of confidence, the name of a TV station, and the name of the guy who ran it.

I parked outside of KCOP-TV, located then at 1000 Cahuenga Boulevard, and walked into a small lobby fronted by one tough cookie of a receptionist. I asked to see Al Flanagan, the station manager, who didn't know me from Adam. But that was okay because I was now supposedly flush with this new kind of boldness. My goal, of course, was to volunteer myself for a job, any kind of job. The receptionist asked who I was. The only thing I could think to say was a flat-out lie: "Mr. Flanagan is a close personal friend of mine." (*Great start—and yet what was I getting myself into here?*) But it worked. She directed me out onto the lot, which comprised two large soundstages surrounding a Mexican hacienda–style courtyard with its own wishing well. I should have tossed a few coins into it as I passed, but I barely knew what I was doing there to begin with!

I found my way to Flanagan's office, where now his secretary also asked the purpose of my visit. And again I somehow mustered enough courage to deliver the same stupid lie: "I'm a *personal friend.*" Of course, the next big concern was how he'd react once he saw that I was a total stranger. I just hoped he was a nice guy. A few seconds later, he emerged from his office—this tall, imposing man who wasn't smiling at all when he said to me, *"Who the hell are you?"* I just spat out my reason for being there: "Mr. Flanagan, I don't know you, but people say you're the man to come see. My name is Regis Philbin. I'm looking for work." He glanced at the résumé I'd handed him, which basically said next to nothing: Born in New York City. Graduated from University of Notre Dame. Sociology major. Just served two years in the U.S. Navy, based in Coronado, California. I mean, what else was there to include? He led me into his office, asked me a few more questions, and then surprised me by saying, "Look, I don't have anything now, but if something opens up, I'll call you." Maybe my blindly brazen—or was it just naively idiotic?—approach had impressed him a little. Who knows? I then told him that I hadn't been home to New York in two years, that I'd like to go see my family again, and asked if he would call me there. He said that he would. I somehow believed him and actually felt kind of triumphant. And so I went home.

Now I should point out that my folks weren't *entirely* unfamiliar with the broadcast world. I had an uncle, Mike Boscia, who then worked as the CBS press agent for Arthur Godfrey (that hugely popular radio and TV persona whose name is now all but forgotten). Back in New York, I told Uncle Mike about Al Flanagan's promise. And Uncle Mike, who knew the game inside and out, was plainly skeptical—especially about anyone on the West Coast end of the industry. "They're all crazy out there," he lectured me. " *'Don't call us, we'll call you.'* That's the oldest line in the book! You'll never hear from him again." Just like that, he'd crushed my hopes—but then in the next breath he brought them right back to life: "Look, if you want a taste of the TV business, let me get you a job as a studio page over at NBC. I know some people. . . ."

And that's how it really started. Hollywood, after all, wasn't the only place to get that break I wanted so badly. On the appointed morning in June of 1955, I would report to NBC and officially enter the world of big-time television. Of course, I was nervous. So nervous, in fact, that I sat for a moment outside of 30 Rock, trying to collect myself on one of those benches that still overlook the lower concourse reflecting pool—the one that, during wintertime, becomes the famous ice-skating rink you see so often on NBC broadcasts. I noticed that all the flags stationed around Rockefeller Plaza were flapping in the breeze, much as they do today. In fact, most everything about that iconic building, forever the home of NBC, has remained the same. Even now, whenever I walk through its massive lobby with those old murals on the walls, it reminds me of that June morning so long ago when I was scared stiff and yet terribly excited to begin this new chapter in my life.

Anyway, that first day, I checked in and got my official page uniform—which had a very familiar military feel to it—and then I was assigned to head over to the Hudson Theatre on West Forty-fourth Street. There, I would work in the second balcony, seating audiences for an already popular new late-night program called *The Tonight*

Show, which starred a multitalented fellow named Steve Allen. I arrived well before showtime, and once I got up to my second-balcony post, I saw that rehearsals were still under way onstage below me. I sat down to watch, instantly awed to find myself smack in the midst of genuine television stars doing their thing. There, planted behind that piano he played so expertly, was Steve Allen himself, kibitzing with his regular comic ensemble—Louis Nye, Tom Poston, and Bill Dana—each of whom would go on to great successes of their own. They were all tossing around very funny lines so effortlessly, honing their material for the broadcast to come. I laughed—and loudly, too—as I sat alone high above them. Then the show's boy-and-girl pair of house singers—Steve Lawrence and Eydie Gormé, who later famously became major husband-and-wife headliners in the business—stood up and ran through a number or two. I was so impressed with their magnificent voices; they were barely out of their teens, and yet they were already right here making a splash in the big time. *My God,* I thought, *how is it that all these people are just so talented, so confident, so professional—and here I am, this nobody page up in the second balcony, waiting to seat their fans?*

I mean, it was clear to me in that very moment: Maybe I needed to rethink this quest of mine. Had I really chosen the right business in which to pursue a career? I began asking myself all over again: *What is my talent, anyway?* That question in particular—to which I had absolutely no answer—was the one that would haunt me for the rest of my life. Or at least for many, many more years yet to come.

Cut to nearly a decade later:

The truth was, I must have had something to offer as a television persona because, for starters, at the end of that 1955 summertime stint as a *Tonight Show* page, old Al Flanagan did in fact call me back to Hollywood. He gave me work as a stagehand at KCOP-TV and eventually tipped me off to a better job that he thought I could pull off down in San Diego. That better job led to even bigger things in that town, including a local live Saturday-night talk show that allowed me to interview all kinds of people, many of them well-known celebrity characters passing through the area. One such celebrity, who held major sway over the culture and who has a chapter all his own in this book, happened to rave about the show after a most memorable guest appearance, and my phone soon began ringing off the hook. Most of the calls were from well-wishing friends, but one came from a Los Angeles agent named Max Arnow from GAC. He was eager to get a load of me in action, so he flew down to San Diego shortly after. I drove to the airport to pick him up. He was easy enough to recognize amidst the rest of the arriving passengers: very flamboyant, very brassy, very Hollywood. I then brought him to the TV station, where he reviewed some of the shows that we'd managed to record on tape (very few copies of my work existed in those days). He seemed to like what he saw, but made no promises. He did say, however, that he would try to make something happen.

Now this was in 1964, when talk shows weren't exactly booming. In daytime, Mike Douglas was becoming an afternoon favorite in national syndication through Westinghouse. And of course NBC's *Tonight Show* ruled supreme in late night. It was then starring the sensational Johnny Carson as host, who had followed the also sensational Jack Paar, who had, in turn, followed the originally sensational Steve Allen. Naturally, I'd never forgotten my first day as an NBC page, watching Steve from the balcony and requestioning all of my ambitions in that thoroughly humbling moment. But nowadays I was watching him on an all-new show, shot in Hollywood and syndicated by the Westinghouse Group. His latest antics were being broadcast out of a studio renamed the Steve Allen Playhouse on Vine Street, across from the Hollywood Ranch Market. This new version of his previous show was wilder and always daring. Whenever Steve allegedly ran out of material, for instance, he would send someone over to the Ranch Market, which housed a huge bulletin board plastered with crazy personal ads from people looking for jobs or for love or for God only knows what. And Steve would call up these people on the air and pry loose screamingly funny in-the-moment conversations with them. Always sharp and spontaneous, his humor never failed to dazzle me. Plus, his happened to be the only national talk show regularly taped in Hollywood at the time, so he got the greatest and starriest guests of any host working. It was wonderful television.

Anyway, my man Arnow, true to his word, had been poking around trying to find me a bigger opportunity in the business. He met often with his young subordinate agents, telling them that I was the next great new talent on the rise. Of course, none of them had actually seen me—but one of them, named Bobby Levine, happened to be in a restaurant across from the Steve Allen Playhouse one night and heard the rumor that Steve was preparing to quit the Westinghouse show. Levine immediately started telling anyone in the restaurant within earshot about this guy named Regis who was doing big things down in San Diego. Steve Allen's executive producer, Chet Collier, turned out to be sitting there at the bar, hearing every word of Levine's nonstop spiel. Chet, having had a few drinks already, made sure to spell out in ink on the palm of his hand the name "Regis" so that he wouldn't forget. The next morning, he woke up, stared at his palm, and called Bobby Levine. Bobby raved on about me even more, quoting the showbiz power-house who had earlier praised me as well. And that did it. Chet and his lieutenants were down in San Diego to witness my very next Saturday-night show. The guest that evening was none other than the glamorous Hungarian movie queen Zsa Zsa Gabor. Chet's gang stayed backstage, watching the live broadcast on the monitor.

Luckily, Zsa Zsa and I hit it off famously, having a good laugh together. Afterward, backstage, she just blurted out for all the execs to hear: *"My God, he's as good as Carson!"* That was all the encouragement they needed.

Next thing, they called and asked me to go to Cleveland to pinch-hit for the daytime star Mike Douglas, who was planning a vacation. They wanted to see me try my hand at a national daily show for a week. Mike, at that point, had never let a guest host sit in for him, never wanted one to either. But he finally relented and I got my shot. His staff was terrific (headed by the dynamic executive producer Woody Frasier and including a young guy named Roger Ailes, who would decades later put Fox News on the map). They even flew in a guest of my own choice, the colorful wrestler Freddie Blassie, who'd been such great fun on my San Diego show. The high jinks actually escalated on the Douglas show: While doing some stunt with Freddie, I inadvertently slapped him on the face. He, of course, blew up and began chasing me around the studio, looking very much like he would kill me once he caught me. The largely female audience screamed in terror! I probably did, too. Finally, we had to stop the chase, but not before he grabbed my hand and pretended to crush it. Except that he did crush it—*Freddie was one very strong guy!*—and accidentally managed to break one of my fingers. (I mean, I *think* it was an accident!) I still have the bump to prove it. But he was a wonderful friend. And we made some great TV there, and elsewhere in later years.

Anyway, the Westinghouse people liked what they saw and wanted to see more. So next they gave me another week—this time in Hollywood, actually guest hosting for Steve Allen himself, the guy whose shoes they seemingly wanted me to fill. They liked how that turned out, too. And then they offered me the job to take over the show from Steve once his contract ended, which was apparently happening *within weeks*! I wasn't counting on that. I would have preferred that we'd created a brand-new show built around who I was and what I did rather than be compared to the remarkable one-of-a-kind man they simply wanted me to replace. The same man I'd watched from the second balcony roughly nine years earlier and who'd left me instantly awestruck on my first day of work in the television business.

What followed, I must honestly tell you, bothered me tremendously. I was flown around the country on one of those promotional meet-and-greet tours, stopping off at the various cities whose stations had been airing Allen's show nightly. And no matter where I went, some TV critic would inevitably ask, "Why you?" I mean, they had never heard of me. They'd cite so many of Steve's great abilities and talents, and then openly ask me, "So what's your talent?" *There was that damned question again*—the one I'd never stopped asking myself, starting well before that first day in the Hudson Theatre balcony.

And I still didn't have an answer for them—or for myself. Never quite precisely, anyway. It just got more humiliating and embarrassing every time someone raised it. It hurt, and I hated it. Worse yet, it also dominated my thoughts. I should have been focused entirely on succeeding at my big break, my new national show in Hollywood. Instead, as I went from city to city and watched Steve's last handful of programs each night on my hotel room TV, I grew more and more discouraged. My hopes had suddenly all faded. On the last night of the tour, the actual Friday before the Monday when I would take over, I was put up at the Mark Hopkins Hotel in San Francisco. I watched Steve's final show. And then I couldn't sleep. At all. Instead, I stayed up until dawn, looking out my window at the Golden Gate Bridge.

Though the show had its moments after I took over, it died within months. Suffice it to say that for me, it was a major heartbreaker.

And what about Steve Allen? Over the years, I met him at many functions, would actually enjoy dinners at his home, had him as my own guest on future shows, and even guested on one of his shows. And every time I saw him, it dredged up the painful memory of following him on that Hollywood Westinghouse show. Steve never mentioned it to me or even gave the slightest clue that he remembered I'd once been his catastrophic replacement. He was always in good spirits, maybe thinking the mere topic would be uncomfortable and that it was all part of the business—that if it hadn't been me who took over his show, it would have been someone else, and at some point, why would it matter in the long run anyway?

But for me, he represented much more than I could've ever told him. His was the very first undeniable television talent I had seen up close and personal in this business. And I mean *tremendously personal*. Starting on that day when I began my own career, wearing my crisp new NBC page uniform and watching him onstage from that second balcony, all the way through the many years to come. I must admit that every time I drive down Forty-fourth Street in New York, past the old Hudson Theatre where I'd once been so unsure of what my future would hold, I always think of Steve Allen. Because he forced me to wonder long and hard and practically ever since—in a way that maybe nobody else could have—about what exactly my talent really is.

WHAT I TOOK AWAY FROM IT ALL

When other people believe in you, they believe in you for a good reason. Don't worry about that reason—just believe right along with them.

To specifically label what you do best is to unfairly limit what you can do best.

Just make sure you know what you absolutely *cannot* do. And don't be afraid to admit it.

Chapter Four

RONALD REAGAN

Probably more often than you'd guess, I catch myself thinking about my early days in San Diego TV and how it all got started—thanks to my rather unconventional work on radio there. Those were the days sandwiched between my stint as an NBC page in New York and the whole Westinghouse debacle in L.A. With the help of Al Flanagan, who'd previously hired me as a pretty menial stagehand at Hollywood's KCOP-TV, I'd now landed a somewhat bigger broadcasting job right back in good old San Diego, across the bay from the Coronado military base where I'd been stationed in the navy for two years. This new job—which is probably hard to even fathom nowadays—required me to cruise the city's streets in a KSON-radio car equipped with both a microphone and a typewriter set up in the front seat, so I could slide over and bang out my report and then broadcast it on the ham-operated mic. Every hour on the hour, I had to deliver a story—it was as if I was on a nonstop news-hunting expedition, always searching for the next "breaking" incident in town. Usually, the blotter that hung in the pressroom of the San Diego police station would have something I could work with—which I'd then go chase down. Not always, though.

Once, with my hourly deadline drawing near, I went to the blotter desperately hoping for something, *anything*! There was something about—are you ready for this?—a break-in of a piggy bank in Poway, a little town, now probably booming, outside of San Diego. Believe it or not, I *knew* it was the last thing I should even consider filing as a legitimate news story. But time was running out! So I wrote an overly dramatic, and hopefully funny, account of how this little piggy bank—holding less than a buck in change—had been busted open and the contents stolen. A piggy bank—*in Poway* . . . for god's sake!

But I wrote the hell out of the story and delivered it like Edward R. Murrow: somehow both somber yet urgent in tone, which made it pretty funny. I just hoped whoever heard it had a sense of humor. Understandably, I never thought stories like that would get me into television. But sure enough, the news guys over at KFMB-TV happened to be listening and wondered, *Who is this character reporting such offbeat kinds of stuff?* They liked it, called me in, and hired me to do regular funny feature stories on their newscast—one every night, no less. And they gave me an 8-millimeter camera to shoot it. I'd go out, film the piece, come back to the station, process the film, edit it, write the copy, and deliver it on the show. The rival station, KOGO-TV, liked what they were seeing, too—and soon offered me an even better job: do my feature story on the 6 P.M. broadcast—and then actually anchor the 11 P.M. news, which was quite a major step up. Also, I asked for, and received, the promise of a Saturday-night talk show, which would begin in early October 1961.

By then I had been inspired hugely by Jack Paar—especially by his gift of connecting directly with that camera lens. I wanted to give it a try, in my own way, and also to have real and lively conversations with guests in front of a TV audience. For this local show, there were no writers, no producers, and, naturally, no budget. Tom Battista—

who became my lifelong friend from the start—was assigned to direct the program. During the week, it was just Tom and I. In between my nightly newscasts, I would try to contact whoever was coming to San Diego that weekend and build my guest lineup, combining visiting notables with our local San Diego celebrities—hoping for an interesting mix. For a few minutes every Thursday afternoon, Tom and I would have a meeting and outline the upcoming Saturday-night show. And that was it. Our whole planning session lasted about as long as a coffee break!

Sometime in 1962, I read in the papers that Ronald Reagan was coming to town. Right away, I booked him for that Saturday night. I had seen him in the movies, of course, as the Notre Dame football hero George Gipp in *Knute Rockne All American*—a favorite of every devout Fighting Irish fan—and also in *Kings Row,* his best acting role ever, as well as in a few so-so westerns. Maybe it wasn't the most thrilling period of his acting career, but he was an established movie star, and I was hungry for guests. The show aired live beginning at 11:15 P.M., after the local news, with a studio audience of around two hundred people. A couple of gung ho San Diego State college students would set up the audience seats beforehand and then stick around to remove the whole setup afterward. (One of them was Bud Carey, who later climbed up the ranks of the business and became general manager of New York's WCBS-TV; he went on to teach his great television know-how at Syracuse University before retiring. The other student volunteer was George Lewis, who turned into one of *NBC News*'s best reporters, covering the West Coast and also several wars overseas for the network through the years. I'm very proud of both of them.)

Anyway—because I probably already knew that hosting a talk show was the job I would always love best—Saturday night was truly the most important night of the week for me. To prepare what I hoped might make entertaining stories for my opening segment, I would think about all the things I had done that week and the interesting people I'd bumped into around town. This was to be my Jack Paar–style conversational monologue material—and I found that it came to me pretty naturally! After that, it was all about bringing out the guests, whether from New York, Los Angeles, or dear old San Diego. Pro football had just been getting started in town back then, and the Chargers were our new franchise team. Jack Kemp was the team's star quarterback and, inevitably, one of our show's first guests. Instead of just sitting on a couple of stools, we passed the ball back and forth during the interview. I was trying hard to do something different with the format.

So along comes Ronald Reagan. There was never a chance before the show to go over what the guests and I would talk about. It was always ad-libbed. My instinct told me this would be the most exciting and spontaneous way to do it. Reagan, as we now know, had been more than just an actor; early on, he'd done some radio sports announcing. So we talked a little sports. Plus, he did portray the Gipper so heroically on film two decades earlier. How could I ever resist that topic? But we never got into politics. Because frankly, it was unthinkable back then that he would go on to become the governor of California and, eventually, the president of the United States! Instead, we talked about his life and career, and also of his spirited feelings about this country and how, just like him, anyone else could achieve the goals they truly wanted. The more we talked, the more you had to like him. I could tell the audience was becoming mesmerized by his optimism. He just made you feel better, gave you hope, made you want to strive even harder to achieve your own goals. He looked great, spoke beautifully, and when he was finished the audience was completely his. He'd talk with such common sense and logic—always with that down-to-earth smile and easy, reassuring shrug. Guestwise, he was simply terrific. I could tell that he was having a good time, too. He left to rousing applause.

After the show I met with my director pal Tom, and we agreed that Reagan was dynamite, the best guest we'd had since we started the show. He had cast a spell. But there was more to it. This guy elevated you. No doubt about it. Tom and I were thoroughly impressed. The next day, Sunday, was gorgeous and bright and I was out on the beach at the Hotel del Coronado, across the bay from San Diego. I almost thought I was imagining things when I saw Reagan come striding through the crowd on his way to the water. He cut a very impressive figure, then plunged right into the ocean, sliced through the powerful waves, and swam out beyond them to a quieter place where he continued to swim . . . for a long time. The night before, I remembered, he had mentioned having been a lifeguard in his hometown in Illinois. He certainly seemed at home out there in the water. Then I spotted his wife, Nancy, walking right down to the shoreline, too, and watching him intently. She became famous for those deeply engaged and adoring looks at her husband during their White House years. Even then, she appeared very much in love.

And so life went on. I left San Diego in 1964 and, three years later, became the second banana on ABC-TV's *The Joey Bishop Show*. And among the first guests we booked was . . . California governor Ronald Reagan! Backstage, Joey introduced me to him. I wondered if Reagan would remember that show of ours in San Diego five years before. Well, he actually did. He was that kind of guy, and he gave me a hearty handshake, telling everyone within earshot how much he'd enjoyed that Saturday-night show we'd done together back then. And I loved it—especially because all of this happened right in front of Joey, who stood there amazed at the easy familiarity of our warm and unexpected reunion.

Sometime after the Bishop show went off the airwaves at the end of 1969, I'd gotten a local daytime show in Los Angeles on KHJ-TV— this was the early seventies, which were wild and turbulent years in the streets of L.A. and in the hearts of Americans in general. But on several occasions, Governor Reagan was right there with me on the program, sharp and dependable as ever during those especially dangerous times. Riots and chaotic rallies were regular occurrences throughout the city and the rest of the state back then, but Reagan remained calm and strikingly firm. Once, in a speech, I heard him actually challenge the malcontents: "If we can't settle things peacefully, then, okay—let's get it on in the streets." He was no wallflower.

Of course, our lives and careers continued. I'd joined KABC-TV in the mid-seventies, and by 1981, Ronald Reagan had become president. Then, shockingly, after only sixty-nine days in the Oval Office, he took a bullet from a would-be assassin. If the bullet had hit an inch closer to his heart he wouldn't have survived. But he did. And in May of that same year, Notre Dame president Father Ted Hesburgh had an inspired idea: *Why not invite President Reagan to deliver a commencement address for the graduating class of '81?* The president had not been seen out among the public since the shooting, and his recovery had been long and arduous—even though he made it look easy with his swaggering wisecracks that charmed the nation. At the time, I was the entertainment editor for the station and, like Father Hesburgh, a similar idea hit me right away: *Why not take a camera crew to cover the Gipper's return to Notre Dame?* I worked out the deal with the news show producer, and off we went to South Bend, Indiana. The campus was alive and jumping that weekend with the graduates and their families—but all the more so because the president would be giving his first speech since the attempt on his life.

And to top it all off, "Knute Rockne" was there to magically watch over everything. That's right, there I was standing with my crew outside the Morris Inn—the only hotel on campus—when a car drove up, and out stepped the great actor Pat O'Brien. Pat, of course, had so memorably played the title role in the classic 1940 movie, alongside Reagan's portrayal of quarterback George Gipp. And believe me, Rockne is still a part of the tremendous Notre Dame legacy. In fact, during the immortal coach's heyday, he was one of the most popular figures in the entire country, inside and outside of football. Over the years, whenever I was covering major Hollywood parties and events, I would always ask O'Brien to deliver Rockne's locker-room speeches for our newscasts. And now here we were together on the legendary campus waiting for the Gipper's triumphant return. What better time to go for it? I approached the car with my crew; Pat O'Brien, at eighty-one years young, was a bit slow getting out and looked a little tired. They probably drove him in from Chicago—hardly a quick commute—but this was a must. It took him a second to recognize me. Clearly he wasn't expecting to see me there, but I gave him my most heartfelt plea: "Pat, we may never get together again on this campus as long as we live. *We must do it again with Knute—and also for Knute!* His spirit is still here all around us. I'm sure he'd love to hear his pep talk one more time—just the way he did it to fire up the team so long ago."

And so Pat O'Brien braced himself, took a deep breath, and let me have it, full throttle, while our camera rolled: *"We'll go inside them, we'll go outside them, and we'll never rest, boys, never until we win again for Notre Dame!"* On and on he went with the speech—and I swear to you, inside my head, I clearly heard the Notre Dame band playing "Cheer, Cheer for Old Notre Dame." It was an exciting moment for me—and for Pat O'Brien, too. I mean, we were reenacting history on sacred ground!

Next day, May 17, was the graduation ceremony—which looked very different from mine there on campus in the spring of 1953. For one thing, I naturally remembered that only a few years back Father

Hesburgh had decreed that Notre Dame become a coed school—and here they were: all of these young ladies in their flowing commencement gowns heading toward the convention center to collect their diplomas. And they looked great. I thought of our own two little daughters—Joanna and J.J.—and imagined how nice it would be for them to one day be draped in those gowns and getting their diplomas here, too. And I'm happy to say that did happen some years later, which was another very special thrill.

As you'd expect, security at this graduation was terribly tight and restricted. Reporters were bunched together. There was no chance to talk to the president. What would I have said, anyway? *"Hey there, Secret Service guy, wait a minute—he did my local show in San Diego twenty years ago. He knows me!"* No, those days were over. Father Hesburgh, who's known for his own warm and fabulous speeches, made a wonderful introduction—and then out came Ronald Reagan. No sign of being wounded, a big smile on his face, he simply gave one of the most stirring speeches I had ever heard. He noted that he was the fifth American president to address a Notre Dame commencement and, soon enough, began to reminisce about his experiences playing George Gipp on film, while giving credit to the now beaming Pat O'Brien for so generously helping him secure the role. But let me share with you a taste of some of Reagan's remarkable words that day—specifically about the invaluable subtext of that Rockne movie, even though it was just a small portion of the president's long and thrilling invocation. . . .

> . . . because it says something about America. First, Knute
> Rockne as a boy came to America with his parents from
> Norway. And in the few years it took him to grow up to
> college age, he became so American that here at Notre
> Dame, he became an All-American in a game that is still,
> to this day, uniquely American.

As a coach, he did more than teach young men how to play a game. He believed truly that the noblest work of man was building the character of man. And maybe that's why he was a living legend. No man connected with football has ever achieved the stature or occupied the singular niche in the nation that he carved out for himself, not just in a sport, but in our entire social structure.

Now, today I hear very often, "Win one for the Gipper," spoken in a humorous vein. Lately I've been hearing it by congressmen who are supportive of the programs that I've introduced. [*laughter*] But let's look at the significance of that story. Rockne could have used Gipp's dying words to win a game anytime. But *eight* years went by following the death of George Gipp before Rock revealed those dying words, his deathbed wish.

And then he told the story at halftime to a team that was losing, and one of the only teams he had ever coached that was torn by dissension and jealousy and factionalism. The seniors on that team were about to close out their football careers without learning or experiencing any of the real values that a game has to impart. None of them had known George Gipp. They were children when he played for Notre Dame. It was to this team that Rockne told the story and so inspired them that they rose above their personal animosities. For someone they had never known, they joined together in a common cause and attained the unattainable.

. . . But is there anything wrong with young people having an experience, feeling something so deeply, thinking of someone else to the point that they can give so completely of themselves? There will come times in the lives of all of us when we'll be faced with causes bigger than ourselves, and they won't be on a playing field.

. . . We need you. We need your youth. We need your
strength. We need your idealism to help us make right
that which is wrong. Now, I know that this period of your
life, you have been and are critically looking at the mores
and customs of the past and questioning their value. Every
generation does that. May I suggest, don't discard the
time-tested values upon which civilization was built simply
because they're old. More important, don't let today's doom-
criers and cynics persuade you that the best is past, that
from here on it's all downhill. Each generation sees farther
than the generation that preceded it because it stands
on the shoulders of that generation. You're going to have
opportunities beyond anything that we've ever known.

Yes, the "Gipper"—now the leader of the free world—came back
that day to give these graduates a rousing send-off that I'm sure each
of them will remember forever. I could see the same effect on these
kids that he had made on our small audience that night in San Diego years earlier. He had spectacular presence.

Back in Los Angeles on Monday's newscast, we presented the
story. There was Pat O'Brien doing Rockne for me; there were the
kids walking around their campus, happy but also sorry they were
leaving that wonderful school. There was Father Hesburgh with his
grand introduction to a president who had almost been killed a few
months before, this former movie actor who so brilliantly portrayed
one of the greatest characters and football heroes ever to play for
Notre Dame. And there was the president himself with his jaunty
walk to the microphone, all charm and grace, delivering that terrific
speech.

Because I knew the story was pure gold, I had cajoled an extra
minute from the news producers for my segment that night, and

then stole another minute from the anchorman to put together what I thought was an unforgettable piece. After it finished airing, I threw it over to Jerry Dunphy, my anchor, to go to a commercial. Dunphy—a pro among pros who had seen just about everything throughout the course of his esteemed news career—was visibly moved. He had trouble collecting himself before getting to the commercial. And then the studio doors flew wide open and our tough news director, Denny Swanson, who in later years was instrumental in launching Oprah Winfrey's monumental career, bounded in. And he was headed right for me! I remembered that I had deliberately *not* discussed this trip with him before I left. I was afraid he wouldn't okay it, since it was a pretty expensive undertaking for a local newscast.

But as he got closer I could see—maybe for the first time ever—that Denny Swanson was actually impressed. He never handed out accolades to anyone, not ever! But he was excited now. "I didn't know you were going back there to do this," he practically boomed. "It was terrific. One of the best stories we ever did. How did it happen?"

How did it happen? How *did* it happen? How in the world could I ever explain this whole long ride of mine with Ronald Reagan—not to mention Notre Dame—to him. Twenty years—from San Diego onward—flashed through my mind. "Well," I said, "Denny, it's really a long, long story. But I'm glad you enjoyed it."

I like to think I won that one for the Gipper, too.

WHAT I TOOK AWAY FROM IT ALL

Go ahead and take a chance on doing surprising things at work (as I did in my piggy bank story, for instance). Attention will

be paid. Eventually, anyway.
Maybe not right away, but someday,
someone will notice.

There's no such thing as a lowly job when
you start in the particular business where
you've always dreamed of succeeding.

Chapter Five

WALTER WINCHELL

Believe it or not, there was a time before World War II when at least twelve different daily newspapers were operating in New York City. Nowadays, we're lucky to have three. As a kid, I was a tremendous sports fan, and each paper had a full array of fabulous sportswriters, many of them now legends. But there was another section of the papers I loved, too: the entertainment pages with their exciting boldfaced gossip columns! There must have been at least twenty of these intrepid columnists doing their snoop-around stuff day after day, and I was always thrilled to read about whichever big celebrity was in town and what adventures they might have been up to. When you live in the Bronx, Manhattan can feel just as far away as Iowa—but those columnists almost made you believe you were a part of everything that was going on right in the city. Of course, the king of all the gossip hounds was Walter Winchell.

The Great Winchell! Nobody wrote like him. He could condense a story into a few lines, sometimes even into a few words, and then came those three dots separating each different item and giving the column a nonstop energy that was irresistible. Exciting reading? You bet. Winchell had started his special style of reporting, practically on a whim, back when he was a young vaudeville performer. (The guy did, after all, have a theatrical personality!) For some reason, he'd jot down notes about whatever intrigue he heard buzzing among the theater types and then tack the notes onto the wall backstage. Immediately, this knack for spilling secrets grabbed attention and caught on—as did he! Now he was the premier go-to guy in New York City for behind-the-scenes celebrity news—in fact, many people believed it didn't happen unless Winchell said it did. He had that kind of power over the public, both around town and all across the country.

Meanwhile, the city was booming, especially after the war. It was a golden time, when television was just being born right here in the heart of Manhattan, and Broadway stages were all lit up with the greatest musicals and plays. Those same shows are the ones that keep returning everywhere as big-time revivals because they were that good. Broadway also had many of those now-forgotten movie palaces where you could see a good film and then, between screenings, watch an even better stage show—five times a day—with performers like Sinatra, Martin and Lewis, Jimmy Durante, and so on. Then there was Fifty-second Street with its string of great jazz clubs clustered along *both sides* of the street, as well as all those glamorous old nightclubs that we'll never see the likes of again. The town was jumping in new and exciting ways. So for the showbiz columnists, every day was another field day. And like clockwork, Winchell topped them all; he could seemingly jam close to two hundred names into any one column! The man was untouchable at his craft.

But now let's fast-forward to the early sixties, when I'd been anchoring the San Diego KOGO-TV nightly newscasts and hosting my Saturday-night talk show. Walter Winchell had always made it his habit to escape New York in the summer, especially in August, opting to cool off in Southern California instead. He loved heading to the Del Mar racetrack, just north of San Diego, about a mile off the Pacific Ocean. The track had been financed by Bing Crosby back in the thirties, and the Hollywood crowd still regularly zipped down there to hang out and bet on the races—which conveniently provided Winchell with lots of ammunition, or at least plenty of boldfaced names for his column. He also liked to hold court in the newsroom of the *San Diego Union-Tribune*, which carried his syndicated column. The local reporters couldn't get enough of the stories he'd spin right on the spot. Naturally, I thought he would be a great guest for my Saturday-night show, but the reality of it intimidated me more than I can express. The local gossip columnist, Frank Rhodes, who was a good friend of mine, encouraged me to just give Winchell a call and ask him. "He'd love to come on," Rhodes assured me.

So I sucked up my courage and called Walter Winchell, and let me tell you, it wasn't easy. I was a nervous wreck. Reading his stuff for so many years had made him something of a god to me. He was the one who had the inside track to Washington for private face-to-face meetings with FDR. He was the one who not only knew every big player in show business but also had the power to make or break most of them. He was the one who Louis "Lepke" Buchalter, the murderous gangster, turned to when he was about to give himself up to the cops—but only if Winchell would walk into the police station with him. Nope, this was no ordinary guest. This guy was a very important figure in American culture. But without hesitation he said yes, that he'd be there for me Saturday night at eleven. I wish I could recall our conversation, but I'm sure I was beside myself over the whole thing. The mere idea of it stirred up a flood of memories— of how, as a kid, I'd buy the *New York Daily Mirror* for two cents just to read what Winchell had to say. Back in those years, there he was—planted every night at the Stork Club, right in the middle of all the glitz and glamour of New York—and now he was coming to be interviewed by *me* . . . on a very local but increasingly popular San Diego talk show.

When he arrived at the studio, he looked exactly the same as he had in all the pictures I'd ever seen of him since the time I was ten years old. He was snazzy as could be in a fedora hat, a dark blue suit, a white shirt, and a matching blue tie. But here's what you also need to know about Winchell, if you don't already: He was quite controversial. He had an enormous ego. A lot of people hated him for that ego and for his shifting politics and even for his successes. And now, face-to-face with him, I felt his electricity. It was almost overwhelming, but there we were on camera in a couple of chairs reviewing his life. It was Winchell talking about Winchell-in-action, and you could tell pretty quickly that it was a topic he enjoyed thoroughly. Out poured his personal greatest tales spanning the old glory days and beyond—classic New York scandals, behind-the-scenes Broadway feuds, crazy antics in the nightclubs, and his lively relationships with movie stars, mobsters, cops, politicians, singers, everybody. Every minute of it was beyond fascinating. At one point, he even got up and encouraged me to join him in an old tap dance from his vaudeville days. He still had it down pat! This was an interview for the ages—and also, very much to my regret, one that's been lost to the ages because it was broadcast live with no tape running.

And then, out of the blue, pandemonium broke loose: It must have been close to twelve thirty in the morning when the doors to our studio suddenly swung open—right in the middle of one of his fabulous stories, naturally—and into the broadcast area marched a procession of firemen, some of them carrying axes. I had never seen anything like it. But I had to interrupt Walter—*which was not so easy to do*—and throw to a commercial break so I could find out what was going on. The fire chief told me, "We have a report of a bomb planted in your studio." Apparently, there'd been some call about an alleged explosive device hidden on our premises that was probably meant to harm Winchell—or at least interrupt him. The firemen began scouring the studio. The crowd was unsettled, but no one made for the exits; they stayed put, loving the Winchell exchange as much as I'd been enjoying it. In those far more innocent days, no one heard much about bombs going off in public places, especially in TV studios.

As the firemen carefully poked around the set, Winchell and I approached the audience. I explained the situation and told them that they were free to leave. Meanwhile, Winchell tried to calm everyone down, assuring them that it was most likely a phony tip from some crackpot trying to shut him up. So nobody panicked—except for one woman, who got up and walked down the stairs to the stage, ready to escape. Winchell immediately went to work on her: "What are you afraid of?" he roared. "You've got both the navy and the marines based right here in San Diego. You can't let these Ratzies, these Nazis, scare you!" She nevertheless kept moving. Winchell pleaded, "Don't leave!"

She looked him right in the eye. "Don't go?" she said. "Walter, I love you, but I'm not going to hell with you!" And out she went into the night. The commercial break ended, but the firemen continued their hunt throughout the next segment of the show. And if you think about it, this had to be something of a historic moment for television, probably never to be repeated again—*a bomb search going on while I continued a live TV interview* . . . with Walter Winchell, no less, who, by the way, picked up his story right where he'd left off, as though nothing at all had happened in between. I was hanging in there, halfway distracted, with one eye on him and the other eye on the firemen. Thankfully, nothing at all suspicious turned up, and the search team had already filed out before we finished the show—at about one twenty in the morning! And keep in mind, we'd been on the air since 11:15 P.M. Quite the unbelievable night. Winchell declared the bomb scare a prank pulled by someone who likely disagreed with his politics and wanted to rattle him. Afterward, the crowd came down from their seats and surrounded him—mostly fans, some not fans, but he loved them just the same. All the commotion, all the excitement—things had gotten very, very New York, right there in serene little San Diego.

Finally, when the studio emptied, I thanked him and tried to say good night. Winchell would hear of no such thing. "Where are you going now?" he barked. "Home," I told him. I mean, I was exhausted—to talk to him, to dance with him, to go through a bomb scare with him—I couldn't take much more! But he wanted to go out for a late bite, and he fully expected me to join him. He was twice my age and still ready to go, whereas I was feeling older and older by the minute. It was nearly two in the morning—an hour when things were still hopping during his regular New York rounds. But here in San Diego I was hard-pressed to come up with a place to entertain him. He settled for a Chinese restaurant, where he continued to tell me stories. This guy was all stamina—he even got up to dance a little more soft-shoe!—while I was fading fast. Meanwhile, other late diners in the place came up to us—some for me, some for him, and most because they just couldn't believe that Regis Philbin and Walter Winchell were hanging out together in an all-night Chinese restaurant in San Diego. I couldn't believe it either. I was now beyond worn-out, but I'm pretty sure that he next asked me to cross the street with him to the *Union-Tribune* office where he wanted to bang out one more column. With regret I still feel to this day, I begged off. We shook hands good-bye on the sidewalk sometime around 3 A.M. I recall the way he straightened his hat, turned, and jauntily crossed the street to go find an available typewriter. I went home drained but exhilarated all the same.

The next day I was surprised to receive a note from him. But Marilyn Monroe had just died mysteriously in Los Angeles and he was now headed up there to pounce on one of the biggest celebrity stories of the year, if not of all time. Then another surprise came a week or so later: I got an actual plug in a Winchell column. It was, of course, dazzling to see my name mixed into his parade of legendary three-dot items. My item read like this:

> Att'n network execs on both coasts: His name is Regis
> Philbin. No. One Rating-Getter in Southern Calif. Via Ch.
> 10 (San Diego to Santa Barbara). He is show-biz from head
> to toenails. Plus style, class, dignity. The only late-show
> personality around, we believe, who matches Johnny
> Carson's way with a guest or a coast-to-coast crowd . . .

I couldn't believe it. I'd made the column. So had my toenails, for that matter. All those years of reading Winchell, and now I had turned up under his national byline, with lots of praise on top of it. Privately, though, it also gave me pause. I was proud, of course, but I had trouble believing that I deserved it. Strangely, I was a little embarrassed, too. In the end, that Winchell plug would lead me to the agent Max Arnow, my first syndicated show, and many great adventures to follow. Yes, it was Winchell I alluded to earlier as the celebrity guest who'd gotten the whole ball rolling for me. And it is to him that I owe a huge debt of thanks.

WHAT I TOOK AWAY FROM IT ALL

There will always be something special
and more impressive to me about newspaper
print than about anything I'm likely to
find on the Internet.

Accepting a compliment from a hero—or
from anyone you deeply admire—is harder
than it really ought to be. Just accept it and
don't forget to say thanks, and it's yours for
the rest of your life.

Chapter Six
SYDNEY OMARR

ll right, as you can probably tell by now, my path has intersected with people who not only impressed, delighted, or inspired me—there have also been those who've just plain amazed me. Maybe looming larger than any other in that category was the late remarkable astrologer Sydney Omarr, whose name is still revered in the mysterious realm of reading the stars via charts and birth dates, numerology, and mystical powers. He was a man who would later tell me things that guys like me should never begin to know!

Anyway, as you're well aware, that plug in the Winchell column did not go unnoticed. And flattered as I was, I also sensed that my life was in for some dramatic changes, probably much sooner than later. I mean, the great Winchell himself had suggested so very boldly that I was ready for bigger things than my beloved little Saturday-night talkfest in quiet San Diego. And though, frankly, a part of me didn't want to believe it—not just yet, anyway—next there would actually come a glowing review of our Saturday show in no less than the showbiz bible *Variety*, as written by correspondent Don

Freeman. (Yes, that would be the same Don Freeman who wrote for the *San Diego Union-Tribune* and whom I'd long admired, even if I never did muster up the courage to talk to him when I first had the chance!) So within a span of just months, I found myself headed to Hollywood to take over the nightly show started by the great and inventive Steve Allen. My debut had been set for the second Monday in October 1964. Here at last—because I had yearned for this moment as much as I'd sort of feared it—was the first truly huge break of my career. It would end up being a break that came and went so fast, nobody ever remembers it. But I, of course, would never forget it, as hard as I may have tried over the years.

For sure, nothing about this supposedly exciting new show resembled anything I'd done in San Diego. No, this was the big time, and suddenly I had a full staff (as opposed to relying solely on myself and my director friend Tom Battista, as I had done before). The staff included producers, talent bookers, and production assistants as well as two writers to load me up with monologue jokes. Well, honest to God, I'd never told a joke on camera in my life! I had always just come out, sat on a stool, and shared whatever stories had captured my fancy during the week. Plus, in San Diego we aired live, which meant I could talk about various things that had virtually just happened hours earlier. But now, for some reason, this new show ran on *a two-week tape delay*. (In those days that's how syndicated programs worked.) No joke writer alive could come up with material that would feel topical or fresh under those circumstances. My television career had always been about immediacy—and now I had to operate in a strange time warp.

And if that wasn't bad enough, Westinghouse had only aligned a grand total of thirteen stations around the country to run the show, which meant we never really had a chance to begin with. But none of us knew that at the time.

Well, I take that back.

One person knew.

And he would make it very clear during the first national broadcast of what the decision makers had jazzily titled *That Regis Philbin Show*. In case you haven't guessed, I'm referring to Sydney Omarr. What's really wild about it all is that he appeared at my own request. I thought it would be fun for our debut airing—plus original and kind of risky—to have an astrologer come out and forecast the future of the show. So we booked Sydney, whose syndicated horoscope column was a staple in newspapers from coast to coast. And on opening night, out he came to give me his reading. I'd supplied him with all of my birth data to work with. And now he was sitting next to me— my very first guest on my first national program. I was quite excited at the prospect of what he would predict.

"So tell me, Sydney," I said. "Win or lose, how are we going to do?" Sydney fixed a haunted gaze on me and said, "This show will fail. There's a fight going on right now behind the scenes as to what direction the show should go. It will not become your show. Others will take it from you. You won't make it."

Well, this had to be an all-time first for an opening segment of a brand-new show. I was, to say the least, humbled and disturbed. But in my heart I knew he was probably right. It just wasn't the same kind of show format for me. I'd already more than sensed that the top brass wanted me to be an altogether different personality than the one they'd discovered in San Diego. Sydney was exhorting me—right on the spot—to take control, to make the show mine, but I didn't know how. And furthermore, it wasn't my decision to make. During a commercial break, he asked if he could see me alone after we were done taping—as if what he had already said wasn't painful enough. And that was when he steadily informed me that the next few years would be the worst period of my life. There would be ongoing drastic changes all around me. In fact, he said, the earth would literally move under my feet. What he was telling me was simply incomprehensible.

Nevertheless, we were renewed after our first thirteen weeks, which came as a very happy surprise. And the patience and loyalty of Chet Collier, my executive producer and Westinghouse's key man on the show, were equally uplifting. He'd seen enough of my work in San Diego to believe in my potential. With the renewal, my confidence once again climbed, if not exactly soared. I felt like maybe we did have a chance, after all. The shows were definitely getting better and better. Feeling just a little bit cocky, I even asked for Omarr to come back. I wanted to hear what he thought now. So he returned, and I said to him, "Sydney, much of what you said was true. We did have storms. We did have some terrible times. But now we've been renewed. We're getting better. I see blue sky ahead. What do you see?"

And Sydney looked at me, his expression dark and soulful, and told me, "I hate to be the bearer of bad tidings every time I'm with you, but this show is going off the air within forty-eight hours."

I winced. How could this possibly be true? This time even the great Sydney Omarr had to be wrong. Somehow we got through the rest of the broadcast. Two days later—actually it was thirty-six hours later—I got the call from Chet, whose voice dripped with gloom. "What is it, Chet?" I remember asking. "Did Henry Fonda drop out?" He was slated to be our top guest that night. Instead, Chet asked me to immediately get over to the Beverly Hills Hotel, where the Westinghouse brain trust had all convened. I rushed over there, and in no time flat, they lowered the boom. We'd been canceled. I was out. They wanted to go in "a different direction"—that notorious phrase that spells certain doom in show business—this time with Merv Griffin. And that was that. Omarr had nailed it from the get-go and reconfirmed it just two days earlier. It was a struggle to get through the show that night, knowing we were dead in the water. My friend Tom Battista was in the audience. I didn't have a chance to talk to him before the show, but one look at my face, and he knew immediately it was over for me. That's how it started for Merv and how it almost ended forever for me.

Worse yet, the rest of Sydney Omarr's predictions came true, too. Personally and professionally, I was in the dumper. In those days, new talk shows were few and far between. It wouldn't be easy to get another show during the next few years, and further, there would be one personal crisis after another. My brave son, Dan, was born with complicated congenital anomalies, and my failing marriage to his mother, with whom I'd already had a wonderful daughter named Amy, finally ended. And as for the earth moving under my feet? That happened, too. In February of 1968, it rained for two straight weeks in Los Angeles. Day and night, it was a heavy, unrelenting downpour. It wouldn't let up. I had a home on a hillside overlooking Universal City, and during one of those rainy days, half of the back-yard slid down the canyon. City officials ordered the house evacu-ated, and when I couldn't pay the bills to shore up the property, I lost the house entirely. No, wait a minute, the city of Los Angeles paid one dollar for the house and what was left of the lot. And I took it. Yes, old Sydney had seen it all, a little too clearly, I'm afraid.

But there's one more Sydney Omarr prediction I need to share with you. It happened on the final broadcast of *The Joey Bishop Show* in 1969. Joey had left the show a few weeks earlier, and a vari-ety of people pinch-hit for him as the remaining weeks wound down. I also hosted now and again during those final weeks, which included the very last broadcast we ever did. And for that particular farewell show, guess who I asked to be booked as a guest? Sydney Omarr. I figured, *Why not? What else could happen to me?* As usual, I asked him about the future, then braced myself—out of habit at this point! And Sydney proceeded to stun me once again, but in an altogether new way. He said, "You will become a household name in America. Your name will be known everywhere. You will have great success."

Well, this was more than I had hoped for. Now I really got excited. Sydney Omarr with good news? What could be more of a pleasant shock? Naturally, my next question was "When, Sydney? When?" He proceeded to tell me that it wouldn't happen right away, that it would take some time.

"That's okay," I said. "I can wait. But how long will it take? Six months? A year? Two?" And he looked right into my eyes and said, "It will take twenty years."

"*Twenty years?*" I screamed. Murderers get out of prison faster than that! Twenty years might as well have been forever! Twenty years would never come, I figured.

"That's what I see," said Omarr with certain resolve. But keep this in mind: His two-decade pronouncement was made in December of 1969. In September of 1988, our local New York morning show had just gone national. And although Regis Philbin and Kathie Lee Gifford might not have been household names by 1989, we were well on our way to making that twenty-year prediction come true. Anyway, we were close enough. Omarr, I'm sure, was very proud of himself.

WHAT I TOOK AWAY FROM IT ALL

Astrology isn't for sissies. Those stars do seem to know things we don't—and maybe never should.

Great things can happen much later than you might have hoped. But even then, great things are still great—and always worth appreciating—so don't give up.

Chapter Seven
CARY GRANT

Throughout my fifty years of hosting talk shows, I've been lucky enough to get to know and chat with so many unforgettable show business greats, some of them bigger than big—icons whose work will live on forever. Though I never did get that chance with one of my all-time favorites: Cary Grant.

But it's not like we didn't try.

And by *we*, I'm really referring to a young man named Marshall Lichterman, who came into my life the day I returned to Hollywood in 1964 to host that ill-fated Westinghouse show. Marshall Lichterman was a holdover from Steve Allen's staff. And although he was really just a kid starting out by doing various mundane tasks around the office, he had somehow become a great fan of mine. So on that first day, he asked if there was anything—*anything!*—he could do for me. . . . For instance, was there any particular guest I wanted him to get for the show, never mind that the talent-booking process wasn't even remotely part of his job! But he was so sincere, so earnest, so unbelievably *persuasive* that I couldn't resist. I thought, *Okay, why not give this hungry kid a chance to show me what he's got?*

"Marshall," I said, probably only half seriously, "let's just shoot for the moon. Let's get the one guy who has never done a television interview. Let's get Cary Grant! I love all of his movies, I love him—he's simply the best there is. So, Marshall, I want you to go get him!"

Why, you may wonder, had I instantly thought of Cary Grant as the perfect target? Well, besides having never seen him in an interview situation, he had made an enormous impact on me in one of the first films I ever saw as a kid, *Gunga Din.* A classic among classics, this movie featured Grant as one of three fearless, brawling, hell-raising sergeants in the British Army stationed in India during the nineteenth century. But moreover, it was also the story of a young water carrier for their troops who wanted desperately to be a soldier, too. And Grant and the actor Sam Jaffe, who beautifully portrayed this water carrier named Gunga Din, had a wonderful chemistry together on-screen.

The movie was actually based on an epic poem by Rudyard Kipling. At the film's great climax, Gunga Din saved the British troops when he climbed to the top of a tower and blew a trumpet to warn them of an impending ambush. Of course, in that moment, Gunga Din became the most important soldier of them all. But earlier in the film, we would see that while the troops were going through their afternoon drills at the base, Din would hide behind the barracks to privately simulate answering all the same commands. He wanted to be something more than he was—he wanted to be a soldier, a good one. One afternoon, the sergeant Grant was playing spied Din doing this and began giving him the same set of commands that the troops had been answering during those drills. Din was proud to demonstrate perfectly all the correct moves he had studied. Then finally Grant's character brought him to "attention," and Din snapped off a proper military salute to the sergeant, who complimented him in that crisp cockney accent Grant was so well known for, *"Very regimental, Din, very regimental!"* For many years afterward I would quietly repeat Grant's bolstering line to myself, usually when something I'd done had gone well; it always made me feel better. Anyway, the sergeant then walked away, while Din stiffened even more so and held firm his salute with a triumphant smile, clearly pleased to have impressed this dashing role model. He was, in effect, a soldier at last. Of course, those who know the film's dramatic ending recall that, after trumpeting the warning to save his "fellow" soldiers from attack, Din was shot down off that tower and fell to his death. Before the final credits rolled, a key portion of Kipling's poem was recited:

> Tho' I've belted you an' flayed you,
>
> By the livin' Gawd that made you,
>
> You're a better man than I am, Gunga Din!

Very moving, very touching. I never forgot it.

And that was my earliest introduction to Cary Grant, whose career continued to dazzle me throughout his parade of terrific movies over the decades—*His Girl Friday, The Philadelphia Story, Penny Serenade, Suspicion, Arsenic and Old Lace, My Favorite Wife, Mr. Blandings Builds His Dream House, An Affair to Remember, Indiscreet, North by Northwest*, and so on. I loved them all, but mostly I loved the way he talked, the way he walked, the charm he exuded. Whenever I stepped out of a theater after any Cary Grant movie, I felt just for a moment—as did so many other men—like I too was Cary Grant. And it was always a great feeling—while it lasted, anyway. (As it is, I've always been accused—especially by a certain cohost named Kelly "Pippa" Ripa—of trying to sound just like Cary Grant every time I attempt a British accent. I guess that's how huge an impression he made on me, okay?)

But now I was in Hollywood, about to launch into my biggest

break to date. And here before me was this intent and purposeful kid, Marshall Lichterman, swearing how he would get my new show off to a great start and bring me Cary Grant. It was fate, I thought. Marshall vowed that Cary Grant would be ours! He so eagerly wanted to prove himself to me that, by God, he actually began to remind me of Gunga Din!

The next day he reported that he'd been able to secure Mr. Grant's phone number. And that he called it. And that he in fact had gotten the great movie star on the line! Well, that's when I found myself both shocked and also very excited. And seeing my excitement, Marshall was by now beside himself. He said, "I told Mr. Grant that this was a brand-new TV show and Mr. Philbin is the new host and his very first request was for an appearance by Cary Grant." First of all, I couldn't believe this young kid was able to get Cary Grant on the phone, much less actually talk to him. But somehow it happened. Unfortunately, he wasn't able to get Grant to commit to the interview. Though Marshall did say that they had a nice talk and that Mr. Grant was very charming. Well, I could see the handwriting on the wall, so I said, "Nice try, Marshall, but I think we should move on to someone else."

But Marshall didn't want to hear that. He would not give up. He needed to show me, to totally impress me! *Hello, Gunga Din!* So apparently he called Cary Grant the next day and practically every day for the next two weeks—and Grant was always charming but remained noncommittal. Of course, I didn't realize that Marshall's pursuit of Cary Grant had continued for as long as it did. When I found out, I was totally embarrassed. Even mortified. "You simply cannot call Cary Grant ever again!" I told him. "You must cease and desist!"

But even after my little tirade, I couldn't help myself: I simply had to ask Marshall, "Just between us, what did he sound like? What did he say during all those calls? Did he ever get annoyed that you kept after him so relentlessly?"

"No," Marshall said. "He never got angry. He always remained charming and patient but firm. And over and over again, he would explain that he just never gave interviews because he feared he would be a terrible guest. He would say, 'Now, please, Marshall, please—explain that to Mr. Philbin and tell him that I wish him the very best for his new show and the rest of his career.'"

And so ended our adventures in trying to get Cary Grant as a guest. I forbid Marshall to ever call him again and told him that if he did, he would lose his job. But Cary Grant has stayed an important part of my life; practically every day I still check to see if any of his movies might be airing on TCM—and if one is, I try to stay home and watch it. Because nothing else will be better on television that night. Of that I am absolutely sure. But let me add just one more thing. I don't care what he said—Cary Grant would have simply been a terrific guest on any TV talk show. Anywhere, anytime.

WHAT I TOOK AWAY FROM IT ALL

All men should study the charm of Cary Grant in the movies whenever possible. You may not become Grant, but you'll be inspired to be a better man.

No really does mean no, especially if the same person keeps telling you so every single day for weeks on end.

Chapter Eight

JACK PAAR

H ow I got to be the way I am—especially in front of television cameras—is mostly due to the inspiration I took from one special man. I've never made a secret of that fact. But in truth, nobody could ever do things the way he did them. It was my mother who first called my attention to Jack Paar. She wrote me a letter while I was in the navy mentioning how impressed she was with his chatty style and personality—and keep in mind, this was well before he became the original king of late night on NBC-TV's *Tonight Show*. Back then, in the early fifties, she'd only seen Jack host *The Morning Show* for the CBS network out of New York, where he worked with a battery of news correspondents and always kept things lively throughout. Before getting her letter, I'd barely heard of him, but now I was very curious. Then, soon enough, our squadron was ported in San Diego, and the TV happened to be turned on in our LSM wardroom, where the commodore was holding his standard meeting. Somehow, maybe out of a little boredom, my gaze drifted toward that TV screen, and there was the show my mother had told me about. The one with Jack

Paar. And I could see that my sainted mother was right again. Paar was a natural. You couldn't take your eyes off him. (For the record, my mother had always been pretty good at spotting talent before they made it big: About a decade earlier, for instance, she heard a sixteen-year-old Brooklyn kid named Vic Damone singing over the radio on *The Carnation Hour*. Right on the spot, she announced he would become a musical sensation—and, of course, he did.)

Anyway, when I came back to San Diego in the late fifties—this time working as a young broadcaster reporting the news—I saw Jack Paar again, but now as host of *The Tonight Show*. And again I was knocked out by him: same spontaneity, same charm, and the same engaging interviewing skills I'd seen earlier. But what impressed me most was his opening monologue. Every night at eleven fifteen he would come out, sometimes sit on the edge of his desk, and just talk into the camera—directly to those of us watching at home. He created an intimacy with viewers like nobody I'd seen before. His openings were never simply a compilation of jokes (although I later learned that he did keep a stable of writers on staff). Instead, he was just telling his audience stories about where he had been that day, who he had met, what fun or crazy mishap he had along the way. To me, he was beyond different and always fascinating. Even though I was just getting my feet wet on the TV news side of things, I'd still been wondering what my future would hold in this business. And then I saw Paar, who made whatever he did on camera seem so personal, so unpredictable, so funny, and mainly so very real. It was marvelous. It was what I wanted to do, and he showed me how. Because in my heart, I somehow felt that I had the ability to do that, too. So with Jack's influence planted firmly in mind—and once I got my own Saturday-night talk show in October 1961 on San Diego's KOGO-TV—I was determined to open every one of those live broadcasts in exactly the same way. I told stories of what had happened in my life during the week, all very similar to the kind of stuff Jack was doing nationally night after night. And happily enough, it came across pretty smoothly for me—so much so that for the next fifty years I've never stopped doing it that way. That is, except for those few detours I made after moving on from San Diego, the most well known of which was my run as second banana/sidekick on ABC's *The Joey Bishop Show* in Hollywood. But even then, part of my job was to banter with Joey about things going on in daily life—although it was mostly Joey's daily life that we were focusing on. It was, after all, *his* show.

Joey, along with everyone else who ever tried, had his struggles competing against Johnny Carson's *Tonight Show,* which was still based out of New York and then as always the dominant force in late night. Carson, of course, had taken over as host once Jack Paar had decided, after not quite five years at that job, to escape the nonstop rigamarole of making nightly television. Starting in late 1962, he opted to scale back and simply limit himself to hosting a popular Friday-night prime-time interview show—which he also later chose to give up, this time after three years. But even then, and for the rest of his post–*Tonight Show* life, he had mainly shunned all requests to be a guest on anyone else's talk show.

But that was all about to change, if only for one unforgettable night. Turned out, not long after we started the Bishop show in the spring of 1967, we got word that Jack had come to Los Angeles to visit friends. Immediately, Joey knew it would be a coup—and would also help make a sizable dent in Johnny's great ratings—to coax Jack into coming on as his guest. He already knew Jack slightly, having gone on Paar's old show a couple times. So on the night that we'd heard Jack had come to town, Joey went to the Beverly Hills Hotel where Jack was staying. And unannounced, knocked on Jack's door, got inside, and pleaded his case. He needed a big boost for our show, and Jack would be it, absolutely. No one had seen him on television for a couple of years, and Joey wouldn't leave until Jack agreed—which to everyone's amazement he did. And to raise the stakes further, we even scheduled Jack's appearance for what turned out to be the very same night that Carson would come back to *The Tonight Show* after a nearly monthlong standoff with his NBC bosses over contract issues; Johnny went so far as to declare that he was done forever with the show, then disappeared from the air, a bold move that commanded headlines for all those weeks. NBC finally gave in to Johnny's demands, but Joey knew that having Jack as his special guest would steal some significant spotlight away from Carson's eagerly awaited return. This, by the way, was what TV people would call "counterprogramming" to the extreme!

Well, when I heard that Jack Paar was booked on our show, I was simply thrilled. I would finally meet this guy who had changed my life, who had shown me how to do it, who inspired me. I couldn't wait to shake his hand and to thank him for what his work and his style had meant to me. The booking was already getting a lot of press. The ratings were bound to be much bigger than usual. But that day Joey's producer, Paul Orr, who years earlier had also been Jack's producer, approached me and said, kind of tentatively, "You know, Joey and Jack are both very nervous about this." Then he added, "I think they would probably feel more at ease if you didn't sit with them on the couch, if you'd just let them go at it one-on-one tonight." I couldn't believe it. All those years, and now I still wouldn't have my chance to thank Jack Paar. That's all I'd wanted to do. Not even on the air, heaven forbid, but during a commercial break, when no one but the two of us would know. I told Paul Orr what Paar meant to me, but he assured me not to worry. "I promise you," he said, "when the show is over I'll make sure you meet him."

So the show went on, with me kind of awkwardly stationed on

the sidelines and well away from the two of them. And yes, they clearly *were* nervous. Both were actually a little hesitant with each other during the interview. And as soon as the show was over—guess what?—Jack got up, rushed to the nearest exit, and was gone into the night! Joey, meanwhile, disappeared directly into his dressing room, probably because it hadn't exactly turned out the way he'd hoped. And that was that. It took me a while to get over it.

To be honest, I never did entirely get over it . . . until at long last I was finally given a second chance to meet Jack. And when I say "at long last," I'm talking about *nearly two decades later*! It happened just a few years after I returned to New York to start a morning talk show that I hoped would lead to national syndication. During those interim years I held many assorted jobs—one of which brought me to Chicago in the summer of 1974 to take over the local morning show on ABC's WLS-TV after its host, Bob Kennedy, suddenly passed away. The producer on that show was a smart, funny young guy named Rick Ludwin, who would eventually become the top executive at NBC for all prime-time specials and late-night programming, among other duties. Anyway, in 1986 Rick called to tell me that NBC was preparing a nostalgic special titled *Jack Paar Comes Home*, to be taped in New York. It would feature Jack presiding over a parade of clips from some of his greatest interview moments. Rick remembered what a fan of Paar's I had always been and asked if I'd like to be part of the studio audience for the taping. My answer, naturally: "Absolutely! I'd love nothing more!"

How great it would be just to see Jack in person again! I was seated about ten rows up, right on the aisle, and directly behind a blond lady who at one point turned and gave me a warm smile like she knew me. I smiled back, but I was sure we'd never met. Then the show started: Jack came out, as charming and spontaneous as always. Now in his early sixties, everything about him looked and felt ageless. There, right onstage in front of me, I could see all of his famous little mannerisms that I'd enjoyed since I first watched him so long ago—plus his electric warmth when telling hilarious "inside" stories and setting up clips of his best exchanges with all those great guests: *"Wait till you see me here with Richard Burton!"* It was wonderful television, all the more special because we were reliving Jack's work right along with him.

Of course, being in his presence also brought back memories of that night on the Bishop show when I never did get to shake his hand. And frankly, it didn't look like it would happen on this night either. But at the end of the show, with the band playing his rousing theme song, "Everything's Coming Up Roses," and the crowd applauding wildly, he began to walk up the steps into the audience—*shaking hands with people on the aisle seats! My God*, I thought, *he's heading right toward me.* Here was my chance! I was terribly excited, but also afraid he might stop after only a few steps up and then turn around to make his exit. But he didn't. He just kept coming! *What luck to have this seat*, I realized. And then suddenly he stopped right at the row in front of me. He bent over and kissed the blond lady, gallantly helping her up from her chair, and together they walked down the steps and out the door. That blond woman was, of course, his beloved wife, Miriam. And while I was happy to see them share his moment of postshow triumph—*it had happened again!* I had come so close . . . but once more, no cigar. I mean, *I swear*—all I wanted to do was just tell him thanks!

For days afterward, I couldn't hide my disappointment. At that point, our program was called *The Morning Show* (just like Jack's was at CBS, in fact, when my mother first spotted him). My producer, Steve Ober, plainly saw my agony over this latest runaway Paar incident and, about a year later, also saw his chance to surprise me. Jack had made yet another retrospective NBC special that was about to air, so one day Steve very quietly booked Jack on the show, partly to plug the special but mostly to finally give me the thrill I'd waited for so long. It was all a big hushed-up secret when, without any warning, Jack simply walked out onto our set. I was completely floored. Jack took the stool next to mine and—as our own studio audience gave him a long huge ovation—I could see he was very excited about being there. But also a bit nervous, which, let's face it, was always part of his charm anyway. Main thing: there we were, Jack and Regis—*together at last!* I was so stunned that I can barely remember our conversation, except that it happened.

On that particular morning, the studio had an overflow of audience members, so we accommodated them by moving some extra rows of seats up to within a few feet of the stage. I remember this because, within seconds, Jack immediately began playing to a group of women sitting to his right. And I was sitting to his left! He barely ever looked at me! I do recall having had a tough time getting his attention. But he did get big laughs—especially with those women to his right. And in a few moments after the segment ended, he was gone again.

But now I was in New York, and Jack was up in Greenwich, Connecticut, just forty minutes away, so fate had bound a real connection to finally occur. Sure enough, a couple of years later, Kathie Lee Gifford, my cohost at the time, was dining at 21, one of New York's top restaurants, with her husband, Frank, and there at a nearby table were Jack and Miriam. They chatted for a little while and the Paars were quite effusive about our show; I guess he probably also remembered his surprise guest appearance with us not long before we went national. Kathie Lee reminded him of how much I admired him. Also, right around the same time, I happened to be talking about Paar with Dave Letterman one night. He said that he knew Jack only a bit; Paar had guested on Dave's old NBC *Late Night* program and they'd communicated on and off. But then Dave just laid it out in front of me: "Why not call him and take him to lunch?"

So that's what I did. Joy and I met the Paars for lunch, and it was wonderful. I would prompt him, and all of those great old stories would just pour out of him. I loved it; it was simply the beginning of a treasured friendship. Soon after, Jack invited us to one of his lively dinner parties at his Greenwich home. And there, I finally managed to corner him for a moment, just the two of us, and privately tell him what he'd meant to me. He heard me, but I could see that he had a hard time taking compliments. But what parties he and Miriam threw! Always full of great names and old friends, so many of them now gone, like comic pianist Victor Borge, and the legendary show-biz caricaturist Al Hirschfeld. Guests were usually split between two separate tables, with Jack presiding at the head of his table as only he could. Famously, he loved to lean in and say to anyone near him: "Tell me something that would interest me." What a challenge! Usually it produced plenty of laughs. But if he'd hear too many laughs coming from the other table, he'd be up like a shot and over to find out who was getting the laughs and why. "What? What?" he'd ask breathlessly. But that was Jack: He hated to miss out on anything.

For the most part, though, he had been living a rather quiet life up there in Connecticut. He dabbled a lot in painting and was quite good at it. Also, every day he would drive into Greenwich to pick out a movie at the video store, and then he and Miriam would watch it during their lunch. We got to know them better and better after Joy and I bought a weekend home in Greenwich as well, not too far from their place. And yes, throughout those years, I could never resist reminding Jack of what he meant to me. But just like that first time I cornered him, it seemed that Jack didn't want to hear it, that it sort of embarrassed him. And yet he was always so complimentary and encouraging about our show. He couldn't get over the fact that we cohosts—whether with Kathie Lee or later with Kelly—never even spoke to each other before the broadcasts, that there was no rehearsing at all, no quick meetings about topics to discuss, that we'd just go out and make it happen live on camera. Of all the people in the world, with maybe the greatest spontaneous mind in television history, *he* couldn't understand how we did it! Coming from him, as you could imagine, I would never know a greater compliment. Ever.

Sometime along the way, during a New Year's Day party at our home, I introduced him to my pal the actor-turned-commentator-host Chuck Grodin, and the two became fast friends. We all would go to the best restaurants in Connecticut and always it was great fun. Jack had never stopped being a superb conversationalist. And there had grown such a great bond between us. Sometimes I couldn't believe this was the guy I'd had so much trouble meeting.

But later, strange and difficult things began to happen to Jack. One day Miriam went into the garage and encountered a snake. She screamed and yelled, *"Snake!"* and Jack grabbed his gun. Well, it wasn't a real gun, but it was one of those things that makes a real loud *bang* to scare off deer. Jack was hoping the snake would react to it like a deer. Well, the snake beat it out of that garage, but the bang cost Jack his hearing in his left ear. Then things turned more serious. Jack had a stroke. It left him unable to speak. It was a tough time, but he could still see you, could still hear you in his good ear, and could still smile at a good joke. So we all tried to amuse Jack and get him through this terrible ordeal. The last time I saw Jack was Christmas Eve 2003. Our Christmas show had been pretaped for that day, so I was already in Greenwich that morning. Joy and I were spending our family holiday in Connecticut, and I'd decided to drive over and wish him an early Merry Christmas. I got there around eleven o'clock, and it was cold and dreary and pouring rain. His nurse answered the doorbell. She said, "Regis, I didn't know you were coming." I told her that I'd arranged it with Mrs. Paar. She said, "Come on in! Jack and I were looking at the show this morning and he was laughing." I said, "Did you really hear him laugh?" She said, "Oh yes, he laughed!"

She led me to the living room, where he seemed to be in good spirits. He still couldn't talk, but he was a great listener. He loved hearing all the stories, all the gossip I could think up. But the problem was how to keep talking, which is a little difficult when the other person is unable to answer and join in. Nevertheless, I plowed ahead and gave it my best, until I had nothing more to say. And then we sat there, looking at each other, listening to the rain, and I began to feel very, very sad. Here was this sophisticated first-class man, one of television's most legendary talkers, who loved nothing more than to engage in conversation. Suddenly that had all been taken away from him. It made me angry as I sat there with him. It wasn't fair. That's what had always kept him going, and now I sensed it was almost over. I finally got up, walked over to him, kissed his cheek, told him I loved him and wished him a Merry Christmas, and then I left. Jack Paar died not too long after that. To this day, I just miss him more and more. I realize how unique and very special he was, and I'm so glad I had the chance to finally say, "Thanks, Jack. You changed my life."

WHAT I TOOK AWAY FROM IT ALL

Emulating the style of someone you deeply admire is a natural instinct. It helps free you to find your own style along the way.

Never stop saying thank you to the people who've made the biggest differences in your life. No matter how much it embarrasses them.

Chapter Nine

BILL COSBY

During the early sixties, it seemed that every time you looked up, a terrific new future star was emerging— somebody bright and original and just beginning to blaze across the culture of our business. Which brings me back so clearly to this story that started one particular Friday night during that long-ago era: I was the anchorman at San Diego's KOGO-TV in those days, and in that last hour prior to airtime, I had been busily preparing for our eleven o'clock newscast. That's when I actually happened to *look up*—just at the right moment—at the office television set, which was tuned to one of my favorite shows, the NBC Friday-night prime-time *Jack Paar Program*, the weekly version Jack had started shortly after leaving the grind of his *Tonight Show* hosting job. It was then, quite accidentally, that I got my first look at the latest comedy sensation suddenly on the rise. There in New York, Jack was in the midst of announcing this brand-new name. He explained how funny and special this guy was and correctly predicted that he would go on to become a major star. And then he introduced the tall and youthful Bill Cosby. I had never seen him, but I had to stop and ask myself, *Bill Cosby—why do I know that name?* Then I remembered, in fact, that I had just booked him some-time within the last few days to be my guest on the following week's Saturday-night interview show I hosted for the station.

I couldn't have been more thrilled that one of Jack's guests would be mine as well—*only a week later*—on my own local show.

And so Cosby came to San Diego and we met for the first time, forming an immediate bond that became a friendship we've main-tained for all these years. (In fact, we happen to share the same personal booking agent, the irrepressible Kenny DiCamillo, who regularly tells me that the Cos always asks how I'm handling the fortunes, good or bad, of my beloved Notre Dame teams.) But back then he had been working in the nightclubs of New York and L.A., and was now appearing with the Kingston Trio at some San Diego hot spot. The wiry Cosby I met must have been in his mid-twenties. He was a well-dressed, great-looking young guy who had a loose-limbed athletic gait and a big open smile on his face. I would learn that he'd served in the navy and then went on to Temple University in his hometown of Philadelphia where he became a track star and also played defensive back on the Temple football team. But he pos-sessed a brilliant gift for comic storytelling, which would serve him so successfully throughout the rest of his long and important career. My show, it turned out, would only be Cosby's second television ap-pearance, but he was made for the medium. He climbed onto the stool next to me that night and we got to know each other with lots of laughs flowing.

But maybe I should point out that many of those laughs had sprung from an idea that occurred to him while he was backstage in our little greenroom waiting to come out. You see, another guest that night was a master hypnotist named Dr. Michael Dean, whose own popular nightly stage show had been the talk of San Diego. And so Bill—who's always had a great eye for anything that he could turn to comic gold—saw his chance to have some fun by briefly mentioning that he'd just been trapped for a while in our greenroom with an accomplished hypnotist. But to drive home this point, he came out and *repeatedly kept falling asleep during our interview!* I'd ask him a question and he'd begin to answer, then suddenly just slump down on his stool and pretend to fall into a trance. It was great fun, with Cosby allegedly passing out throughout the course of our chat. All these years later, however, I do sometimes ask myself: Had the hypnotist really cast a spell on him backstage? Did I bore him to death on the show? Or did he just fake falling asleep that night in order to get all those laughs? Whatever it was—and let's bet on its having been brilliant ad-libbing—it made for an unforgettable appearance, and was enough to prompt anyone who saw our little talk show that night to remember the name Bill Cosby. Over time, however, that was going to be inevitable anyway.

But here's something also worth remembering: Those were rather tense and racially divisive years in this country, yet Cosby never touched the subject in his routines. His onstage persona had nothing to do with skin color. His objective was to entertain, to be funny, to make you laugh no matter what your racial heritage. He gently forced his audience to connect only with his warmth, his playful personality, and his indisputable talent. He always wrote his own stuff—personal childhood yarns or great reimaginings of so many things we all took for granted. His wonderfully detailed and hilarious version of the old Noah's Ark biblical story, for instance, was the centerpiece of a comedy album that became a runaway national sensation. His voice, his inflections, and his nuanced material could make the whole family laugh together—and families did, everywhere. Subsequently, color barriers dissolved a little bit more every time this happened.

And then, of course, Hollywood took special notice. NBC signed him to do a caper show called *I Spy*, which featured two guys—one black, one white, both equal partners—working together to solve cases. They struck gold with the fun chemistry between the wily Cosby and the dashing actor Robert Culp. I believe it was Bill's first real acting job and he was terrific. But for the TV business, it had been a bold move—practically unheard-of in those years—this simple pairing of what could be considered impossibly diverse costars on a major prime-time program. I thought Cosby did more for race relations with that show than anyone else could have attempted in any medium. But later on, he made even more important strides in this area.

In 1984 he debuted *The Cosby Show,* a remarkably popular NBC sitcom focusing on an upper-middle-class African-American family—a successful doctor and wife raising five kids in bustling New York City. The Huxtable family, as they were called, had the same problems as everyone else, trying to instill key values in their kids and find day-to-day happiness in a complicated world. Oddly enough, even in the mid-eighties, this represented groundbreaking television—the depiction of an upscale black family was an altogether new concept for viewers. But week after week, year after year, it ranked as the number one, most-watched show in the Nielsen ratings. Never heavy-handed about matters of race, it provided more insight to viewers, who might've been less-than-enlightened people, than almost all of the equality lectures in history could have ever done. Cosby was setting an example and still getting giant laughs—always in a smart, wholesome way that makes most of our current sitcom crop look trashy by comparison.

So at the earliest height of all the racial yelling and screaming in this country—and then in the decades to follow—Cosby was always doing things his way. He didn't have to tell you he was a black man—he showed you what kind of a man he was with a great, relatable style. On *The Cosby Show,* he was doing his job—as both a comedian and an actor—by playing a loving husband and a wise father.

And during the eight seasons the series ran, he showed us all how it should be done. All the people watching couldn't help but say to themselves, maybe in a totally new way, "Hey, that family is just like mine." That, I think, was Bill Cosby's message to the country, and it couldn't have come at a better time.

So it's understandable that through the years, Bill Cosby became an icon in this country at an age earlier than most. He still goes out there onstage and sits in an easy chair and entertains the audience just like he always has. And he still works clean as a whistle. That's another thing I like about him. Over the years many comedians have succumbed to constantly using the old f-word in their routines. Only a few have chosen not to use it at all: Cosby, Rickles, and Seinfeld don't, and that's because they don't need to. But of course, the f-word is everywhere in our society—movies, Broadway stages, songs, and practically everywhere else you go. In comedy, it's become such a crutch for so many stand-up performers; the reason why is that they *know* the audience will laugh, for sure, when that f-bomb drops. At first it was a shock for people to hear it from any professional entertainer. Now, it seems, the public has almost been trained to respond to it. For example, the other night at a stage play, I heard a character use it to describe a girl's date: "He had a face like a f— fish." The audience screamed. The same line, minus the f-word, would have been simply: He had a face like a fish. Descriptive. But no laughs. The truth is that it's the easy way out. But it's so sad, isn't it?

I say these things because you should know that nobody feels more strongly about the topic than Bill Cosby. (The scolding calls he used to make to steer young Eddie Murphy away from blue language are now legend.) Anyway, it's been almost fifty years since that night in San Diego, and he's been my guest many more times since then—but during one appearance on the morning show just a couple of years ago, we started reminiscing about that first show back in the sixties, and damned if he didn't doze off again! Of course he was just kidding—*I think*—and said he still blames that hypnotist for the whole thing. But I know better. It's Bill Cosby getting his laughs—a sound he may know better than just about anyone else alive. You've gotta love him and also thank him for all he's done to cause the best kind of color blindness in our world. But really, I doubt we'll ever be able to thank him enough for that.

WHAT I TOOK AWAY FROM IT ALL

A cheerful, relatable voice in the face of social turmoil will help dissolve that turmoil much more effectively than a strident, angry voice.

There is no f-word more powerful than *funny*.

Chapter Ten

JOEY BISHOP

I'll admit it right off the bat: taking this particular job went against my every gut instinct at the time. But working as the sidekick announcer on ABC-TV's new late-night entry, *The Joey Bishop Show*, would turn out to be both a true revelation and quite an education for me—in more ways than I can probably count. And most importantly, I was about to find out at last—in no uncertain terms—what my true talent was. Yes, that cursed question that I could never quite answer—the one that especially tortured me in those weeks before I replaced Steve Allen on my short-lived Westinghouse show—still plagued me. As it happened, the Bishop offer came out of the blue during a time when I was down in the dumps. By then, I was barely getting by, doing only a local once-a-week nighttime interview show on Channel 11 in Los Angeles. But believe me, I was plenty thankful I had that.

I knew that Bishop, in the many months before his show debuted in the spring of 1967, was looking to hire a sidekick announcer, someone to play the role of Ed McMahon to his Johnny Carson. But I never once thought about it as a career opportunity for me. So I kept focused on my Channel 11 show, where one night I had scored a coup by having as my guest the hottest, toughest, most controversial radio guy ever (in those days, anyway): Joe Pyne. He was an ex-marine who got around on one leg, with only the support of a cane. So tough was he that he was rumored to gargle with razor blades. The only reason I'd gotten him as a guest was that he was very interested in meeting a faith healer who'd been on my show a few weeks earlier. The faith healer, who worked his miracle cures somewhere deep in the Philippine jungles, had stirred quite a following of ailing Americans; apparently, they'd flock in droves to this remote location where the healer would preside before a roaring fire and cure all their ills. Well, I didn't know it at the time, but Joe Pyne happened to be in the throes of battling cancer. He had seen the interview and reached out to us, asking how he could find this strange miracle man.

My producer made a deal with Joe: We'd personally set him up with the healer if he'd come be a guest on our show. Now Joe Pyne *never* did an interview on any show. Most people were afraid of him. I mean, *truly afraid.* But I was intrigued with the possibility. So we sent Pyne off on his venture to the Philippines, with the promise of his spending an hour on my show to talk about it when he returned. And true to his word, he did just that and came on the show brimming with a fire all his own. He recounted how he had flown all the way to Manila, was met by the guides we'd arranged for him, journeyed deep into the jungle to the secret spot where the cure-all bonfire raged, and saw all these hopeful tourists gathered round it, singing and praying through the night with the healer. Joe was at once totally turned off, thought it was all nonsense, and left the scene without ever trying to connect with the man.

I said, "Joe, you went all the way deep into that jungle, saw the guy, and never approached him?"

"That's right," Joe said. "He's a phony, a fake, should be

arrested. . . ." And so on. But since we'd opened our conversation with this topic—which he'd instantly shot to pieces—there was now another fifty minutes of airtime we had to fill. I figured as long as I had him, I'd dig deep into his life, his experiences in the Marine Corps, and his explosive career in radio. He was terrific—we had one of those great interviews where you know you've gotten more than you'd ever hoped for—and I left the station feeling pretty good that night.

Next day, my agent called and said, "Joey Bishop saw your show last night. Apparently he liked it a lot. He'd like to see you as soon as possible—like this afternoon." I was pleasantly shocked, but also had never quite stopped reeling from that whole Westinghouse experience, and I was still feeling quite angry at myself for having made the wrong career decision by taking that job. I wasn't looking for further disappointment. So I said, "No, forget it. Tell them thanks, but no thanks. I don't want to go through that again."

Reluctantly, he asked, "Are you sure?"

"Yes, I'm positive."

And I hung up. Then, of course, came the afterthought: *Wait a minute. There's only one other late-night show on TV . . . Johnny Carson. So why not Joey Bishop?* I had seen Joey pinch-hit for Johnny several times on *The Tonight Show* and he was always pretty good. ABC was ready to get into the late-night business and saw Joey as their best bet. Now he was searching for the right sidekick, ideally somebody whose energy would balance Joey's low-key but rather biting persona. The fact that he had seen and liked what I did with Pyne the night before was flattering in itself. Plus, I thought, he's a bona fide member of the legendary Rat Pack: the official court jester to Sinatra, Dean, and Sammy! It was Joey who had created so much of the Pack's onstage patter and long-standing routines during their heyday. I heard my mind thumping: *What's wrong with you? Are you actually turning him down before you even meet him?* And as for sidekicking, I realized that so many wonderful opportunities had happened for Hugh Downs and Ed McMahon, even while they worked as *Tonight Show* second bananas. Also, what about all that national exposure on network TV! All these things raced through my mind as I lunged for my phone again to try to catch my agent, hoping against hope that he hadn't already turned down the job. His line was busy. *Oh my God, he could be making the call right now.* I waited a few seconds and tried again. Still busy. I began beating myself up: *What, am I crazy passing this opportunity by? What else is there for me that's bigger than this?* Again, feeling the regret building, I thought, *Well, I've done it again—yet another wrong decision!* I dialed once more. This time I got through. I instantly yelled into the receiver, "Tell Joey's people I'll be there this afternoon!" And then I held my breath and prayed for him to say that he hadn't called them yet. He assured me that he hadn't, and I was on my way.

I got there right on time. Bishop was seated at a desk in his office inside the Beverly Hills headquarters of the William Morris Agency. He was dressed casually, wearing an orange sweater and his inimitable hangdog expression. But he was very complimentary when I walked in. "I saw your show last night. You've got a lot of talent."

When he said that, I couldn't help but recall how the question of my talent had haunted and hurt me over the years—and how humiliated I was to always have some halfhearted response: "I don't know . . . I'm not sure."

And then I thought, here was none other than Joey Bishop, a very savvy guy who'd been around this business for a long time—and he'd just told me that I had talent. I got excited. I wanted to hear exactly what he thought it was. So I got up from my chair and said, "Really? What *is* my talent, Joey?" I sank back down in my chair as he stood up and looked at me for a long time. Clearly, he wasn't expecting that question, but realized that he had to answer it. This was almost ironic: Here I was, applying for a job on his show, and suddenly I'd put *him* on the defensive. He stood there before his first-floor window at the old William Morris office on that November afternoon. I remember seeing a tree outside that window, its branches blowing in the California breeze. The longer he took to formulate his answer, the more I just stared at that tree, hoping it might ease his pressure.

Finally, he turned to me and announced, "I'll tell you what your talent is." I couldn't wait to hear it. "*You*," he said, definitively. "*You . . . are a great listener.*" Ohhhhhhhh . . . a great listener—that was my talent! I don't know what I was expecting. But that was it? I guess I was hoping for more than just learning that I had the ability to hear and absorb whatever someone else was saying to me. But I accepted it. And later I would come to understand what he meant—about how important it is to stay present in the moment and be aware of the nuances of every conversation, especially while on TV. I suppose I mumbled some kind of thank-you. And we continued. He remained very cordial and kind and finally told me straight out, "I like you."

Then he asked me to go get a cup of coffee at the drugstore around the corner at the Beverly Wilshire Hotel and come back in an hour. I did as he suggested, turning over in my head exactly what all of this might mean for me—and still wondering if it was really the right kind of fit. When I returned to his office, I found a different Joey than the one I'd left an hour earlier. Now he was surrounded by his manager, Ed Hookstratten, his agent, Norman Brokaw, and his brother and assistant, Mel Bishop—all of whom were silent and not especially friendly. Immediately, I grasped what had happened. These guys were trying to warn Joey against hiring me. There must have been some yelling in the interim; Joey's face was beet red. Clearly they'd been telling him that I was wrong for the show. That I was a talk-show host, not an announcer. That I would probably try to steal the spotlight away from him by injecting myself into conversations he'd be conducting with his guests. That I would probably throw him off track, that it could be a disaster with Regis—and that's exactly what Joey told me, while working himself up into a near frenzy.

"How do I know this is not going to happen?" he screamed at me. "How do I know you'll be able to sit there on that couch, night after night, without trying to butt in, and just keep your mouth shut?"

I rose to my feet, suddenly full of quiet confidence, and said, "I'll tell you how you'll know . . . *because I am a great listener."* I thought this echo of his earlier compliment would get a laugh. But there was nothing. He stared at me with no indication that he even remembered saying it. I thought, *Well, that's that.* I then simply wished him good luck and walked out the door. A few days later I received a call telling me I'd gotten the job.

That's how it started with Joey, and before I knew it, there I was night after night meeting all the stars I'd seen on-screen and read about in the papers. From John Wayne and Kirk Douglas to comedians such as Danny Thomas and Jack Carter and all the guys in between—and even some of Joey's Rat Pack pals like Dean and Sammy. But not Frank—never Frank. That was a topic of great speculation backstage. *Why not Frank?* Joey never brought it up, but whatever the reason might've been, it was obviously a sore subject. Sinatra, after all, had done *The Tonight Show* a few times when Joey would pinch-hit for Carson—but not *The Joey Bishop Show.*

Anyway, for me, it actually was a wonderful job. I didn't have to worry about prepping for the interviews. Once in a while I could sneak in an ad-lib, which sometimes got a big laugh—and also a withering look from Joey. So—guess what?—I didn't do that too often. But it was the late sixties and Hollywood was still classic Hollywood. Most of those great stars were older than me—the ones I'd been watching all my life. I mean, suddenly there was Jimmy Durante himself, right in front of me, banging away at the piano, throwing his song sheets across the stage while pleading with Bill Bailey to come home. But it was more than a starry playground for me; it was a chance to meet and befriend some of these legends who would later be guests on my own shows. There, for instance, was Joan Crawford, who'd had a few drinks before coming out on-stage, talking about the old days with Clark Gable—she called him King the whole time. And I'll never forget one incident with Buddy Hackett, who was among Joey's best friends. Joey had urged Buddy to tell one of his long trademark shaggy-dog story jokes, and reluctantly, Hackett went into it. It required an extended buildup before he would get to his big payoff punch line. And finally, when Buddy had hit that moment just before coming in with the killer line, I saw Joey reach from under the desk and squeeze Buddy's leg. Hackett stopped talking and looked at Joey, who then delivered the payoff line himself and got a tremendous laugh, then quickly threw to a commercial break. Hackett was furious. They almost came to blows, but it was a lesson to me about just how competitive comedians can be, regardless of their love for each other.

Then there was the night Barbra Streisand agreed to come on the show. Well, not really *on the show.* Joey, as it turned out, would have to go up to Hollywood Boulevard and the Egyptian Theatre to interview her on the red carpet before the premiere of her very first film, *Funny Girl.* Streisand had made a Broadway sensation of the musical before doing the movie version, and already she was considered the newest, hottest star in Hollywood. Even back then, however, she had been gaining a reputation for being somewhat difficult to deal with. Joey resented the whole idea of having to go over there to do the interview before our own show started taping. For some reason, I was invited to come along—but he was plainly annoyed throughout. Of course, no one knew how big a star Streisand would become. Nevertheless, we fought our way through the crowds on

Hollywood Boulevard and met her on the red carpet. The cameras were all set up. There were confused discussions about who would stand where for the interview. The fuss made no one happy. Finally we lined up with Joey in the middle, me flanking him on one side, and Barbra positioned on his other side. Just before the cameras rolled, Barbra exclaimed, "Wait, you weren't listening to me! This is not my good side. I want to be on the left." And Joey said, "But the left side is my best side." There was a silent standoff. They each had their own battery of producers and handlers on the scene, and now everybody froze. I should have kept my mouth shut, but I couldn't resist. Somebody had to break this tension! So I shouted out, *"But what about me? I want the left side, too."* The crowd around us laughed, but there were no laughs from our two stars. Not even a smile. I'm sorry, but I still think it was a funny line.

I should point out that even though maneuvering a couple of blocks over to that theater for the Streisand interview didn't please Joey, he and I were no strangers to strolling the streets of Hollywood together. Joey, as no doubt you've figured out by now, was a complex guy, forever interesting to be around, but he also had a pretty hot temper—which, quite frankly, was nearly ready to blow at any given moment. Keeping him loose became an ongoing priority. On the afternoon before our very first show, in fact, our producer, Paul Orr, came to me and said, "Joey's restless. Why don't you take him outside and go for a walk?" So I popped into Joey's office and very offhandedly said, "Joey, why don't we go for a walk today?" He just glared at me. "What?" he barked. "I've got a lot of things on my mind! I can't be worrying about taking a walk! Forget it!" So I went back to my desk, and five minutes later, Joey wandered up to me wearing a Windbreaker and said, "Let's walk."

From that moment forward, in fact, it would become our daily ritual. Like clockwork, every afternoon around three, we would walk from 1313 North Vine Street all the way up to Hollywood Boulevard, then all the way over to Cahuenga, and finally all the way back down again. It took about fifty minutes, and invariably it allowed Joey to clear his mind. And for me, it was one of the greatest pleasures of my entire *Bishop Show* experience: walking and talking with this veteran comedian, soaking up his knowledge and his terrific inside showbiz stories. I'm quite certain that those walks taught me more about the careful construction of telling a funny story—the little intricacies of how to set it up, how to pay it off, and the value of some colorful digressions along the way—than just about anything. Every day I learned something new, including how to be truly gracious to fans and viewers, no matter how irritable a mood you privately might find yourself in. I thought it was remarkable how Joey could overcome an ugly funk and suddenly become a charming prince to whoever greeted him on the street.

Meanwhile, those days marked the official beginnings of what would decades later become known as the Late-Night Wars. Back then it was just us versus the unbeatable Johnny Carson; Merv Griffin would try his luck over at CBS a couple of years later and soon enough fall by the wayside as well. But I'm sure Carson's New York–based *Tonight Show* staff compared our nightly guest lists and saw that, while Johnny drew his share of celebrities in Manhattan, we had a near-endless choice of Hollywood superstars. A few times a year, Carson would come out to do his show at NBC's Burbank studios, not far from our home base. Those weeks always gave him an extra boost. We were, of course, never able to catch Johnny in the ratings. He had a five-year jump on Joey, plus the NBC network was much stronger than ABC's back then—and let's face it, *The Tonight Show* was already a firmly established American institution, starting with Steve Allen, continuing with Jack Paar, and on through Johnny, who'd become something of a major icon by then, anyway.

Still, we'd been fighting the good fight for fifteen valiant months on the air, when Joey had sprung a notion on me that would become probably the strangest footnote of my entire career. One day, while we took our walk up Vine Street, he started fretting about Johnny coming to town again in a few weeks, which meant the certain downturn of whatever regular viewership we had. The big guest stars would abandon us for Johnny's Burbank visits, no question. And that's when Joey told me of a plan he had to steal the spotlight from Johnny—*and I was to play an essential part in it.* He said it was a foolproof old show business trick.

I couldn't wait to hear what it was.

Until he told me what it was.

The plot, as he laid it out, was simple: On Johnny's first night in town, I would announce to Joey and to the audience that I'd heard murmurings from on high and elsewhere that my presence was weighing down the show and hurting our chances. And then, in a selfless display of loyalty to him, I would bravely walk off the show, brokenhearted, in full view of the audience, and disappear into the night. He said it would make for instant headlines and lure viewers away from Carson to follow our drama for the rest of the week. I was stunned. I was sure I'd look like a spoiled brat who felt unappreciated by his bosses, someone who was behaving badly because he couldn't stand it anymore. Sort of like that childish old pouting routine "I'm taking my marbles and going home!" I hated the idea. But Joey loved it. "You could make things interesting," he told me with a smile that felt more like a direct order. Which it was. I dreaded everything about that approaching night—and yet I couldn't get out of it. He stressed to me from the start that it was temporary. "Just know that after a few days, I'll make sure you come back," he'd say. Still, when Johnny finally came to town, I was upset at having to execute Joey's rather devious little plan. In fact, every day beforehand, I grew more and more anxious as Bishop grew more and more enthusiastic about it: a devastated Regis walking off the show! It hadn't been done since Jack Paar left *The Tonight Show* in a huff over an NBC network edit of one of his jokes! That got enormous attention at the time and to this day remains a historic television moment—*except Jack really meant it when he stormed off that night!* But like it or not, I would do as I was told.

And so, on that night—for the record, it was Monday, July 8, 1968— I interrupted Joey toward the end of his monologue with something I just had to tell him. I've never seen a tape of it, and at this point I never want to. But what I told him went approximately like this: "Joey, I've been hearing things in the hallways. Things like maybe I was wrong for this job, like maybe I was holding you back, like maybe I should leave the show. And maybe they're all right. Maybe you could do better without me here. So I tell you what—I'm going to go. . . ." Joey immediately protested, imploring, "Regis, Regis, don't leave. I want you to stay!" Then he couldn't resist making a joke: "If you leave, they might find out it was me hurting the show and not you!" But I kept on with the charade and mournfully said, "Anyway, thanks for giving me a chance, and good luck to you." And with that I shook his hand, turned, and headed offstage. The whole thing ate up about eight minutes, but it felt like forever.

Well, as predicted, the audience was shocked; they groaned, and some even applauded (for what, I'm not sure). But it was too late. I was gone. I had taken one for the team. And I actually did briefly feel sort of choked up in that very strange and surreal moment. The first person I saw as I walked off was the fine singer Vic Damone. He was the opening guest, waiting backstage to go on. Vic, I'm sure, was looking forward to coming out and knocking them dead with his great voice. He thought it was a joke—or hoped as much. He said to me, "You're coming back, aren't you?" But I was too embarrassed to stop walking. I said, "No, Vic, I'm not." And I kept going as Vic went ashen-faced.

All week long Joey repeatedly mentioned my absence in his monologue: "Where is Regis? I wish he'd come back. I went looking for him today at the beach. I hope he's all right." That kind of thing—never too serious, and usually tossed off in casual little throwaway asides to the audience. The press, of course, pounced all over the story. Joey stoked the fervor by telling Kay Gardella of the New York *Daily News* that he'd heard me sobbing in my dressing room after the walk-off. Never mind that I'd left immediately and gone out for drinks with my office mate and closest friend on the show, the writer Trustin Howard, to try to make sense out of what had just happened. But Joey played it for all it was worth. *A tearstained Regis leaves!* Meanwhile, the public reaction to the walk-off turned out to be a real eye-opener. Viewer mail poured in on my behalf, outraged that the network had somehow forced me out the door. ABC immediately issued a disclaimer, pointing out that its executives had nothing to do with the situation: "We feel that Regis Philbin's statements were unwarranted and had no basis in fact." The tone of it wasn't exactly remorseful, but at least the big bosses made sure to distance themselves from the drama. Anyway, by Friday it was over: Our producer called and said I should come back on Monday night's show.

I felt like such a jerk. I don't remember what the ratings were during that crazy week, but I'm sure Johnny rolled over us anyway. I asked the producers if Joey could possibly mention the outpouring of fan mail and maybe express that ABC was pleased to have me back as well. I even reminded them all again just before Monday's show: Could Joey please just reintroduce me by making it clear that I was returning due to the public outcry on my behalf and that everyone was very happy about it? I'd hoped that, at least, would make me seem less like some sort of unstable, oversensitive idiot who'd just disappeared for a week to go sulk.

So of course I held my breath standing backstage, while Joey introduced me near the end of his monologue. Except he neglected to offer the audience any of the reasons for my return that I'd so desperately requested he give. His only comment on the subject came abruptly, in one quick line: "Well, all's well that ends well, folks. Here's Regis!" His whole demeanor about the episode couldn't have been more dismissive—almost like "Let's get it over with already and get him back out here." I was surprised, disappointed, and angry all at once. In fact, I felt even more ridiculous than when I had walked off in the first place. So out I strode and said something like, "Yes, I'm back now. Everything is going to be okay." And Joey added, "For a nice Catholic kid from Notre Dame, you're a real troublemaker." And so the show went on, as though none of it had ever happened.

Now, more than ever, I knew the TV critics would want the real inside story about this Regis walk-off/walk-on business. Was it my idea? What had I really wanted? Was it a raise? Were my feelings really so hurt by rumors? Did I truly do it as a display of loyalty to the host? Well, I couldn't give Joey up. I couldn't spill the beans and say it was all an old show business trick Joey put into motion in order to eclipse Johnny Carson's Burbank visit. For years, I had to keep mum, be evasive, and usually just admit that yes, I really did take all those rumors to heart, that I had briefly believed the less-than-great ratings were somehow at least partially my fault. Even in my first book, which was published sixteen years ago, I couldn't quite tell the bald truth behind the walk-off drama, and again I put most all the blame on my own self-pitying. I've danced around it during interviews throughout my entire career. But now, of course, Joey and Johnny and so many others from those days are all gone. Nobody remembers. Nobody cares. I don't hear about it anymore. But it's one of those things I've never forgotten, and I have come to the conclusion that the joke was really on me.

I've mentioned that the writer I had drinks with after my walkoff was also my best friend at the show. He went by the name Trustin Howard, but he'd started out years earlier in New Orleans as Slick Slavin, a stand-up comedian with a very good reputation. When applying for his writing job on the Bishop show, however, he changed it for fear that Joey wouldn't like the idea of another comic performer writing his jokes. Comedy writers are a special breed, all too accustomed to taking the fall if their material doesn't consistently score for the star. Naturally, some nights go better than others, but after the bad nights on Joey's show, crisis was bound to follow. Joey was particularly tough on his writers, calling them on the carpet and demanding to know why they thought they'd given him something funny when it had somehow died onstage. Trustin and I shared an office all the way across the floor from Joey's, but still we could hear through the vents in the ceiling how Joey raged at writers who'd supposedly failed him. We called it "yodeling." I'd thank God that I wasn't one of them, while Trustin would slowly turn white as a ghost and quietly say to me, "Reggo, this isn't good. The man is wild. Why? Why does it have to be like this?" And then he would get his own summons to go face Joey; his shoulders would slump, and he'd get up from his desk and take what we called the "Death March" down that hall. As it happened, all of the writers were eventually fired or quit, but at the end of the show's run, Trustin was the last original writer left. I was very proud of him. Then again, Joey had never found out about Slick Slavin. If he had, it might've spelled Trustin's doom much sooner.

Finally, one night in November of 1969, the inevitable happened. Joey's temper had gotten the best of him, and after a furious phone call with the new ABC chief, Elton Rule, it was over. He told Rule that he was done. This time, ironically enough, it was Joey's turn to walk off. He didn't have to do it that way, but he did love his dramatic endings. So at the outset of the last show, he announced his departure this way: "I am going to leave you, and if there's anything I can think of or say, I'll ask either Johnny or Merv to let me on their show to say it. I can't think of anything now. I do want to apologize to you people who came here perhaps to be entertained and had no knowledge you were going to hear a sermon or a long speech." But it wasn't that long a speech, and he quickly finished by adding, "I am now going home to have dinner with my wife and a few friends. I just want to say one thing before I leave. About a week ago, I asked ABC, 'Could I have a little time off?' I think they're ridiculous." That got a laugh, followed by long applause, as he turned to shake my hand and left me in charge of hosting the rest of the show. And as he walked off, who do you think was standing backstage waiting to come on shortly afterward? You've got it: Vic Damone. Poor Vic. Twice he was on the show, and both times, someone had dramatically walked off before he came out to perform. But somehow we all got through it. I closed the show with the words: "That's it, ladies and gentlemen. What else is there to say? I'll never be surprised by anything else as long as I live. Good night to you. And good night, Joey."

I could have just said, "All's well that ends well," but that was hardly the case at the time. In fact, Joey Bishop had taken me in during a low ebb in my life and given me a new lease in the business. Not to mention the education that came along with it. There were so many invaluable lessons, not the least being how important the role of straight man—or set-up man—is to comedy . . . and also to just plain good storytelling. I had learned right away that he relied on me to come out and feed him, to keep that opening segment of the show moving briskly, to spark his great spontaneous wit. And it really was pure spontaneity out there most nights. After a while, I knew exactly what he wanted to hear, what he needed, and he grew to expect nothing less from me. Although he was never one to dole out compliments, I'll never forget something he told me on one of our walks not long before the show came to its end. He said, "I heard from Dean Martin yesterday. Dean said what we do together every night is the best seven minutes on TV." I'd never told Joey that I was a big fan of Dean's for fear of the jealousy it would stir. But I was thrilled to hear that. Especially because Dean, of all people, would have understood our dynamic in ways few others could, after his own ten years of playing set-up guy to Jerry Lewis.

But in the end, let's just say that Joey Bishop was a tough task-master. He wanted everything to be perfect, and for those seven minutes together every night, I hope I came close to meeting that expectation. I never forgot for a moment that he was the king of the quick comeback line. Nobody did it better. Both of us did what we had to do, and I was proud to be a part of it.

WHAT I TOOK AWAY FROM IT ALL

Learn what you can from old mistakes, but don't dwell on them too long or you may miss out on some truly great opportunities.

When pressure gets the best of you, remember to take time out. A brisk walk can clear the mind and leave you ready to laugh again.

Chapter Eleven

DEAN MARTIN

You probably have no idea how much I depend on Dean Martin. There's never been a morning for as long as I can remember—at least over the last fifteen or more years— when Dean hasn't sung to me both before *and* after every single one of our *Live!* broadcasts. Of course, I've talked about him every chance I've had during our Host Chats, but what you probably don't know is that I've kept his music playing almost constantly whenever working upstairs in my office above our studio. In fact, people have called my office a shrine to both Dean and Notre Dame, and I guess that's pretty much the truth. Mixed with my Fighting Irish mementos, Dean is spread all over the place. People keep sending me these treasures that can't help but delight me: great photos of him, stacks of his tapes and CDs, a half-dozen bobble-head statuettes, an automated singing doll, and even a life-size cutout of him laughing and looking terrific in a tux with his tie tugged loose. I happen to get a wonderful feeling hearing his smooth, playful voice. Like nobody else, he was the personification of relaxed, carefree ease; you couldn't rattle old Dean. Nothing shook him. He just had that special aura. So whether at work or at home, I keep Dean and his music near me at all times.

But now let me tell you about the first time I was ever near Dean himself, up close and personal. Somewhere during my high school years, I'd read in the papers about a new radio singer who sounded very much like Bing Crosby. Well, that's all I had to hear. I tuned in that night, and sure enough, it was absolutely true: This new voice had that same remarkably mellow and romantic Crosby sound. He'd been working at the many nightclubs in and around New York City back then, but hadn't yet broken through. At least, not as a solo act. But then, all of a sudden, he found himself on the same bill one night with a comic named Jerry Lewis, and somehow they began kidding around together onstage. Next thing you knew, they became not just the team of Martin and Lewis but in fact the hottest act in all of show business. They were all you heard about—everywhere! The power of their popularity (especially once they started making movies together) has probably never been matched.

Anyway, in those days, after high school prom dances, it seemed that kids always wound up at one of the many nightclubs in the city. And as it happened, after my Cardinal Hayes High School prom in June of 1949, five friends and I took our dates to the famous Copacabana to see Martin and Lewis, who that same year were just hitting it big on radio together. It was already an exciting night—all of us dressed up and feeling kind of sophisticated—not to mention that this would be my first time going to a nightclub. I remember how Jerry Lewis came out shrieking and breaking dishes he grabbed from busboys. People were howling at his crazy antics, and then Dean entered singing, so cool and in control, the total opposite of Jerry's chaos. He was tall, handsome, and, for the one who was supposedly the straight man of the team, he was just as funny as Jerry. *This guy is dynamite,* I thought. *He can do it all!* It was a revelation to me. Later in the show, he crooned a special love song full of deep feeling and aimed it directly at a beautiful blonde sitting ringside. Sometime that same summer, I read that he and that blonde, Jeanne Bieggers, had gotten married. You'd hear him talk about her for years to come—"my Jeannie," he always called her.

All through Notre Dame I followed Dean: *The Colgate Comedy Hour*, his terrific Capitol Records albums, all those movies with Jerry. And in 1956 they came back to the Copa for what turned out to be their last live appearance together. It was truly sad—maybe the greatest comedy team ever was breaking up. I knew Dean was a fabulous talent, but I wondered how he would do without Jerry. Well, you all know what happened. Each of them became separate sensations, but Dean soared in new and special ways: first, as Sinatra's right-hand man—the second in command of the legendary Rat Pack (which, of course, included Sammy Davis, Jr., Peter Lawford, and a guy named Joey Bishop); and then, especially when his NBC variety show took off in the mid-sixties, as a stand-alone performer, without having to divide the spotlight between himself and a partner or any of his Rat Pack pals, he was still simply amazing. Naturally, he also excelled with every kind of guest who appeared on his program. He could dance beautifully with the Step Brothers, sing unforgettable duets with the likes of Bing or Frank or anybody, and somehow always manage to be funnier than all the top-line comedians who joined him onstage. I loved that show, as did so many millions of viewers, making his program unofficially the NBC network's very first Thursday-night "Must-See-TV" series. In fact, I was fortunate enough to attend a few tapings of the show back then and was always mesmerized by his easy, debonair presence. He had a magic all his own—the looks, the voice, the timing, and he was also a bit mysterious.

You never did see much of Dean around Hollywood. If he wasn't working, he was always on a golf course—or else at home with his large family or appearing in Las Vegas. One night, he made a brief surprise visit to *The Joey Bishop Show*, while on a break from shooting the blockbuster movie *Airport*; he was still in costume—wearing his full pilot's uniform. He walked out, got big laughs from the audience, and was gone again before you knew it. Then, about a decade later, when I was the entertainment news editor for the local ABC station in Los Angeles, I went to do a piece from the set of *The Cannonball Run* picture, starring Burt Reynolds, in which Dean and Sammy Davis, Jr., had cameo roles. I saw my friend and Dean's longtime agent, Mort Viner, standing outside of his star's trailer. He said, "Why don't you go inside and talk with Dean? He's all alone in there." Before that moment, I'd never had the chance to talk with him, just one-on-one. So I climbed the steps, opened the door, and there he was sitting in a booth. He gave me a nice hello and I sat down opposite him. We got along fine; he could put you at ease just like that. So at ease, in fact, that I found myself telling him about my prom night at the Copa and how I'd followed his career from the very beginning. And then, to demonstrate what a longtime fan I was, I launched into a story about one of his earliest records, made for the Apollo label with the Sammy Watkins Band. The song was called "One Foot in Heaven," and I told him how it saved my life during a summer break from college. At the time, I was working the midnight shift at a Long Island plastics factory making venetian blinds. I hated the job, hated the midnight shift, hated going to that factory. But every night, to get myself revved up before heading out to the job, I would play "One Foot in Heaven" over and over again on my old turntable. You see, he had that ability to spark my mood even then!

But as I heard myself talking, I began to wonder why in the world I was telling him that story. I was probably boring him to death. There was so much more to talk about. So many things I wanted to ask him. Then I thought, *My God, it's now 1980! That record came out nearly thirty-five years ago, and it was never a hit anyway. Why was I bothering him with this trivia?* But I was already deep into the story and now desperately looking for a way out of it. And suddenly Dean said, "Regis, why don't you sing it for me." Now there was no escape. So I sat there opposite Dean Martin, the two of us all alone in his trailer, and sang "One Foot in Heaven" to him: "One foot in heaven when you hold me sweet, / One foot in heaven right on Angel Street. . . ." He listened carefully, and when it was over, he said quietly, "You know, that's a nice song, Regis, but I never did it." Then a production assistant rapped on the door, and Dean had to return to the movie set. I left the trailer feeling absolutely ridiculous. Here was one of the great heroes of my life—the guy every other guy wanted to be like, and I was no exception—and yet I'd just wasted so much time going on and on about a minor song he didn't even remember singing! I felt like such a jerk.

So the years went by, and slowly, over time, you heard less and less of Dean. He'd already been retreating from public view before his handsome son, the actor-turned-pilot Dean Paul Martin, died in that freakish Air National Guard jet crash in early 1987. After that, Dean all but disappeared. Frank and Sammy tried to lure him out of his shell a year later by plotting a Rat Pack reunion tour. It didn't work; Dean left the tour after only a few performances. Stories of his ill health circulated, but he'd just decided to live a very quiet life, always sticking to his unassuming ways. And yet he still made it a point to get out for dinner every night. His chauffeured Rolls-Royce delivered him always to the same restaurant, La Famiglia, on Canon Drive in Beverly Hills, at the stroke of six thirty. He sat alone most of the time. He wanted it like that. But at least he was out among other people, and was kind and gracious to anyone who came over to say hello. That was one very good sign that he hadn't given up.

Sometime during that period, my good friend Bill Zehme, the well-known writer from Chicago, revealed to me that we shared the same feelings about Dean. We both wanted to see him for ourselves, one more time. Zehme said he'd even gone to La Famiglia on a few occasions and Dean was in fact always there, like clockwork. He'd always dine alone, Zehme confirmed, but never seemed lonely. Soon enough we made a plan to meet in Los Angeles and then go see him together. I had come to town to play myself (of course) on an episode of Garry Shandling's HBO talk-show send-up *The Larry Sanders Show*, and Zehme arranged a trip out there during my stay. We set up a date to have our eagerly awaited dinner at La Famiglia—which turned out to fall on one of the strangest evenings I'd ever experienced in Los Angeles.

For one thing, the city seemed to be totally deserted. On our way over to the restaurant from my hotel, we barely spotted another car on the street. I had never seen it so quiet. And the reason was this: Everybody was at home glued to their TV sets, watching O. J. Simpson attempting to escape arrest in that famous white Bronco driven by his friend Al Cowlings—with at least twelve police cars chasing them down the freeway. As helicopter cameras followed the action from above, it was a television news spectacular, pure drama every second. Immediately, Zehme and I were worried that, of all the nights we could've picked to go see Dean, O.J. now had all of Los Angeles sitting on the edge of their couches staring at this chase . . . and maybe Dean was one of them. I couldn't believe our rotten luck.

Nevertheless, we parked and walked across the street to the restaurant, hoping against hope that Dean hadn't broken his nightly ritual. "Well, if he's there," Zehme said, "he'll be sitting in his booth just to the left of the front door as we go in." I stole a quick glance to the left as we entered and saw someone sitting there, *alone,* across from the bar, where the TV was of course tuned to O.J. on the loose.

We couldn't stop to stare, but it *had* to be him; it was his booth, after all! Surprisingly, the place was far from empty—and the music that was playing softly in the background? Naturally, it was all Dean's. We chose a table across the room, but in direct view of—yes, it was him—Our Man. Well into his seventies, he still had that great thick shock of hair, which was only specked with gray. He wore a big pair of black eyeglasses that slid down his nose a little. But what a presence he continued to have, the kind you can feel when you're near it. Completely content and relaxed, he sat there watching the Simpson story unfold on the TV, a cigarette in one hand, a tumbler of whiskey in the other, and a dish of pasta in front of him.

During a commercial cutaway, I finally screwed up enough courage to go over to him. I reminded him of who I was and he was very receptive. "Regis!" he said softly. I mentioned my work with Joey Bishop in the late sixties, and he said, "Yes, I remember—you and Joey." He also said that he'd seen Kathie Lee and me every now and then on our morning show. I told him I still loved him, always thought he was the best—"Dean, you know, you're still the greatest"—and shook his hand. He had that timeless, proud look about him. He knew exactly who he was and what he'd done in this business. He gave me a nod, a smile, and said good-bye. It was quick. That was how he wanted it. A few minutes later, I looked back at his booth and he was gone.

But that short exchange meant everything to me. I was happy to have at least gone up to tell him one more time how much his work and his life had touched mine. Because, unfortunately, we do miss those chances all too often with the people we've so appreciated before they're suddenly taken from us. Dean died Christmas morning of 1995, about a year and a half after we saw him at La Famiglia. Fate being what it is, he died the same day, and at the same time, that his mother had twenty-nine years before.

In the years that followed his death, Dean's popularity seemed to skyrocket even more—his music sold millions of units with all kinds of repackaged CDs hitting the market. His voice was all over movie soundtracks and television commercials, helping to sell products from cars to coffee to overnight delivery services. But one day, almost nine years after Dean left us, I got a call from Greg Garrison, the legendary producer of all of Dean's terrific NBC shows, who knew well of my admiration for his guy. He asked, "How would you like to host an infomercial for a collection of DVDs featuring the best moments from all of Dean's old NBC variety shows over the years?" Previously, Greg had done well with a similar set of DVDs of *The Dean Martin Celebrity Roast* series (which had become so popular in the early seventies). But this was a whole package of all those unforgettable musical numbers and all the amazing guest stars, doing what we would never see them do again in our lifetime. Up till then, I had turned down all infomercial offers that came my way, but this was special. This was Dean.

I jumped at the chance and I loved every minute of doing it—all on a Los Angeles soundstage that had been dressed to resemble the original set of Dean's show, with actual pieces that Greg had kept in storage for so many decades. Throughout the taping I couldn't get enough of Garrison's stories about this man, whom he also cherished, and about how he'd guided Dean through every movement of every show, especially because Dean was never one to rehearse anything he did on camera. In the end, that infomercial we made was, in my opinion, one of the best ever produced anywhere—never mind that I'd had the privilege of hosting it. Garrison had chosen and edited the most thrilling and hilarious moments from those classic shows; it was an assemblage so entertaining that the thirty-minute pitch became like a show unto itself. Everyone said that if you accidentally tuned in, you couldn't tune out—and they were right.

Suddenly, it was just so refreshing to see that kind of television again, the greatest variety show ever—and one that only Dean Martin could have presided over.

But Garrison had one more surprise for me, something I didn't ask for or would have ever imagined possible. He had an idea for a big finale to the infomercial that he would create through the magic of modern television technology. He wanted to simulate Dean and me together, dressed in our tuxedoes, running down those original winding steps that looked like piano keys—something Dean had done so many times at the start of his show—singing a duet of the great old number "Baby Face." I remember being knocked out when I arrived at the studio early that morning and saw the famous lighted staircase glowing on the dark set. He led me through the moves, and what you ended up seeing was Dean and me, side by side, laughing and singing and finally landing on an original pair of the high-backed stools where Dean always finished the song that he'd started up at the top of those stairs. This is a funny business I work in, where anything and everything can happen. But I never would have dreamt of performing a bouncy duet with Dean Martin. And even though he wasn't really there—not that I didn't *feel* his presence, because I swear that I actually did—it was one of the biggest thrills of my television career. Plus, what a beautiful bookend to that prom night at the Copa so many years ago when I saw him for the very first time!

But I should also mention that, about a month after we shot the infomercial, a huge box arrived in my New York office. It came from Greg Garrison, and when I opened it, lo and behold, there was one of those same high-backed stools that Dean had sat on to start his show each week. The same one I'd perched myself on during our magical duet. And whenever I need to feel a special jolt of Dean's easygoing aura, I climb up onto that stool, and after a moment or two, I always feel better, all over again.

WHAT I TOOK AWAY FROM IT ALL

No matter what your musical tastes,
I swear that listening to Dean Martin sing
will calm you and boost your energy at
once—without fail.

If you are grateful to someone who's brought
your life even a little joyfulness, and if you
have the chance to tell them so—do it! It just
takes a second, and you'll never regret it.

Chapter Twelve

DON RICKLES

The name Don Rickles began catching my attention back in the late fifties. At the time, believe it or not, he aspired to become a serious actor, and had just made his movie debut with a small dramatic role in the Clark Gable–Burt Lancaster submarine picture *Run Silent Run Deep*. But by then, showbiz insiders knew there was nothing serious or silent about this one-of-a-kind guy. Already his reputation had caught fire as a young, brash comic who'd been tearing it up across the major nightclub circuits, sending shock waves and also drawing raves, whether in Miami, New York, Los Angeles, or eventually, of course, Las Vegas. There, at the Sahara Hotel, his after-hours lounge performances truly put him on the map, especially when Frank Sinatra and his gang of pals made a habit of dropping by to catch Don in action. I remember later on reading that mid-sixties classic *Esquire* magazine story "Frank Sinatra Has a Cold," so beautifully written by Gay Talese, who'd followed Frank and company into one of Don's shows and described Rickles as "probably more caustic than any comic in the country. His humor is so rude, in such bad taste, that it offends no one—it is too offensive to be offensive."

Sinatra fell in love with him years earlier when entering a Miami club where Don greeted him from the stage: "Make yourself at home, Frank. Hit somebody!" They would become great friends for life, and to this day, one of the most famous stories to ever come out of Vegas happened during the sixties when Rickles walked up to Sinatra at a restaurant and asked for a favor. Rickles had been sitting at a table across the room with a young lady he was trying to impress. So he told Frank it would mean the world if he could wait a few minutes and then come over to their table and say hello. The girl, he said, would be knocked out. Sinatra agreed to play along, and after a while he strolled over—with every eye in the place on him—and gave Rickles a warm and cheerful "Hi, Don, so good to see you!" And Rickles turned from the girl and said, "Not now, Frank. Can't you see I'm busy?" That story gets laughs even after being retold a thousand times, and I still love it.

Anyway, as I said, I'd been hearing early buzz about this fierce and funny Rickles character back when I was just a young TV reporter in San Diego, still a couple years away from starting my local Saturday-night talk show. But I was always on the lookout for an entertaining story to use on the newscasts. And one day I heard that Rickles was coming to town—not to perform but to meet, for some reason, with the Advertising Council of San Diego. It was a lunch gathering set at the upscale US Grant Hotel, and since the town was a much less thriving place in those days, the council had no more than about fifteen members. I got myself invited and took a seat at the far end of the long table where I could keep a close eye on Rickles, who sat at the head. As the council went over its business, I could see that Rickles was clearly wondering how in the world he'd gotten involved with whatever these dull, serious older businessmen wanted from him. Here was the hot rising star of the club scene stuck with this rather humorless bunch who, I'd guessed, probably hadn't even heard of him yet. I waited anxiously for Rickles to go to work on them. I could tell he couldn't wait to bite into those advertising guys and then get out of there. Finally he was introduced. He stood at the table and, one by one, demolished them. I had never seen anything like it. He just ate them alive. He didn't know them, of course, but how they were dressed, who their clients were, their whole life existence—everything about them—was now being examined by Rickles in the most hilarious way. To the letter, he was everything I'd read about—and I loved him immediately. After the massacre, I timidly approached him and asked for an interview. He was not thrilled about it, but we went outside in the sunshine where my camera crew was set up and we began. He started with my name. *Regis.* He had never heard it before. It was fresh meat for him. He beat me up pretty good on the sidewalk that day and I still loved it. I marveled at his attack, his perception, his style of humor. He had a way of sizing you up and then letting you have it like you never had it before. He was sensational.

Last year, on our show, I asked him if he remembered that interview and got the same Rickles I'd first met those fifty years earlier—pure Rickles: "Yeah," he said, his eyes rolling up into his head. "You had a blue tie. And I had brown cuff links. I didn't forget it. And that's how our life began. And now I can't dump you. I'm trying to get rid of you, and I can't."

Our next go-round came after I left San Diego for my first national television hosting job (yes, the Westinghouse debacle). My producers asked me who'd I love to have on my new show. I began with Don Rickles. They called his manager, Joe Scandore, who made a deal not for one appearance but for three. I was thrilled. I didn't think he remembered me, but I didn't care. This was the guy I wanted on my show. I knew enough to position us on two stools facing the audience up close. *Let them share the pain*, I thought. I knew what fun he would have with them, and it worked. They were his sitting ducks, in row after row. He gave me the best experience that I would have on that show.

A few years later on *The Joey Bishop Show*, Don was booked as a guest, but Joey was leery of him. Rickles was unpredictable. He would get off on an opening rant about me and then turn to Joey. That meant it was Joey's turn to take the heat. Comedians, as I've mentioned, can be very competitive when sharing the spotlight, and Joey, who was as competitive as they got, knew that whatever he'd say to Rickles would be turned around into a joking attack on him. So Joey went on the defensive. He realized that the less he said to Rickles, the less ammunition Rickles would have. Finally, at one point, he actually said nothing. At all. The silence was deafening. I was getting nervous until Rickles leaned over to Joey and said, "What's the matter with you . . . *are you a mute?*" I never forgot that line and the laughs it produced, which I'm pretty sure did not thrill Joey.

The sixties brought quite the influx of comedians from New York to Los Angeles, which was, after all, closer to Vegas, where stand-up jobs were so often popping up. Plus, in L.A., maybe they could get a movie, maybe a TV series or regular guest shots on other shows. It was a new world of opportunity. One of the best results of this westward movement was the way they would assemble for all the showbiz banquets or luncheons or, funniest of all, the Friars Roasts, which featured all the greats—Jack Benny, George Burns, Danny Thomas—the list could go on. Most of them had marvelous stories that they'd perfected over the years. Routines that were built line by line, with steady laughs in between, and as each story progressed, it would get funnier and funnier until they reached the punch line, which was usually a scream. Everybody who took the podium was dynamite, but the one who would always close the show was Don Rickles. And that's because no one could follow him. And they all knew it.

In the seventies, I'd gone back to news and become the entertainment director of KABC-TV. That meant a routine of doing movie reviews and also regular interviews with Hollywood stars. My favorite target to chase down, of course, was Don. I tried to make a point of covering most every function he attended, and our interviews dependably became great fun for both of us. Soon enough, we got to be friends. I found him to be a classy guy, always very well dressed, and he had a lovely wife, Barbara, who was perfect for him. Once I took a camera crew to Las Vegas to spend an afternoon in his suite with him before his show that night, talking about his life and his recent trip to England with Bob Hope for a royal performance and how Bob held his breath when Rickles got up to speak before the queen. Everything worked out—even the queen laughed. But I noticed, then and always, that everywhere Rickles went, there, too, would be his dear friend and valet, Harry Goins. Harry was a sweet, quiet man who'd met Rickles when he was a bartender at the old Slate Brothers Club on La Cienega Boulevard in Los Angeles, where Rickles had played many times. Don formed a warm bond with Harry and told him if his break into the big time ever came, he would take Harry along with him. Well, one day when that break arrived, Don did not forget his promise. He called Harry, and they were together from that point forward, with Harry keeping Don's life organized both at home and on the road. Harry was family, even a part of the act. One thing I learned during that Vegas trip was that despite all of his antics, Rickles was the kind of friend who stayed loyal and faithful.

Anyway, our Vegas interview stretched into a three-parter, which concluded with the cameras following us down in the elevator to the Sahara Hotel's show room, by way of navigating through the massive kitchen, where Rickles gently chided the help with threats of deportation, and then on to the side of the show room to capture those waiting moments before his grand entrance. Finally, with that trademark trumpet blaring his toreador theme, he made his way like a bullfighter through the raucous crowd, which was already on fire, cheering him on, wanting their inimitable Rickles experience, which he was about to unleash on them.

So went our Hollywood days, but even after I returned to New York in 1983, our relationship continued to grow, both on and off camera. Every time he passed through Manhattan we'd do another interview, and eventually began something of a ritual where we'd go at it, one-on-one, in the Bull & Bear saloon at the Waldorf-Astoria Hotel. We would each take a bar stool, and once the tape rolled, no one would be safe—the camera crew, Gelman, the bartender, whoever was around him. Rickles was always dynamite, starting the very first time we did it back in 1994. He then happened to be on the road with Sinatra, who was also headquartered at the Waldorf, which made for an irresistible topic. That exchange went like this:

> DON: Sinatra's up in his suite, and I said, "Frank, you wanna come downstairs with me and do Regis Philbin?" He threw up his breakfast.
>
> ME: What if we went upstairs and barged in on Frank? Don, I've never asked you for anything. I'd love to see Frank. How about it?
>
> DON: You have two daughters, right? Would you like to see them again?

Over the years when he came to town, we always found time to go dine with our wives, Barbara and Joy, among other friends and new acquaintances. One night he wanted to go to Rao's, the most difficult restaurant in New York to get into. Located way up in East Harlem, it had for many years been a notorious gangster hangout, and even now, it still maintains that original mystique: the same tables and chairs, the same bar, the same slightly forbidding charm. Happily enough, Sonny Grosso, one of the New York cops who broke up the French Connection gang, invited us to join him at his regular Monday-night table there. Naturally, Rickles loved the place, and the small, exclusive crowd was thrilled by his presence. In no time, he was on his feet doling insults out around the room, with everybody loving it and Don loving it even more.

Somewhere along the way, with the help of the famed William Morris agent Lee Solomon, I developed my own nightclub act. Slowly, it began in the waning years of the Catskills resort show rooms, then moved on to New Jersey's Club Bene, before I started becoming an opening act in Atlantic City for the likes of Steve and Eydie, Sergio Franchi, Tony Bennett, and, yes, God help me, one weekend with Don. Having seen him at work and knowing him all those years, the idea of suddenly sharing the same stage with him gave me the terrors. Just knowing he'd be backstage watching me perform was almost enough to keep me at home hiding under the bed. But he was wonderfully encouraging in private. On the other hand, since this was such a major kick for me, it made for a fun chance to tape an interview with him during the course of our special premiere, weekend engagement together. I would ask him to give a review of my act, something we could run on *Live!* the following week.

Here, for the record, is a little snippet from that warmhearted appraisal: "Hey, Regis, can I tell you something?" he began. "If we work together again, so help me, I'm going to the VA, and I'm going to ask to be sent back to Vietnam. The war's over, but I'm going to just stay there in the jungle and blacken my face so nobody finds me. I never want to see you again, Regis. Really. Don't come around anymore." Of course, I was cracking up, even as he started playfully shoving me out of his dressing room. Not that he was finished with me yet: "The voice is weak! You stink! How's that, Regis? You stink. You're not good. You stink. And stay out of my life, Regis. *I never want to see you again! I hope you get a boil on your neck!*"

But the double billing of our acts was terrific fun—I loved it— and through the years we worked together at various places all over the country. Those were nights I will always remember. The show he'd put on backstage was just as good as whatever happened later onstage, with Rickles in his formal shirt swaddled under a bathrobe, minus his pants. (It's the old-school showbiz rule: Pants go on last, before heading to the stage, so the pleats won't be disturbed.) Sometime before, Harry Goins had sadly passed away, and Don luckily enlisted the help and watchful guidance of Tony Oppedisano, known to all as Tony O, who had accompanied Sinatra, in his later years, all over the world as his road manager and dedicated compatriot. But by now, Frank was gone. So were most of those great comedians from the sixties. But here was Don Rickles, heading toward his mid-eighties, still going out there onstage and firing away at his multigenerational audiences, giving them what they expected, a brash and feisty night full of laughs, the way no one else ever could.

And as the years go by, I realize more and more what a beautiful friend he is. We still work together now and again. And we talk on the phone all the time. If he doesn't hear from me for a while, he'll call up and start yelling at me, half seriously, about keeping in steadier touch—but only showing again what a wonderfully sensitive guy he really is. A true gentleman—and gentle man. I couldn't have ever imagined Don as my friend fifty years ago when I sat in on that San Diego advertising meeting, but that's the way it worked out. I never did stay out of his life, after all. And I love him.

WHAT I TOOK AWAY FROM IT ALL

Loyalty to others tends to ensure that your loyalty will always be returned in kind.

Know how to take a ribbing, especially from people who obviously care about you—as well as those who do it for a living and mean you no harm. It's really a compliment that they thought enough of you to talk about you in the first place.

Chapter Thirteen

JOHN SEVERINO

This is a business where the same person can keep coming back to be a key part of your life over and over again. Especially from behind the scenes in those executive suites—which was where this particular guy repeatedly brought about some of the most important changes my life has ever known. For sure, he was fiery and unpredictable, which our special relationship eventually would reflect through the years. *Oh God, would it ever!* But maybe I should have expected that long before we actually worked together. I mean, the first time we literally crossed paths, he signaled to me, as only he could, that he was nobody's pushover. . . .

So how about this for a first impression: As I've told you, when I left San Diego in 1964 to take over Steve Allen's national Westinghouse program, the big bosses insisted on parading me around that October on a promotional tour of all the cities whose stations would be carrying our show. First stop was Boston's WBZ-TV, a very important station in the chain. As the plane landed at the airport there, I looked out the window and saw a high school band lined up on the tarmac playing the Notre Dame fight song. I was not used to this kind of fanfare, to say the least, and felt my panic rising when the Westinghouse vice president Jim Allen told me that these kids had been trotted out there to salute me, never mind that they had no idea who I was. I was totally embarrassed. Then came a procession of cars through the rainy streets of Boston on the way to the Ritz-Carlton Hotel. That's when I began to spot what turned out to be WBZ employees standing on every street corner leading to the hotel, each of them holding up a placard saying: *"Welcome Regis! You're going to be great!"* Riding along in the car with a group of upbeat Westinghouse and station execs, I was overwhelmed and even touched by this display of support—in the rain, yet! But then something happened to bring me back to reality. There was one guy out on a corner who wasn't holding up a sign as we drove by; instead, I saw him hold up something else. Yes, it was his middle finger. I couldn't miss it. I asked the execs, "Who was *that* guy?" They said, "Oh, that's John Severino. He's starting a new job at ABC Chicago tomorrow, but we asked him to come out here today to greet you along with everyone else. And he's probably not too happy about standing out in the rain. Don't worry about it. You'll never see him again, anyway."

Those, by the way, are the sorts of offhand statements that people like to call "famous last words"—the kind that never turn out to be even close to the truth.

Now let's skip ahead ten years, during which time the *Bishop Show* had come and gone, and I had been picking up work wherever I could—from hosting a weekly talk show on KHJ in Los Angeles to doing the same thing on Saturday nights for KMOX-TV in St. Louis, which, I'll confess, made for quite a rugged ongoing commute from my L.A. home. And there was the six-week stint filling in for an ailing Denver sportscaster, too. You get the picture. Then, like a flash, it was on to Chicago where I'd just gotten an urgent call from WLS-TV station manager Chris Duffy. He needed me to immediately come and take over the local early-morning talk show as the summer (and possibly more permanent) replacement for its popular host Bob Kennedy, who had suddenly died. When I arrived—wouldn't you know it?—the general manager and top boss there was a guy named . . . John Severino. Turned out, however, that my first day in Chicago was (*once again*) to be his last day at the station: He would leave town within twenty-four hours to go run KABC-TV in Los Angeles. Anyway, he watched my first Chicago show that final day before heading west and told Duffy that he very much liked what he saw. (Apparently, giving me the finger ten years earlier had less to do with his opinion of me and more to do with getting soaked in the rain!) Frankly, I was lucky that he'd still been there and was able to see me do my thing, if only for that one morning. Somehow, whatever he enjoyed about my work then stuck in his head and would pay off for me in a surprising way months later. Because at the end of that summer in Chicago, I didn't get the permanent replacement hosting job after all. Bitterly disappointed, I returned to Los Angeles, again with no prospects for work. Many bleak weeks followed until, on the Wednesday morning before Thanksgiving, I got a call from John Severino's office at KABC. Could I come in and see him that afternoon? I was both stunned and thrilled. So I showed up at his office promptly at four in the afternoon only to see that his secretary, Verla, was a girl I had known way back in the fifties during my KCOP stagehand days. (See? *All* kinds of people keep turning up again when you work in the television business.)

Verla said that Mr. Severino had just returned from a luncheon party and was waiting for me in his office. I opened the door and walked in. The room was dark. Shades pulled halfway down. He wasn't at his desk. I turned to look around, and there he was lying on his couch. *That must have been some party at lunch,* I thought. "Oh, hi," I probably blurted. "I didn't see you there." Severino cut right to the chase. He said, "Can you do the same crap David Sheehan does?" Sheehan was one of the first reporters in the country to critique movies on local newscasts; his work in town over at Channel 2 had always been top-notch.

I said, "You mean review the movies?"

"Yeah," he answered, barely opening his eyes.

"I'd love to do it," I said.

I needed that job and was about to continue my pitch when Severino simply said, "Okay. Be here Monday. Check in at the newsroom that morning." And that was that. It was back to scale pay, just like I was starting all over again. Nineteen years in the business—*and* . . . *I* . . . *was* . . . *starting* . . . *all* . . . *over* . . . *again.* Still, I did need that job. Which would not only include movie reviewing but also general entertainment reporting. I hit the ground running that first day: I took in a movie, rushed back to the studio, edited a clip, wrote a review, and delivered it on the 6 P.M. news. Then I hurried home for a quick supper with Joy and the girls before having to dash off with a camera crew to cover some star-studded Hollywood event for the eleven o'clock news. After a few months, the station sales manager told me the news ratings were up and viewers seemed to enjoy what I was doing. Everybody was happy.

During the next year, though, the host of the KABC morning talk show decided to take a job in Atlanta. And that's when I saw my opportunity. I went to Sev and reminded him that that's what I really did, and what I had always done best—hosting talk shows. He did recall liking me in that role on his last morning in Chicago, which was why he'd hired me here in the first place. But, he said, there'd been an upward ratings spike in our newscasts, on which

I'd become such a dependable team member, and he didn't want anything to interfere with that. So I told him I could do all three: the ninety-minute talk show in the morning, the movie review for the early-evening broadcast, and an entertainment-world piece at eleven at night. Yes, a fifteen-hour day. And I did it. But it didn't take too long before the morning show, *A.M. Los Angeles*, became a big hit. And even though the news ratings had never been higher, I was wearing down hard with this killer schedule. So after a year of pounding away on that all-day-and-night treadmill, I went back to him and admitted I couldn't keep up the breakneck pace. I was running out of steam. He took me off the eleven o'clock news, but he didn't like doing it one bit.

Now most people feared Sev. Probably for good reason. He was a fierce and calculating competitor, bursting with gruff Italian machismo. He could chew out anyone who displeased him like no one else I've ever encountered. He was a tough guy all right, but from the start he was very supportive of me, maybe because I had gained a little national recognition working with Joey Bishop on our ABC network a handful of years earlier. Who knows? Every afternoon at five, after I got my movie review ready for the six o'clock news, I would go over to his office to shoot the breeze with him. He would set up a tray of cheese and crackers and serve up a couple of cold Cokes and we'd have a lot of laughs.

But one afternoon during our regular bull session, I happened to notice that Paul Moyer, one of the station's big-time anchormen, was out doing a run-of-the-mill live field report on the five o'clock news, direct from a sweltering Santa Monica playground, about its being one of the hottest days of the year. I couldn't believe it. This was not a story worthy of Moyer's stature as a major newsman.

"Sev," I said, "why is Moyer out there doing that kind of a report?"

"He's been a bad boy," Sev said ominously. "I want to remind him that he's an anchor, and should feel lucky that he's not still just some street reporter."

"How long are you going to keep him out there?"

And suddenly, in a loud and angry tone, Severino barked, *"Until he learns his f—ing lesson!"*

I never knew what had prompted that punishment, and didn't want to probe, but eventually all was forgiven and Paul returned to his anchor desk. Clearly, though, you didn't want to mess with Sev. I knew how fortunate I was that he always seemed to take my side when problems arose. For instance, over the years I'd had troubles here and there with various newly hired producers about the opening segment of our morning shows. The uninterrupted eighteen-minute-long Host Chat would simply freak out some of these antsy producers—to them, it felt like an eternity of meandering airtime, no matter how entertaining it was. But I knew that's what had always worked best for our show. I remember when KABC brought in a smart young guy from San Francisco to take over producing the show. His name was Ron Ziskin, and right off the bat, he thought the opening should be shortened. Rather than get involved in an argument upon his arrival, I decided to get my point across in another way. I took him over to Sev's office to properly introduce Ron to our inimitable general manager. And that's when I also casually mentioned to Sev that Ron wanted to shorten the opening—which, by the way, had become so popular that even many of our station employees would pop into the studio to grab some quick morning laughs during our freestyle banter. But now here was a new guy, determined to cut it back, timewise. Almost on cue, Sev leaned in close to Ziskin's face and, pointing over toward me, told him in a firm whisper, *"Do it his way."* And then he grabbed each of Ziskin's cheeks, gave them a little twist, and again with that whisper added, *"Kapish?"*

"Jeez," Ziskin said as we walked back to our studio. "I fear him." Then he asked me, "By the way, what does *kapish* mean?" With a straight face, I explained to him, "It means *'Or else you die.'*" Of course it really means "Do you understand?" But I couldn't resist, and Ziskin never brought it up again.

No matter that Sev and I maintained a strong relationship back then, he turned into a sly and cunning businessman whenever my contract renegotiations would roll around. I didn't have an agent in those days, so I had to do my own bidding. It was no contest. He'd split a piece of paper into eight pieces—four for him, four for me. He'd then have me write on each piece what I thought the increments of my annual pay raises should be over the next four years. And he would do the same on his four slips of paper. He'd say, "Whoever's numbers feel fairest will be the winner." Of course, I was grateful for any kind of pay hikes at all, and so, for some strange reason, he won every time.

And there was something else that happened during my seventies stay at KABC-TV. My then *A.M. L.A.* producer, Frank Kelly, said one day, "Why don't we take a camera crew and do a live hour before the Academy Awards as the nominees walk the red carpet." The Oscars, after all, was an exclusive ABC telecast. Our preview show would only be for our station in Los Angeles—perfect for that Hollywood-happy market. It was a great idea. In those days, the academy put up some bleacher seats for the movie fans right in front of the long red carpet with ropes on either side. The likable and well-known reporter Army Archerd would stand at the foot of the carpet. As a longtime columnist for *Daily Variety*, everybody in the business knew Army. He was a favorite among actors and actresses, many of whom would never talk to any other reporter but him. One by one, he would announce who was arriving: "Ladies and gentlemen, here's that wonderful actor Richard Burton." There would be polite applause, and once in a while an audience member might shout out, "Hi, Richard." Nothing too raucous.

Meanwhile, we would be waiting at the other end of the carpet. This was still the era when real movie stars commanded Hollywood, not just new faces in teen magazines, and they handled themselves with class and poise. It turned out to be a special night. The ratings for our preshow broadcast were sensational. The next year the station even gave us a second camera for the red carpet show. And yes, I did ask some of the ladies, "Who did your dress?" I just *had* to know.

The following day Howard Rosenberg, the TV writer for the *Los Angeles Times*, would spend his entire column beating my brains out, along the lines of "What a ridiculous idea the whole thing was. Regis Philbin talking to Fred Astaire . . . how dare he." Howard killed us every year, and I've got to admit he was sometimes quite funny about it. But the show was such a big success that it spawned what you now see every single Oscar day, as about twenty-five cameras from all over the world are aimed at the star entrances, while dozens and dozens of TV producers and their assistants run all over the carpet grabbing their next glittery guests. It's a combination of hysteria and madness, and I know how it started. I was there. Long before it became this mob scene. Too bad, Howard Rosenberg is no longer at the *Times* to report on all that insanity now. He'd have a ball with it. Better them than me.

But back to what seemed like my all too one-sided contract negotiations. After six years at KABC, with the ratings flying higher than ever, John Severino was rewarded by being named president of the entire ABC television network. He would run it all from the company's New York headquarters. I hated to see him go. At an enormous good-bye party, he thanked everybody for making ours the top-rated station on the network, but especially singled out me and Jerry Dunphy, the main news anchor. I was touched and happy to get that kind of recognition but also knew that I'd miss Sev very much. Meanwhile, months went by and my contract eventually ended, but there'd been no call to come in and renegotiate with the station's new general manager. So I pondered what kind of strategy I should take: *Do I just go in there and say "Let's talk" or wait for the new manager to call me in?* I decided to let him call me. I was going to win one of these negotiations someday, I vowed. But before anything happened, my phone rang and Grant Tinker, one of the most astute and respected executives in all of television, was calling me with a bombshell of an offer. He was taking over the presidency of NBC, had faithfully watched my morning show for seven years, loved it, and now wanted me to come over to do the same thing for them—across the entire network. I was beside myself. All these years I had yearned for just one more crack at going national. And this was it. My KABC contract had expired. Nobody had called. I was free to walk off the lot. Still, it was tough to tell the general manager, Tom Van Amburg, that I was leaving. He got very upset and instructed my producer, Frank Kelly, to escort me off the premises immediately—without a chance to ever go to my office one last time and gather my things.

But that was nothing compared to Severino's reaction from New York. He was furious and embarrassed to have to explain to other ABC execs how this could've happened, how my contract could have expired so easily under the new KABC management. But rather than focus on the oversights of his successors in L.A., he made me his primary target of revenge. That night he called me from New York, his voice low and menacing as he unleashed a tirade of language that would curdle blood and other fluids. He had taken it personally, *very personally,* and told me so in no un-certain terms. Let's just say—if I might now try to clean this up for you—that he claimed that I had, um, *violated* him in such a way that he could never forgive me, nor would he ever forget what I had just done to him. And he kept repeating this over and over again until the hair on the back of my neck began to stand up. I even thought I detected vague threats of professional retribution. Sev always sounded as if he had a little touch of the Italian mob capo deep inside of him, which is probably what made him such an effective leader. But this rant was terrifying, stirring up enough of my Irish Catholic guilt to leave me shaking. He knew exactly where your most vulnerable buttons were located and just how to push them. It was tough falling asleep that night after that call. Same thing held true for lots of nights to follow.

Also, he'd made it quite clear that my new NBC show was destined for failure. And in this case, he was right. There was no way to do a fresh 9 A.M. morning show live from Los Angeles; we would be relegated to a one-day tape delay, and worse yet, the show was cut down to thirty minutes even before we got on the air. My opening segment had always run nearly twenty minutes; it was the lynchpin to our success at KABC (and of course, later in New York forever after). Without that easygoing, extemporaneous, and newsy opening chatter, all we'd have was just another show; the rigid time strictures would simply defeat any chance we had to succeed. It was a recipe for doom—and also a loud and horrible echo of the Westinghouse fiasco. Severino had predicted we'd be gone in six months. He hit that one right on the nose. Six months would, in fact, be the total life span of the show, before the plug was mercifully pulled.

My friends were stunned but, at the same time, knew I was never going to make it being crammed into a half-hour format. My cohost, the terrific Mary Hart, was hired the very next day to anchor *Entertainment Tonight*, where she stayed for thirty years and became iconic in her own right. Meanwhile, I went into seclusion. I lived in the doldrums daily with nothing to do. Nothing, that is, except become a master at playing Pac-Man video games, which happened to be our daughter J.J.'s obsession at the time. When she was at school each day, I commandeered the machine for hours on end. Here I had gone from being the king of Los Angeles morning TV to this reclusive and lost Pac-Man addict. But I could only welcome the distraction, while waiting for another shot at . . . anything.

One night deep into this grim period, Joy and I attended a lavish wedding party for producer Duke Vincent, the number two guy in Aaron Spelling's organization, which had created so many major hit series that continually lit up ABC's prime-time schedule. Anyway, it was a beautiful tented backyard affair held behind a lovely home in the exclusive Holmby Hills section of L.A. I should have known that many important ABC executives would be there, and of course I should have expected Sev to walk in, too—but when he did, I still was somehow taken by surprise. Very quickly he spotted me and came over to tell me—in a not so friendly way—to meet him over in a dark corner of the yard in a few minutes.

Naturally, we hadn't talked for many months, probably not since his last call gloating over my NBC morning failure. Our rift was no secret to most anyone who knew me. But my friend Mike Srednick, who had just caught sight of the two of us having that initial exchange near the buffet line, was convinced that peace between us could be restored and he rushed over to tell me so. He was sure that in the next few minutes Sev was going to invite me back and it was all going to be great again. While I stood waiting in that secluded corner of the yard and Sev ominously walked toward me, I could see that Srednick had strategically positioned himself close enough to watch, if not hear, this momentous conversation that was about to take place. Srednick, bless him, even had both of his thumbs hoisted up in the air, predicting a victorious outcome.

Meanwhile, here was Sev, my former beloved boss—whom I un-wittingly "betrayed" because KABC hadn't gotten around to of-fering me a contract to continue my local morning show, whereas Grant Tinker had promised me his whole network, very much to my regret, of course, in retrospect—now glaring deeply into my eyes for an awkward moment. And as Severino began to talk, I knew that Srednick was prematurely celebrating my return to Sev's good graces. What Sev had to say was not good at all. It was as if no time had passed between conversations—he just picked up where he'd left off on those torturous late-night phone calls he'd made to me after my NBC deal was completed. (He had been relentless, expressing his utter disgust with me during those early weeks.) As he had vowed previously, he vowed once again, this time face-to-face: He would never forget what he believed I had done to him. Over and over again he repeated that immortal Italian quote—that chilling phrase describing the worst thing you can do to an Italian male, or any male—signifying the end of our long, great friendship. (My pal Srednick was beyond stunned to have misread the moment so completely.)

And that was also the end of that night's wedding party for me. There was no point in even trying to return to the happy festivities. Instead, I returned to my lingering unemployed Pac-Man hell, won-dering what would become of my so-called career. As it happened, nearly two years had passed since the NBC nightmare, and several months since my gruesome backyard square-off with Sev. Now it was January of 1983, and quite unexpectedly I received a call from a New York–based William Morris agent named Jimmy Griffin, whom I'd never met. But he informed me that he'd just had a meeting with John Severino. On a hunch—with me planted firmly in mind—Jimmy reminded Sev that the local New York WABC-TV morning show had tanked miserably since the departure of its veteran host Stanley Siegel. He knew that this was nothing less than an enormous humiliation for the most prestigious station on the whole ABC network. But he also knew, to some degree, how Sev felt about me. Maybe he didn't know just how terrible the breach between us had gotten, but he took a shot anyway. In the middle of his pitch, he said very earnestly, "If you think with your head and not your heart, Sev, you *know* Regis can turn your mornings around here on Channel 7." I will always be indebted to Jimmy for that one line, which, I think, brought about my return to New York City.

Because somehow, Severino's head must have grasped what his heart had for so long refused to accept, much less consider.

Sev told Jimmy to have me call him, which I did, expecting the worst and receiving not a warm but at least a straightforward and businesslike proposal. He suggested that Joy and I come to New York for a long weekend to explore the idea of possibly moving there. He also mentioned that even he hated New York, warning me, "It's cold and it's dark and ugly here. I just want you to know that." I said I knew that, but I didn't care. So shortly afterward, on Presidents' Day weekend that February, we arrived on a Saturday night and checked in at the legendary Plaza Hotel. At the time, ABC kept an upper floor reserved for guests and network affiliate honchos, so we were terrifically impressed; this, I sensed, seemed to be the star treatment. Along those same lines, great seats had been set up for us at Broadway shows like *Dream Girls* and *La Cage Aux Folles*. It was all very exciting, but Severino did have a point: After spending all those years in California, the weather in New York seemed colder than ever. The snow was piled high and dirtily in the streets. And of course, we worried about how Joanna and J.J. would ever get used to these gray concrete canyons, jammed with people rushing in all directions at once. We also looked at some potential apartments that might suit us. They all seemed so small and cramped. No doubt we would miss our good-size home under the warm sunshine, our backyard with the pool, the green lawn and the palm trees in front of the house. It became a monumental decision to make, and at the end of the weekend we were beside ourselves trying to fathom whether the lifestyle change was the right choice. Really, it was simply driving us nuts.

Finally we decided that we just couldn't make the move. We'd have to stay in California; this cross-country urban shift would clearly be too traumatizing for our family to stand.

But how could I tell Severino? I would have to go see him in person—for the first time since that awful backyard encounter, no less. So I went over to the ABC building on Sixth Avenue and entered his office prepared to deliver the bad news. He was cordial until I told him I couldn't take his offer. Then he and his chief network lieutenant, Mark Mandala, started in—these two passionate Italian big shots—working me over, but doing it in the most peculiar way. They started carrying on as though I weren't even standing in the same room with them.

"He could be a big star here!" Mandala yelled out, like he was convincing himself of the fact.

"But he don't wanna come here!" Severino yelled back, reverting to old-style street grammar, as he did whenever getting himself heated up.

"The people would love him!" cried Mandala.

"What's the matter with you?" said Sev. "Don't you hear him? He don't wanna come here!"

"He doesn't know what he's missing!"

"Don't you understand? He don't wanna come here!"

It all began to sound like something out of *The Godfather*. And that's the way it went until I finally decided to insert myself into the conversation. After all, this was me that they were arguing over. I spoke of the problems that troubled us most about moving east, so they might better understand: the comfortable house I would be leaving, the school situation for the kids, the physical uprooting of our lives, the New York weather, noise, sirens, etcetera, etcetera. But I was no match for these two Italians (even though I'm one-half Italian myself). In fact, they began to speak strictly in their native language and were getting louder and louder with each sentence that I didn't quite understand in the first place.

Then Severino stopped and stared at me for a long time. I thought to myself, *Good God, he's not going to lapse into that scary "violation" diatribe again, is he? Because I couldn't take it.* But instead he spoke English, and of course, being Severino, he had another plan to dangle before me. In a suddenly friendly tone, he said, "Ehhhh, here's what we're gonna do. We're gonna give you a clause in your contract that nobody else has ever gotten. We are gonna call this clause 'The Misery Clause.' You work here for one year, then you come to me after that, and you say to me, 'Eh, I'm miserable!' Then you can leave and go back west . . . or we can talk some more about a new contract that you'll like even better."

I got excited. Usually, in my previous Severino contract go-rounds, I'd be stuck with four-year deals with no escape hatch. I very much liked the idea of giving myself a chance to try out New York for a year, and if we didn't take to it, we could get out and go home. I figured that Joy and I and the girls would know by that time whether we could adapt to this whole new way of life. I convinced myself to think of it as a kind of vacation. But then my mind began to hedge again. They saw it in my eyes, and that's when they swept in for the kill—making me an offer I couldn't refuse, in true *Godfather* terms. They would fly me home every other weekend during the summer. I could live in the meantime at the Essex House in a nice suite overlooking Central Park. We were getting close. I took a chance on asking for one more perk. I told them my sainted Italian mother had been born on Fifty-ninth Street; her father worked on the Hudson River as a stevedore. It was just a few blocks from where my new home station, WABC-TV, was located. She hadn't been back to New York in years. My folks had relocated to the West Coast not too long after my career began out there. How she would love to see her old Fifty-ninth Street neighborhood again, I told them, and the Church of St. Paul the Apostle on the corner where she'd gone to mass every Sunday. . . .

There was quiet in the room when I finished. Sev and Mandala looked at each other. Then Mandala walked over toward me, reached into his pocket, pulled something out of it that looked like a plane ticket, and slammed it onto a table beside me. *"This,"* he cried out, *"is for Mama!"* (Of course, God only knows what or who that ticket he produced so suddenly was actually for, but Mandala sure had Sev's same flair for the dramatic!) She would get her homecoming trip to New York from L.A. as part of the deal.

And so it was a deal, all based on a contract with an unheard-of Misery Clause. I headed back to the Plaza, where Joy was waiting for me in the Oak Room bar. When I'd left her earlier, we had agreed—after a long, tortured weekend of weighing all the possibilities and potential problems—that we'd stay in L.A. Now I was going back to tell her that we were staying in New York for at least a year. She was stunned, although a part of her—her shopping part—loved the idea. On the flight back to California, we alternated between feelings of triumph and despair. Were we really doing the right thing?

As we drove up Plymouth Street in Hancock Park, where we lived, it was a beautiful sunny day, and we could see both of our girls playing out in front of the house near one of the palm trees. The sight was such a far cry from the manic city whirl that we'd left just a handful of hours earlier. My heart sank all over again. I thought maybe we couldn't make the switch, not even for a year, not even with a Misery Clause.

But, you know, we did it. It wasn't easy. There was another brand-new show to start up, with plenty of problems to overcome. But on that first Monday in April of 1983, we got our *Morning Show*, as it was then called, going and going strong, too. And it's been a dependable hit for the last twenty-eight years.

One night, earlier in this very year, Joy and I were out in California again, where both of our girls now live, and we were invited to the Severino home in Encino. It's the same beautiful house that he and his wife have held on to since the seventies, back when we were in the midst of our happy KABC years of big ratings and easier living. There in the garage still stood the same big blowup photograph of Sev as a guard on the University of Connecticut football team. And Sev . . . well, like all of us, he's older now, but he's still a little menacing, in maybe a sweeter and gentler way. But that night we started reminiscing over most of these stories I've just shared with you. And he laughed and laughed, and so did I. Somehow all of that terrible drama we struggled through so long ago really didn't mean a thing anymore. The truth is, we still love each other very much. And we probably always did, even all through those few years of temporary darkness.

Love like that, you know, can be a funny thing. *Kapish?*

WHAT I TOOK AWAY FROM IT ALL

Passionate people are often unpredictable people. If you choose to follow them, be prepared to ride their waves.

In business, think first with
your head, and soon enough your
heart will follow the same path.

Chapter Fourteen

COACH FRANK LEAHY

Well, the time has come for me to take you back to where my heart and my spirit were truly formed—and have also happily remained ever since. That's simply the way it goes with this particular place. Because no book of mine about people who've inspired and impressed me most would be complete without stories I've drawn from what is probably the greatest long-standing influence in my life: the University of Notre Dame, in South Bend, Indiana. I suppose that if you know anything at all about me, you were expecting this. And of course, you were absolutely right.

But to this day, I can't tell you how much I love to walk people around that gorgeous campus for the first time to let them discover its unique magic—those whispering ghosts of triumph, that certain electric vibration in the air, that peaceful feeling of goodness. It's just a very sacred place to me. Even all these years after I graduated, it's still the kind of place that makes you want to be better than you are in every way. It somehow challenges you to aspire to even greater heights than you'd imagined for yourself. I think about so many of its legends—along with all the priests, the faculty, the students, and the coaches I've met there—and I know that they live inside me always, and unforgettably. For sure, its never-say-die influence has helped me overcome a lot of pitfalls I've encountered in the course of my lifetime. Or, to put it another way: I don't know what I would have done—or who I actually would have become—if I hadn't attended Notre Dame.

My first exposure to the school came when I was about nine and my uncle Mike took me to see the great film *Knute Rockne All American*. Yes, the one where Ronald Reagan was the Gipper and Pat O'Brien was Rockne, which made such an impression on me. I was just a kid but couldn't miss seeing, right up there on the big screen, all the passion surrounding that place and its true-life football heroes. After the movie, which we'd both enjoyed plenty, Uncle Mike offhandedly said, "One day maybe you'll go there. . . ." Of course, I never believed for a moment that could really happen. My life was in New York, rooted especially in the Bronx. That's all I knew. I'd never gone west of the Hudson River, and Indiana sounded like it might as well have been a foreign country. But I was already becoming a big sports fan and had known most all the legends of Rockne and George "the Gipper" Gipp and the Four Horsemen. Still, the mere idea of seeing this place called Notre Dame felt as unlikely as setting foot on the moon.

Next thing I knew, though, Notre Dame turned up right in front of me, right there in the Bronx, no less! This was in the fall of 1946 when my Catholic Youth team happened to be playing a game in Macombs Dam Park, directly across the street from the original Yankee Stadium. Around noon, I noticed an enormous crowd pouring into the stadium, followed by a long gray file of West Point cadets. That's when I remembered that it was the day of the big Notre Dame–Army game, a pairing that was then and always would be a rivalry for the ages. At that time, the Army football team was a national phenomenon—thanks largely to their two renowned Heisman Trophy winners Felix "Doc" Blanchard and Glenn Davis, also known as Mr. Inside and Mr. Outside. In their two previous meetings, they had crushed the Irish; the mortifying scores were 59–0 and 48–0. But now Coach Frank Leahy had returned from the war, and the Irish were bitter and furious about those major lopsided defeats. I don't remember the score of the Catholic Youth game I played that day, but afterward I rushed home to hear the Notre Dame–Army match on the radio. It was a nail-biter of epic proportions, ending in the remarkable tied score of 0–0—and it would go down in history as one of the classic football standoffs of the twentieth century.

Three years later, it was college time for me. I mentioned to my parents that I'd been thinking about staying in New York and applying to Fordham. But my father surprised me by pushing hard for Notre Dame. He had served several years earlier in the Marine Corps with the immortal Notre Dame legend Ed "Moose" Krause, who'd returned to become a line coach for Frank Leahy, and would later go on to take over as the school's athletic director. My dad recounted to me that while they were carrying out a mission off in the jungles of some Pacific island, Moose would hold the marine officers spellbound with his tales of Rockne and the Gipper and the lore of Notre Dame. My father was instantly hooked by the great history of the school, and felt that I would thrive there. One phone call to Moose paved the way. He pushed for me, and I got in. That was the first great turning point in my life.

And so, one Sunday in early September 1949, I got on the 6 P.M. westward-bound train at New York's Grand Central Terminal—and off I went clattering toward exotic and faraway South Bend, Indiana. It was an all-night train ride, but there would be no sleeping for me. I was scared stiff! We arrived at six o'clock the next morning and were met by buses that took us to campus. On the way up Notre Dame Avenue, someone yelled out, "There's the Golden Dome."

That's me, of course, flanked by my parents on the hallowed grounds of Notre Dame in 1953. They were happy I graduated . . . and relieved I'd given up the idea of singing.

Notre Dame's football coaches impressed me so much over the years. The first one I met, Frank Leahy, later appeared as a guest on my first TV show.

I love this picture
of Lou Holtz
honoring me
as his assistant
coach for the
day at a halftime
scrimmage. (Well,
why wouldn't he—
we won the game,
didn't we?!)

This photo of Joy and me with Ara Parseghian and his wife,
Katie, at the 1971 Cotton Bowl in Texas is another favorite.
It was a great day for the Irish.

I was a young ensign in the Navy when I met Major Bill Rankin (pictured on the right with me before a quick flight over Southern California). When he and another formidable major, Keigler Flake, ordered me to pursue my dream career in TV, I didn't dare argue.

My first job as a roving reporter entailed driving around in this 1240 KSON News vehicle rigged with all kinds of crazy equipment.

I later had my own show on KOGO TV in San Diego, where I covered events around town like this one at the Old Globe Theatre, which is still one of the most prestigious theaters in the country.

I had great fun
with guests such
as Ronald
Reagan. (Who
knew he'd become
president one day?)

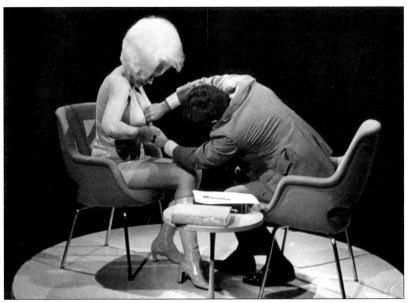

And more fun with the beautiful bombshell Jayne Mansfield. (Well,
maybe not as much fun as this picture suggests—I was just adjusting her
microphone. I swear! Well, somebody had to do it.)

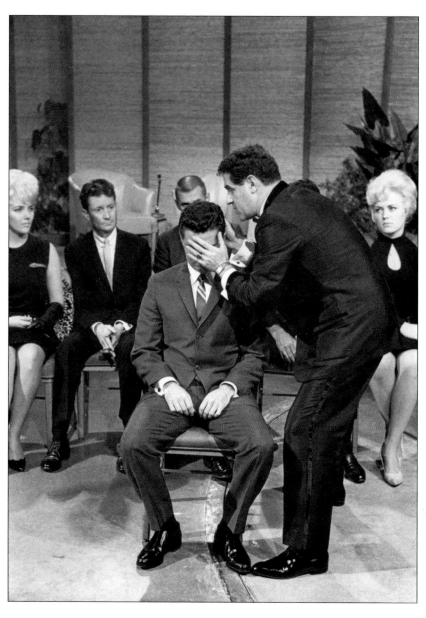

And who could forget the famed San Diego hypnotist Dr. Michael Dean . . .

But it was guest Walter Winchell, the celebrated gossip columnist from New York, who really helped launch me into the big time by mentioning me in his column!

In the sixties, I became second banana on the late-night *Joey Bishop Show*.
Jimmy Kimmel, who decades later broadcast his own show up the block
from our studio, wasn't born yet, but he was watching from heaven.

There's Joey and me looking at the bulletin board at the
Ranch Market on Vine Street during one of our daily
pre-show walks. Steve Allen got lots of great material from
the messages posted there and lots of laughs, too.

Making your boss
look good is a job
requirement. Here I
am taking that role
seriously just before
showtime. (If Joey
didn't look good,
inevitably it was my
fault!)

But I was lucky to meet many entertainment greats through Joey. Here we are with comic genius Jack Benny, who I used to listen to on the radio . . .

with my idol Bing Crosby and his wife, Katherine, shortly after I sang to Bing (he was just getting over it) . . .

and with the one and only Don Rickles. Notice how Joey Bishop backed away, leaving me to die out there?

Here I am with Don several years ago backstage before a show. You should
see him with his pants off and his bathrobe on. He's beautiful . . . in his
own way.

You may not remember this, but Mary Hart was one of my co-hosts for a nanosecond in 1980 before she hit it big on *ET.* (Also shown here is Rick Ludwin, my producer in Chicago during the summer of '74 and now EVP of Late Night and Primetime Series for NBC.)

That's my first co-host on *A.M. Los Angeles*, Sarah Purcell. If you're wondering, we're both doing our best John Travolta impersonations.

My *A.M. Los Angeles* boss, John Severino, was responsible for some of the biggest changes in my career. That's Sev in the center . . . and yes, I'm dressed like Henry Winkler as the Fonz on *Happy Days* this time.

When Sarah left, Cindy Garvey came on the show. Nothing but beautiful blondes for me!

Sure enough, there it was shining in the glint of sunrise, looking like a beautiful postcard image. I landed in dorm room 222 of Zahm Hall, which was planted close to the Golden Dome itself. And that's how it all began for me.

That first week on campus also brought with it the opening game of the season—against Indiana. I attended my very first football rally on Friday night before Saturday's game. It was an event unlike any I'd witnessed—this thunderous show of sheer confidence, raising the rafters of the old fieldhouse, where basketball games and these pep assemblies always took place. The revered football squad filed, one by one, into the balcony seats above us. They looked enormous and tough, which of course they were; most of them were already hardened war veterans now in their final year at school. Then the coach stood up—the legendary Frank Leahy himself, who'd never lost a game since his return to Notre Dame in 1946. He began to speak in a voice that could cut through steel. This was a serious, no-nonsense guy who had a magical way with a motivational turn of phrase. He directed a portion of his remarks at the freshmen in the overflowing crowd, telling us in particular of the university's wondrous tradition and of the spirit that would soon consume us, and also what Notre Dame would mean to each of us later in our futures and how we should enjoy every moment of our time there because we would never again experience a place like this for the rest of our lives. (That, incidentally, pretty much summed up everything I've believed ever since.) With each declaration he made, I'd feel my scalp tingle and more goose bumps rise. He simply inflamed us and, frankly, I was ready to go join the team that very instant—to make that tackle, catch that pass, run for that touchdown! We began to cheer the coach onward, one sentence after another. I had never felt such wild enthusiasm in my life. And so, through the hypnotic power of Frank Leahy, Notre Dame had begun to overtake my soul so deeply that it would never let go.

Leahy had played tackle for two of Knute Rockne's five national championship teams in the late twenties and early thirties. Once during that period, as fate would have it, Leahy was injured at the same time Rockne was taken ill, and the two shared a hospital room for a couple of weeks, where they talked about nothing but football. Rockne spoke and Leahy listened. Leahy asked the questions and Rockne gave him the answers. Neither one could have known that Leahy would one day be considered Rockne's next truly great successor as a Notre Dame head coach. After he graduated, Leahy started as a line coach at Georgetown, then moved to Michigan State. He took over as line coach for five years at Fordham University with Vince Lombardi at the helm and then accepted the head coaching position at Boston College, where he lost only two games in two seasons. That's when Notre Dame quickly brought him back where he belonged in 1941 until the war took him away again a few years later. He became a lieutenant in the navy and returned to coach in 1946. Now here it was 1949, and his team was mainly composed of war veterans (no longer fresh-faced high school recruits), all of them still young men, who'd been aged by the rigors of fighting for their country. But then, Leahy was a master of psychology and motivation, which equals coaching genius. And together, this group hadn't lost a game since they landed back on American soil.

So, yes, when I got to the school, they had gone undefeated for three straight seasons. And we freshmen were beyond impressed by those players on that '49 team. They were older than us, for sure, and had an air of invincibility. We respected them to the point of awe. One player, in particular, who stood out on that great team was "Jungle Jim" Martin; he'd been a First Team All-American left end, but when Leahy suddenly needed a tackle, he chose Martin. And just like that, Martin made All-American at that position, too. His co-captain that year was the tough right end Leon Hart, who is one of only two linemen to ever win the Heisman Trophy; it was, you see, an amazing team. But I confess, Jungle Jim completely fascinated me. He would walk the campus like the heroic ex-marine that he was, and I'd find myself watching him from a distance until he'd disappear into whatever building he was headed toward. He was a rugged blond with a crew cut, and was also the heavyweight boxing champ of the school two years in a row, not to mention a superb swimmer. In fact, he swam so incredibly well that during his military tour, the navy would take him by submarine to a position off the Japanese-held island coast of Tinian and then bring him up to the water's surface, where he would swim his way, in the dead of night and all alone, to shore. There, he'd reconnoiter the island's beaches as a prelude to the marines' landing a few days later. Then he'd swim back to the spot where he'd left the sub and just wait, treading water and hoping it would reemerge to collect him. I was so taken by the guy that I actually wrote a story at the time about Jungle Jim. Years later, I had him as a guest on my San Diego TV show and decided to read the story to him on the air. He was genuinely moved by it, and I was happy I had the chance to do it.

But Jungle Jim and Leon Hart and most all of those tough veterans graduated after that 1949 season, leaving the following year's team depleted and weakened. It showed early on. In fact, in the second game of the 1950 season, Purdue upset us on a dark rainy September day, handing the Fighting Irish its first loss in five years. *Five years!* It had been so long since Notre Dame had lost a game, the whole student body had no concept of defeat. We'd never once seen the team lose a game. It was a shock. A real crusher. The score had been 28–14. We all just sat in the stands after the game, rain pouring down on us. The pain was staggering—an altogether new sensation, crazy as that sounds. Up till then, every Saturday had been a celebration. It had been the most dependable day of the week.

For some reason, a bunch of us wandered outside to the locker-room door of the stadium, where the team would exit. We began to call for Coach Leahy to come out. Maybe he could explain this awful turn of events and tell us what it was that had just happened. As we stood there getting drenched, the crowd grew larger. One student climbed to the top of a nearby tree so he could get a good look at the scene below. That big proud tree, by the way, had stood symbolic and firm during so many postgame celebrations. But now it anchored this wet and mystified assemblage.

Finally, the door opened and there was the coach, looking more haggard than any of us had ever seen him. He had never lost a game at Notre Dame. He didn't make any excuses or give us specific reasons why we were beaten. Instead, he told us about defeat and how sometimes during our lives we, too, would be defeated by something or someone. We would lose out or take it in the chops and it would hurt—but we should use what happened on this day to remind us that a defeat can always come your way. He explained that what had occurred on the field that day should only make us stronger, make us want to win even more, make us understand that that's what life is all about. It was all about getting back up again. Then suddenly it didn't hurt so much. I moved away from that tree renewed and hopeful all over again. We all did. And I never forgot his speech in the rain, especially whenever those inevitable moments of loss came along in my life.

Like Jungle Jim, I later convinced Coach Leahy to come on that Saturday show of mine in San Diego. My respect for him had always been just so profound, and now I faced him, man-to-man—although he was, of course, a truly great man among men. This was really such a deep and personal privilege for me, even though it was being broadcast live to the public. Especially because I was able to look right into his eyes and tell him, as best as I could muster, what he and Notre Dame had continued to mean to me. But still, he could never really know what an impact he'd made on all of us with his speech that day in the rain. I'm sure it was a day he wished had never happened. But even then, I was so grateful that it did happen. And that his words about the importance of loss had been not just necessary but also driven home so powerfully. I always thought it made me a better man.

WHAT I TOOK AWAY FROM IT ALL

The world you know in your youth is only a tiny sliver of the world that awaits you beyond. And it's all there for the taking, when you're ready.

Remember, whatever or whoever inspires or moves you enough to give you goose bumps at the time is very likely to mean more than you know over time.

When heartbreak is a brand-new sensation, know that you've only just begun to live your life. Pain passes, and when it does, it often leaves determination in its wake.

Chapter Fifteen
COACH ARA PARSEGHIAN

Okay, just to be clear with you: I would remain grateful for the invaluable wisdom I had absorbed so early on from the great Coach Leahy. Losses, as he predicted, cannot be avoided during the course of our regular everyday lives. And yes, each setback that we suffer makes us stronger and better individuals. That much I did come to know well, or have at least tried my best to embrace, along the way. But I might as well tell you now—when it comes to Notre Dame football losses—there is only so much that I'm capable of accepting. To this day, I cannot speak after an Irish defeat, not for many hours, anyway. I sulk and I mope, quietly heartbroken, or else I pout and gnash my teeth. It can be very embarrassing, really. I just do not take it well. And Joy, meanwhile, cannot stand the way I don't take it well. She has told me so in no uncertain terms. Even when I think I'm taking it in stride I can be unbearable. I understand completely. *And believe me, I'm sorry!*

But let's go back to where I left off—simply because loss had soon enough, and quite shockingly, become the status quo after Frank Leahy retired from coaching in 1954. Notre Dame, in fact, wouldn't see another coach like him for ten agonizing years. And it showed. The football team went into a serious decline and the fan base sank with it. Even though Leahy had helped me understand the essential meaning of defeat, it was still like a knife in my heart every Saturday when we consistently lost throughout that decade-long drought.

Meanwhile, a new young college coach from Akron, Ohio, had landed a job helming the Wildcats of Northwestern University in Evanston, Illinois, which is located just north of Chicago. Many times each year this man would drive between Akron and Chicago on that Indiana interstate highway, always glancing up to see the Golden Dome as he passed Notre Dame, and never dreaming that he'd one day become the next bona fide legendary head coach there. His name was Ara Parseghian, and he was beginning to make a respectable football program out of the perennially hopeless Northwestern team, whose own school newspaper had been pleading, out of sheer humiliation, for them to drop out of the conference. But Parseghian wouldn't let them quit, and even with that mostly mediocre team, he was beating Notre Dame with stunning regularity. In fact, he beat us four times in a row. And that, as it turned out, was enough to prompt Notre Dame's president, Father Theodore Hesburgh, to hire him away and make him head coach in South Bend. Parseghian arrived too late in 1964 to do any fresh recruiting; he would have to make the most of a team with five consecutive losing seasons—a team that had lost seven out of nine games the previous year. No, this was not the Notre Dame team or tradition America had once revered. Not even close.

Ara really didn't know what to expect from the students, who were already pretty gravely down in the dumps about football. But on a cold February morning with a couple of feet of snow still on the ground, a crowd of three thousand poured out of the dorms and classrooms to surround and welcome him. He stood there in the center of the campus outside of Sorin Hall ready to begin with a simple hello, but the group started to cheer, and that cheer grew into a roar—and that roar, I was told by Notre Dame's sports publicity director Roger Valdiserri, lasted ten full minutes. They wouldn't stop. It was evident that everyone wanted him to deliver more; they wanted their old Notre Dame back, and they hoped that he would be the guy to do it for them.

Of course, I was hoping as hard as all the rest of them. My friends during those years had witnessed how badly I'd reacted to that unending string of losing seasons and naturally thought I was either ridiculous or insane. But out in California they couldn't begin to know what I knew about the old days on that field. So I stayed in close contact with Roger, who'd been a classmate of mine in the fifties. Right away, I peppered him with questions, wanting to know everything about Ara.

"What's he like?" I asked immediately.

"Intense," Roger told me. "Very intense."

"What time does he get there in the morning?"

"Around five A.M.," Roger reported. "While the rest of the campus is asleep, he's there at his desk with his coffee, plotting and planning."

I liked the sound of this guy right away, but what could he do with the same team that had won only two games the previous season?

As it was, Ara's hiring coincided with my own major new career shift to take over that national syndicated late-night show from Steve Allen in Hollywood. By the time I'd settled into that job, such as it was, Ara had already won his first three games, and then the fourth and fifth. I felt the excitement build from all the way out on the West Coast and had an idea. I wrote Ara a letter to congratulate him on what was happening. I told him that I truly believed he could win the next five games and then the national championship as well. I also said that I would love to interview him for my show on the Sunday following the game against the University of Southern California Trojans, which was still a handful of weeks away. He very kindly wrote back, saying he couldn't promise an unbeaten season, but sure, he would meet with me when the Irish came to Los Angeles for the USC game. And then, just as my gut had told me, he won the sixth game, and the seventh, and the eighth, and then the ninth. He was on a roll and grabbing the attention of the nation.

After that 9–0 start, he even landed on the cover of the November 20, 1964, issue of *Time* magazine. The story declared that Ara was *the* coach to put a new coat of gold on the Dome. I couldn't have agreed more. *Time* reported:

> Handsome and raven-haired, Parseghian could pose for anyone's image of the spirit of Notre Dame—wearing Leahy's shoes and Rockne's suit. He has to win because the laundry bill is too high when he loses; his wife has to change the sweat-soaked bedsheets each morning. . . . For Ara Parseghian, the man who cannot stand to lose, the day begins at 5:30 A.M. with four cups of coffee, usually ends with a tranquilizer and the *Late Late Show.* Even when he eats, he has a pencil in the other hand, diagramming a play. Is there something he has forgotten, some minuscule detail he has overlooked, some new way to win? There has to be, there always is at Notre Dame.

A week after the *Time* story was published, that final game of the season had arrived—our Los Angeles showdown with the team's longtime archrivals at USC. All eyes were on Parseghian. I was thrilled for this young coach who'd so suddenly changed everything at Notre Dame after a gruesome ten-year dry spell. The fans and the students would be on top of the world. We'd be playing for the national championship just like back in the old days, and I would be the first to sit with him the next morning and tell him how proud we all felt. We had arranged to meet for our celebratory interview on the 50-yard line at the Coliseum at 9 A.M. on the Sunday after the game.

The Trojans have never been easy to beat. The rivalry dates back to the Rockne era. The games are always tough—especially those played out west in that Coliseum, which is still one of the largest stadiums in the country. The USC band is big, too. Impressive and always noisy—and most annoying of all, even when they stop blaring away, the drummer continues to beat his drum steadily, over and over and over again, like a grim warning . . . a surprise attack just waiting to be unleashed on the opposing team. And then, of course, there's that Trojan Warrior mascot who gallops in on a sparkling white horse, prompting the crowd to go crazy. As the ominous drumbeat, all the while, keeps *pounding, pounding, pounding.* It's downright scary. Well, I suspect many of you know what happened that day. The game went back and forth. Then, deep into the last quarter, Notre Dame was winning when USC began a drive downfield with less than two minutes left on the clock. And that drumbeat just kept thumping. And thumping. And I had a miserable feeling churning in the pit of my stomach. And sure enough, with one minute and twenty-eight seconds remaining, USC scored on a pass from Craig Fertig to Rod Sherman, and they won the game by three points. Instant cataclysm.

I watched Ara's shoulders slump on the field. I was beyond tears. I couldn't believe that after achieving the impossible, after winning every game thus far, Ara and Notre Dame would lose in the final minutes of that championship game. I was sure it was all because of the drummer and that white horse, and I thought, just for a minute, that I would go hunt them down and . . . but never mind. I didn't do it. Frankly, I could barely move.

That Saturday night was a terrible night to be a Notre Dame fan in Los Angeles. The city was dizzy with celebration. But then came

Sunday morning and my interview with this tremendous coach who'd just had his heart broken. I arrived at the Coliseum about ten minutes before nine. My cameraman was set up on the 50-yard line. I would have understood if the coach didn't feel like talking—which, as I've told you, is how I handle such losses. But I walked to the 50-yard line and waited for him anyway. How strange it was to be in that cavernous place when, just hours before, there'd been such a fierce struggle on the very turf where I now stood. A light wind was rustling the empty cups and newspapers left behind in the deserted stands where bedlam had broken loose among the crowd of ninety thousand fans who'd witnessed one of the great Notre Dame upsets in history, their all-but-certain national championship taken from them in the last moments of the game. The place felt eerie. And then I saw the limo we'd sent for Ara drive through a gate onto the field and stop at one of the goalposts. I had told the cameraman to start by panning the Coliseum seats and keep the camera rolling as the coach emerged from the car and walked out to meet me midfield. It made for both a haunting and stoic image of a very proud man, symbolically getting back up on his feet.

Our interview turned out to become a minor classic in Notre Dame circles, with so many requests for copies to play at University Club functions all over the country. For sure, it was quite dramatic to sit there with Ara in that vacant stadium as he recounted the game nuances and those shocking final moments and the pained locker-room scene afterward. He said that not since the assassination of President Kennedy had anything hurt him so much. But while it was a terribly sad morning for both of us, it was also the beginning of our long-standing friendship.

Ara, of course, pushed through his loss that day and continued to coach so many unforgettable Notre Dame football games for another ten years. I was there for all the rest of those drumbeating, hard-fought contests he had with USC coach John McKay, for better or for worse. Joy and I also went to the great Cotton Bowl games in Texas, all so exciting with Joe Theismann as Notre Dame's quarterback. Ara's coaching prowess was always amazing to see. One of his greatest moments came during the 1973 Sugar Bowl game against Coach Paul "Bear" Bryant and his University of Alabama Crimson Tide. Both teams had gone undefeated that year, and met for the first time on this stormy New Orleans night with heavy rain, strong winds, and lightning strikes in the skies above Tulane Stadium. We took a friend with us to that one, the actor-writer Jason Miller. Most famously, he played the young priest in *The Exorcist,* but also wrote the Pulitzer Prize–winning play *That Championship Season.* At the time, however, he was writing a piece about Ara for *Esquire* magazine. Before the game, Jason walked out to midfield, where Ara was standing, for a quick conversation. When he returned to the sideline, I asked him, "How was Ara?"

"Intense," said Jason. "God, is he intense." Which was saying something, because Jason Miller was plenty intense himself. As it was, Notre Dame caught Alabama by surprise in the closing seconds on a daring play from deep in Irish territory. Somehow, through the storm, we connected a 36-yard pass and won by a single point. But that was Ara for you. He had beaten the great Bear.

Those were joyous times for the Irish, but in 1974 I found myself in a downward streak. I had been out of work for nearly a year. Hollywood had become a dead end, and real-life responsibilities were closing in from all sides. Joy and I already had Joanna and were then expecting Jennifer. Money was tight. As I've mentioned, I'd been trying to make ends meet with a variety of jobs around the country. That was the same summer I got the emergency call from Chicago to take over the two-hour-long WLS-TV morning show whose host had died. I filled in for a couple of months and got a very positive reception; in the fall, they would name a permanent host. I wanted that show so badly and really thought I had it nailed. I'd gotten some great guests, such as one of my boxing idols, Chicago's middleweight champ Tony Zale, and even Ara drove in from South Bend early one morning for a special appearance with me. It was great fun and I loved my stay there, which happened to be Joy's hometown, making the idea all the more appealing. But at the end of the summer, the station had to make a decision and instead went with Steve Edwards from Houston. He remains a terrific broadcaster who became a great friend of mine years later in Los Angeles, where he still reigns as the local king of morning talk shows.

But it hurt. God, did it hurt. I had felt so confident about the job that I'd already told my friends and family back in Los Angeles that it looked like we'd be moving to Chicago. So when I got the bad news, I was shocked. Well, more like *devastated*. My spirit was all but destroyed. My hopes were in ruins. I got in my rental car and, instead of turning north on the expressway toward O'Hare Field for what would be a miserable flight home, I turned southeast and instead headed toward nowhere in particular. I just couldn't bear the idea of going back to L.A. like this. I kept driving and soon found myself on the Indiana Skyway and then on the Indiana Turnpike, growing more and more despondent by the minute and by the mile. I kept driving, and nearly a couple of hours had passed. That's when I saw the first exit sign for South Bend—thirty miles ahead. I immediately thought of Notre Dame. Maybe I had actually been thinking of Notre Dame all along, following some sort of internal compass. I will never know the answer. I knew that school wasn't yet in session, but the team would be well into preseason practice. That meant that my friends in the football program would of course be there: George Kelly, the linebacker coach; Tom Pagna, the quarterback coach; and all the other great coaches—but most of all, Ara. I figured that I could use a little cheering up, a little time to begin trying to make sense of what had just gone so wrong.

It was a sunny late August afternoon when I swung off the

expressway and got myself onto Notre Dame Avenue, heading toward that lovely campus. There, up ahead, was the beautiful Sacred Heart steeple and the Golden Dome towering above all else. I turned right and slowly approached the stadium, the House That Rockne Built. There was the locker-room door where Frank Leahy had stood in the rain twenty-four years before and told us how to handle defeat. There was the tree, taller than ever, which the student had climbed to get a full view of that unforgettable moment. All of it came back to me. I went straight to the coach's locker room and heard myself explaining the bad news to the invincible Ara Parseghian, telling him that I'd lost out on getting the job in Chicago. I told him that I'd had enough, that I just wanted to quit—which is something you do not say in the presence of that man.

Because Ara wouldn't hear of it.

"I won't let you quit," he said. "You must never quit." He promised, "There will be better times ahead."

He threw some Notre Dame sweats at me and told me to get out on the field and go catch some passes. I walked out on the practice field and felt better almost immediately. I jogged around the track a little, ran some modest wind sprints. All of a sudden it was great to be back—right there where I had learned so much about character and ambition. I was feeling that old spirit again. I almost felt like I'd never left. I caught some passes and watched Ara and his coaches put a clock on the incoming freshman quarterbacks, checking their speed and agility. One of them was an eighteen-year-old Pennsylvania kid named Joe Montana, who came in last. Joe wasn't very fast, but he sure could throw. Nobody knew he would become the next great Notre Dame quarterback.

But in the course of that afternoon, most of the anger and frustration I'd felt earlier had evaporated. My legs were tired from the team workout, but my mind was clear. I wouldn't quit. I'd keep going. Just like Frank Leahy had said, this defeat was only going to strengthen my resolve. And Ara had made sure of that. Whatever had brought me back to Notre Dame that day had simply saved my life.

I went home and waited. Three months later, John Severino had installed me as the entertainment reporter on KABC-TV, which was where the special journey that would eventually bring me to the life I live today truly began. And once I landed that job, I wanted to call Ara to tell him the good news. Before I could reach out, however, I learned that he'd been diagnosed with a heart condition. The doctors were suggesting that he retire for his own safety. All that intensity, all that charisma, all that work had taken its toll on him. But what a legacy—he had brought Notre Dame football back from near extinction, he made thousands of friends, he had been a great role model.

So the years went by—during which Ara himself did some work in television—and I had come back to New York and started building the morning-show franchise that has continued ever since. But one day I got a call from Ara, who told me that he needed some help telling the world about a deadly disease that I had never heard of—a disease named Niemann-Pick. Ara had become involved with the cause under the darkest of circumstances. He had discovered that he was the gene carrier for this devastating affliction, which skips a generation and passes directly from grandparent to grandchild. In his case, all four of his grandchildren were then in peril, and now Ara was asking if I might find a way to throw a much-needed spotlight on this rare and terrifying condition. He wanted to sponsor a campaign to research the disease and find a cure. He and his wife, Katie, first talked about it on my show. Viewers were stunned, having also never heard about this disease before. Naturally, the Notre Dame family staunchly got behind Ara, who has since appeared everywhere he could, spreading the message with everything he's got.

Like he said to me so many years ago, "You must never quit."

And he hasn't. Now the Parseghian Foundation supports twenty-five research groups all around the United States, the U.K., and Canada—each of them making great strides. He and his family have campaigned tirelessly for years to raise the funding necessary to keep exploring possibilities, and in fact, new drug compounds have been developed that actually slow the progression of the disease. But as of yet, there is still no cure. Most tragically, three of Ara's grandchildren have succumbed, but the oldest still lives, even though he, too, is a carrier. This sort of horror would have broken the spirit of many families, but the Parseghians have stayed the course and continued the fight. And Ara, at eighty-eight, keeps trying to win this battle once and for all. God knows, he excels at the art of winning. He has helped so many people in his lifetime, and now we all want to help him win this one. We all love him.

WHAT I TOOK AWAY FROM IT ALL

When difficult times arise, don't lose sight
of how far you've already come and of
all the better times that have helped
sustain you along the way.

After a terrible setback, the true test is how
you face the next day: Get up, show up,
and I promise you'll soon begin to cheer up.

Chapter Sixteen
COACH LOU HOLTZ

I need for you to indulge me here—*just one more very special time*—so that I can tell you about someone else I also happen to love, someone who is almost impossible *not* to love, unless you've once found yourself opposing him during a big-game showdown. But then again, he's the kind of guy who would win you over even after he'd won over you—as in beaten you and your team's brains out. I'll swear this to you: Even if he'd never become part of the legacy of Notre Dame coaching greats, I still would have wanted Louis Leo Holtz (or, as I like to chant, "Lou! Lou! Lou!") to become a part of my life. Which he is, and for which I am very grateful. Really, I would have felt the same way about him if he'd instead been a tax accountant or an insurance salesman. Although thank God he didn't become anything other than what he was, and continues to be. He radiates a remarkable sense of magic unlike any I've ever encountered. His spirit, his wisdom, his kindness, and his standards—simply as a man—are just that infectious.

How infectious, you ask?

Well, let me share with you a journal excerpt of sorts, returning us to Friday, September 9, 1994: There I was, back in South Bend, where the campus was pulsing with that electrifying one-of-a-kind Notre Dame pregame anticipation. It's called a pep rally. I was one of the speakers. This was the evening prior to the next afternoon's season opener, always a thrilling time, and for the sake of posterity (and also a book I'd been working on), here are some notes that I happened to put together shortly afterward. It ought to give you just a small taste of how Lou had been capable of inflaming me. . . .

> Lou Holtz has asked me to speak at tonight's pep
> rally. I'm ready! I'm always ready for Lou. The crowd
> is big, noisy, hopeful. I get up, take a deep breath, and
> holler: "In the last two years, we've had two fabulous
> football teams, yet neither one of them could win the
> championship. They came close. They deserved it. They
> earned it. They didn't win it. So now we have this team
> and they know better than anyone else that this is their
> season. Their year! Their chance! Their turn to bring
> a national championship back to Notre Dame, where
> it belongs!" I've got the crowd roaring. "We have three
> things on our side: the greatest sports fans in the world,
> the greatest tradition in sports, and the best coach in
> college football. Let me tell you how good Lou Holtz
> is: You could kidnap him on the day of the game. You
> could tie him up, blindfold him, hide him in a cellar in
> Goshen, Indiana! And he would still outcoach the other
> guy!" The crowd goes wild. The band plays the victory
> march. Lou speaks and brings down the house. We're
> all on fire.

Lou, you see, was all about fire—and a bunch of other terrific qualities—and his fire was always ignited in that proverbial nick of time. But to backtrack here for a moment, there were still plenty of good times to be had for the Irish when Coach Dan Devine followed strong on the inimitable heels of Ara Parseghian, winning the national championship with star quarterback Joe Montana in 1977, as well as the Cotton Bowl the year after. But as these things go, once Devine left in 1980, Notre Dame again fell into a tailspin. One we couldn't get out of either. I was back to kicking wastepaper baskets in my office after losing games. This sort of behavior continued pretty consistently from me for more than a few years. It got exasperating, let me tell you. One day, before a televised Notre Dame game, I called my friend Andy Sidaris, who had directed so many college broadcasts for ABC-TV, and I asked him if there was a coach out there who could bring us back. Andy said, "Let me put my color guy on with you." So he handed me over to the game analyst Frank Broyles, a good coach who later became the athletic director at the University of Arkansas. Like it was yesterday, I remember Broyles saying to me in that sweet southern drawl of his, "Regis, there's only one coach in America who can bring Notre Dame back to where you want it to be, and that's Lou Holtz." While I had heard of Lou Holtz, I wasn't all that familiar with his career. But Frank Broyles was pretty convincing, and I soon began repeating what he said to me wherever I went, to whomever would listen. I'm sure it had nothing to do with what happened, but one day not too terribly far down the road, Lou Holtz was named the next head coach at Notre Dame.

Before coming to South Bend, Lou had been recruited by the University of Minnesota to build up their struggling football program and was succeeding in bringing that team back up the ranks pretty quickly. But luckily, his Minnesota contract had a clause that said if Notre Dame ever called, he'd have to go. Well, I was thrilled when he arrived at Notre Dame for the start of the 1986 season. I called my old classmate Roger Valdiserri to find out what Lou was all about. Besides sharing that he was of medium height, very slender, and had a patch of blond hair on top of his head, Roger told me about Lou's first introductory team meeting. Now the squad he had inherited was, at that point, not only mediocre but also a bit lazy and maybe even not all that interested in football anymore. They were talking loudly as Lou walked into the room and took his place up front, where he waited to speak to the players seated before him. Two hulking linemen sat slumped in the front row, laughing raucously among themselves, with their feet casually propped up on the stage.

According to Roger, Coach Holtz looked down at the two of them and growled, "Get your feet off the stage and sit up straight. Listen to me and look at me. Look me straight in the eye!" And then he gave the group a riveting analysis of what he thought was wrong with their playing and what his plan was to correct the problem. None of them had known that Lou Holtz was such a passionate and inspirational speaker. So yes, they sat up straight that night and listened, too. They realized that this man was going to be something special, a different kind of leader. For starters, he had all of the names removed from the backs of the players' jerseys to drive home the importance of team effort over individual achievements.

Lou worked the team hard in the first year. They finished with five wins and six losses. The six losing games added up to a difference in score of only eleven points, so you know they were heartbreakingly close games. The second year, 1987, was already better. Toward the end of the season, they were eight and one. But then they lost the last three games on the road to three excellent football teams that year—Penn State, Miami, and Texas A&M. The final score of the last game was A&M 35, Notre Dame 10. This, after the Irish had grabbed an early 10–0 lead. It left a bitter taste in Lou's mouth. He didn't understand how they could've blown such a lead. He had disciplined them. He had earned their respect. But he wanted something more from them during the next season. He wanted perfec-

tion. Perfection means everything to Lou Holtz. He began his third
year of coaching at Notre Dame with that in mind: perfection. When
he took the stage at the first team meeting of that '88 season, this is
what he told them—which remains, as motivational words in life go,
perfection in and of itself:

> I want you to pay close attention to what I say because I
> don't want any misunderstanding about how I feel. I'm
> here to win football games for the University of Notre
> Dame. Not some of our games, not most of our games—I'm
> here to win all of our games. Every doggone one of them.
> We aren't here to come close. We are here to win every
> single football game we ever play at Notre Dame from this
> point forward.
>
> I want you to be the best, the very best in all areas
> of your life. I want you to be the best student you can
> be, I want you to be the best person you can be, I want
> you to be the best football player you can be. The only
> reason a person should exist is to be the best he can be.
> To play at Notre Dame is to reach perfection. I'm basically
> a perfectionist. I've heard all the reasons why you can't
> reach perfection. I'm here to tell you something. We are
> either going to reach it or we're going to come so close that
> the average person won't know the difference.
>
> Perfection at Notre Dame will not be demanded. It will
> be expected. I don't ever expect to lose another football
> game as long as I'm at Notre Dame and I sure don't expect
> to lose one this year. Less than perfection is a personal
> embarrassment to me, to you, and to this university. We're
> going to write another chapter in Notre Dame football
> history. We're going to reach perfection in football the
> same way as the university seeks perfection in every facet
> of the school. We are not asking for perfection—we are

going to demand it. Don't expect us to lower the standards to satisfy people who are looking for mediocrity, because that won't happen. Mistakes are a thing of the past. We expect perfection and we're going to get it.

I want to tell you what this football team is going to be. It's going to be tough. It's going to be physical. It's going to be relentless. We will look adversity in the eye and we will turn it into success. That's perfection. I'm sure there are people in this room who say right now, "Tell us what we have to do because we're willing to pay the price." On the other hand, there may be some in this room who will say, "We just can't do it." I don't care who questions our ability to succeed as long as they aren't members of this team.

Over the years, I've had the good fortune of hearing many of Lou's speeches to his teams as well as to some of America's biggest captains of industry. Whether or not you play football for him, you can't help but get fired up by the sheer conviction Lou Holtz turns loose on any group. You want to be the best player, the best company boss, the best anything you can be in his presence. Not only can he motivate you, he can entertain you. Believe me, I've heard all the great comedians throughout the decades and I assure you that Lou Holtz more than holds his own when it comes to getting the big laughs. He's not only wise about football, but also about everything else life tends to throw at us. You can give him your toughest personal problem—one so difficult that you don't know where the real answer lies—and Lou will listen to it, analyze it, dissect it, and give you the most effective solution. He'll tell you what is right and what is wrong, what is good and what is bad. He is one terrific human being with a pretty flawless life compass. He comes with layers upon layers of great gut instinct and rational thinking powers. I've pondered his remarkable gifts for years, curious to discover just what makes him Lou Holtz.

So a number of times, I've accompanied him back to his hometown of East Liverpool on the Ohio River, which is a fairly typical midwestern town, except for the unusual fact that it seems to be run more or less by the local mortician, Frank "Digger" Dawson, who simply reveres Lou. As does the general population of East Liverpool; he's their proud son and everlasting hero. They built a museum to showcase all his awards and trophies and photographs and everything else a legendary coach accumulates over a lifetime. It's quite a sight to behold. They've even installed an elevator to help the handicapped and elderly visitors see all the exhibits on the upper floor. With Lou's help, they also regularly raise money for scholarships that send the town's kids off to college.

One day I stood in front of that museum on Main Street with Lou as he pointed out his old haunts. "See the candy store on the corner across the street? That's where I hung out as a young guy." It looked, in fact, just like the candy store, Mac's, where I hung out as a kid in the Bronx, on Morris Park Avenue, across the street from my grammar school, Our Lady of Solace. I kind of liked that coincidence! Lou's son, Skip, who happens to be a terrific young coach now at the University of Southern Florida, told me that his dad had long ago played linebacker on his high school team, even though he weighed only 140 pounds. But he made up for what he didn't have in size with what he carried in fierce passion. I read somewhere that Lou prayed to God every night to make him bigger and stronger so he could continue to play football. Lou had been an altar boy back then and sometimes wondered why God didn't seem to be listening to those prayers. Only years later did he realize that God had most likely heard him, but had a different plan in mind, pointing him in another direction of the field instead. Better than just playing the game, God apparently wanted Lou to capitalize on his passionate spirit and become a coach. It was a plan that would work out pretty well for everyone.

You want another clue as to how the Lou Holtz spirit works? Well, early on another day when I'd gone to East Liverpool to help celebrate the anniversary of his museum, I had an afternoon date to drive twelve miles south to Steubenville, Ohio, where I'd been asked to be the grand marshal of a Dean Martin birthday celebration parade. Lou insisted on joining me, which meant that he would have to leave his own function in East Liverpool a little early. I tried to convince him to stay, but he wouldn't hear of it. I think it was his way of thanking me for being on hand for his anniversary party. So we drove to Steubenville together while he reminisced about all the times he'd ridden there by bus to play Steubenville's high school football team, which called itself the Big Red. Lou said they never did beat that team. Dean's commemorative birthday celebration, as it turned out, would begin later with an afternoon mass in the church where Dean, too, had served as an altar boy. Yes, just twelve miles downriver—and twenty years apart—Dean and Lou each performed altar boy duties while growing up in their respective and very similar small Ohio hometowns. And in time, both would become men who, different as they could be, achieved immense stardom in the professions they pursued. I kind of like that coincidence, too. In fact, something tells me that they would have thoroughly enjoyed each other's company. The image of that combination can't help but warm my heart somehow.

Anyway, Lou and I have never lost touch through the years, as our friendship has only expanded. Whenever he's in New York, we always find a way to get together. Which brings to mind one particular New Year's Eve a handful of years ago. He had called ahead to tell me that ESPN needed him to come to town and join its panel of studio commentators during the New Year's Day bowl games. He'd asked whether Joy and I would be around the night before, so that maybe we could ring in the New Year together. Well, as it happened, we would not only be around but would actually be hosting the Fox network's special New Year's Eve celebration, direct from Times Square. I asked him to be a guest on the big broadcast and suggested that we all go out afterward. He happily agreed.

Now I had heard about the highly cautionary post-9/11 situation that's taken hold in Times Square on New Year's Eve, but until you find yourself right smack in the middle of it, you have no real idea how rigid the rules have become. From three o'clock in the afternoon, there is a total lockdown on the thousands of celebrants who decide to come watch that ball drop from high atop One Times Square at midnight, while the dancing in the streets commences. In our new world of vigilance against terrorism, the police force has no choice but to take tight command over crowded events like these, meaning that once you arrive there, you must stay where you are and not roam around. For the remainder of the day. That's the order. That's the new world.

Meanwhile, our Fox broadcast had stationed us on the second floor of a restaurant directly across the street from the Marriott Hotel, where Lou was staying. When I learned of all the restrictions that were being enforced, I realized that he would have a major problem getting over to our side of the street. I kept watching the crowd in front of the hotel, people packed in four-deep, with nobody allowed to move one way or another. Finally, I spotted Lou stepping outside of the hotel on this cold night, standing there with his blond hair and glasses, wearing a dark overcoat. I wanted to yell across the street to him, but of course the noise was deafening. I wondered how in the world he would ever be able to make his way through the gridlocked tangle to reach our televised home base. I could see him. I just couldn't communicate with him. Then a New York cop saw him, too, and recognized that the great Lou Holtz was standing alone, trapped on Broadway, a half hour before the ball was to drop. The cop asked Lou where he wanted to go, and Lou pointed toward our building, looking a little hopeless. (Hopelessness and Lou Holtz, by the way, have absolutely nothing in common.) The officer turned out to be a fan. He quickly called over five fellow cops, and with three of them flanking Lou on each side, they escorted him through the mob and across Broadway. It was quite a sight, and I only wished that we'd had a spare camera to capture this display of utter respect from New York's Finest—for a guy who had brought triumph back to South Bend, Indiana, several years earlier when it had been needed most.

I had, of course, missed Lou terribly when he finally left Notre Dame after the 1996 season, which had been his eleventh in all. Under his command, he had coached the last Fighting Irish national championship team (the 1988 crew that had been spurred on by the hair-raising Perfection speech), and also the last Notre Dame Heisman Trophy winner, Tim Brown. He had been robbed of another national championship by some very questionable refereeing at the Orange Bowl contest on New Year's Day 1991 against Colorado; the Irish's Raghib "Rocket" Ismail had made a sensational 91-yard touchdown run that was called back for a "phantom block" that only one official allegedly saw. But after all those intense years, Lou had become worn down by the same tremendous pressure that eventually overcame all other legendary Notre Dame coaches. And yet what unforgettable victories and records he's left in his wake. His total of 100 wins ranked second only to the great Knute Rockne's 105. He had reignited the spirit of the campus all over again, and frankly, he has so far not been replaced, much less even closely matched, since his departure from the helm. However, our latest coach, Brian Kelly, also from Ohio, has all the goods to make the Domers happy again.

Still, I've always wondered what made Lou so great. Setting difficult personal goals surely didn't hurt. I once read that long ago he actually wrote out a bucket list of 108 things he wanted to accomplish in his lifetime. Among them, he wanted to coach at Notre Dame. He wanted to win a national championship. He wanted to jump out of an airplane and parachute down to earth. He wanted to learn magic and demonstrate it on Johnny Carson's *Tonight Show.* (He did make it onto the Carson show for a terrific 1991 appearance but, alas, didn't get to pull off any of his magic moves.) At lunch during this past year, I asked him how many of those 108 feats he had so far accomplished. He told me 102. He's still working on the last six, and I wouldn't bet against him. Nowadays, he's a regular on ESPN during weekends in the fall, talking college football with Merle May, and once in a while he even does a little stand-up comedy as well as a few magic tricks in pretaped skits. He's still great fun to watch. He also continues to speak at Notre Dame convocations, and remains a favorite at major business seminars across the country, being the masterful motivational speaker he's always been. All of us alumni remember him and wish he had never left. He brings back fond memories of Friday-night pep rallies, when he'd move the crowds and literally will his teams to win games other coaches might've secretly thought impossible. He loved Notre Dame and we loved him.

To this day, whenever I have an important challenge in front of me—whether it's a new TV project I'm embarking on, a tough personal decision I have to make, or even something silly looming ahead like a crucial tennis serve—I still think of him. I'll bounce that tennis ball over and over again, sizing up my serve, and right there in my mind's eye, I see Lou Holtz in his sweater and Notre Dame hat, telling me that he wants me to hit it right. He wants me to win. He wants me to be perfect. I love him for that. Of course I'm still not perfect. But he keeps making me try.

Thanks, Lou. And incidentally, if anyone in this life is actually perfect at being exactly who he or she ought to be, then that person could only be you.

WHAT I TOOK AWAY FROM IT ALL

Get yourself near people who exude great enthusiasm and watch how it rubs off on you.

If you approach any task with perfection as your goal, it will always bring you that much closer to truly achieving it.

Chapter Seventeen

KATHIE LEE GIFFORD

I 'm still not exactly sure how or why this happened to me. But of course it did happen, and frankly, it's sometimes hard to remember what it was like before it all started. Not that I'm complaining. I'm just talking about the fact that—for the last *three and a half decades* of hosting morning television—I've continually had a woman seated to my immediate left. Rooted firmly, poised at my elbow, fixed to my side, always glowing shiny and bright. Actually, there's been a small full-time parade of these gifted ladies, one after the other, each beautiful, each sharp-minded, each ready to pounce on the next inadvertent stupid remark that might come out of my mouth, taking me to task, and not letting me forget about such remarks too quickly either. Where would I be without them? Where would they be without me? All right, they'd be doing just fine, but what memories we would have all missed out on—me and them and, I'm thinking, our viewers, too. You get the picture. It's a picture that I guess I've shared primarily with six of them—and two, in particular, most famously of all. By that, of course, you must know I mean these last two—that pair of back-to-back dynamos who both became cottage industries unto themselves as I sat to their immediate right, fighting for my life, morning after morning after morning.

As for the first of those two forces of nature, the one whose name sits up at the top of this chapter . . . Well, she was right there at that major moment of blastoff, on September 5, 1988, when people across the country suddenly began to get a glimpse of what I'd been doing locally at the start of every weekday, more or less, since 1975. And what I've always somehow just kept on doing—up until lately, anyway. Yes, she had been my cohost and copilot for three years already when our little New York–oriented WABC-TV *Morning Show* took flight that September to become the nationally syndicated *Live! With Regis and Kathie Lee* program. And what a life-changer that was. For both of us. Next thing we knew, our names and personalities became so hopelessly intertwined that wherever either of us went—and I mean *anyplace* in our actual separate off-camera lives— people couldn't understand where the other one of us was. All we heard, over and over and over again, was *"Where's Kathie Lee?"* and *"Where's Regis?"* Somehow they couldn't understand why we didn't move around perpetually fused together twenty-four hours a day. It was a sign, of course, that we'd caught on as a combo in maybe the biggest way possible, which was a wonderful thing, to be sure—but oh, the questions . . . I once wrote out my definitive all-purpose response because, honest to God, *I couldn't take it anymore:*

Where is she? How is she? What's she like? Her. Her! HER! All right, let's get this out of the way! In answer to the most asked questions of my life: She is irrepressible, indefatigable, unsinkable, ambitious, a whirlwind, and, frankly, she is the one who's really out of control. She's feisty and fearless, brash and loving, sentimental and shameless, generous and demanding. There's more than one woman here. Forget about Sybil—there's a whole platoon of Kathie Lees, and they never get tired. Never!

What's funny to me is that long before anyone cared, there was one especially significant answer to the question of Kathie Lee's whereabouts when we were not together that ought to be noted here. To rewind the tape a little bit, it just so happened that she had been working out in Los Angeles back when I was just getting my local KABC-TV morning show off the ground. Her name then was Kathie Lee Johnson, and she was a budding multitalent who sang (*it's hard to believe, I know*) on the updated version of the old game show *Name That Tune*, in addition to having other pursuits in the business. But as fate decreed it, she found herself regularly tuning in to that morning show of mine, which no doubt helped to give her a very early understanding of what I was all about and also what our future together would someday entail. "When I first saw Reege on TV in Los Angeles," she later said, after the two of us had been cohosting together in New York for about a decade, "I couldn't figure out if he was adorably obnoxious or obnoxiously adorable. I still can't. I just know that he is the absolute best at what he does. . . ." Those years in the mid-seventies marked the dawn of a whole new era in talk television, and—although neither of us could have known it then—it was a dawn that would somehow bring her into my life and plant her to my immediate left further on down the road . . . when we'd actually be ready for each other.

Because all of a sudden, out of nowhere and yet everywhere all at once, it was happening: a gradual format switch that hardly anybody remembers, but I always will. The time had arrived for the two-headed, double-teaming phenomenon of male-and-female cohosts. My KABC general manager, the inimitable John Severino, explained it all to me, just as I was about to take over hosting the station's daily ninety-minute *A.M. Los Angeles* program in 1975. (That's when I was also still juggling entertainment reporting duties on both the 6 P.M. and 11 P.M. newscasts.) Sev told me that television, like the rest of the world, was changing. It was all about balance and equality and individual points of view and so on—but the bottom line was that there would be male and female cohosts or coanchors on all talk and news shows, effective immediately.

It was something new for me, to say the least. Sev then told me about his first choice of cohost for me: She was an up-and-coming sensation at the very same San Diego station where I'd in fact gotten my own start, KFMB-TV. Her name was Sarah Purcell. She'd been hired as a secretary, and when the AFTRA union went on strike, the station substituted for the on-camera people who had walked off the job those folks in the office who didn't cower away from the broadcast spotlight. Sarah happened to be a good-looking blonde with a terrific personality and a winning smile. She jumped in to pinch-hit for the town's number one weather-forecast personality, Bob Dale, who was a folksy midwestern guy from Ohio with a warm, humorous approach. He was just a pure TV natural. San Diego loved him, but Sarah, the secretary from Indiana, was soon making a major impact all her own. Since the weather in Southern California hardly ever changes, the forecast person has to offer up some entertaining antics besides simply reporting the very predictable meteorological numbers, and she magically pulled it off. So magically, in fact, that Hollywood heard about her, and just like that, Severino gave me my first cohost.

I wanted, of course, to keep the style of my opening segment just the way it had always been since that original Saturday-night show in San Diego. The one where I just ad-libbed stories that I'd collected about the various things that had happened to me throughout the week. That part of the show turned out to have been a consistent favorite feature for so many viewers back then. But this was a daily show—*with a cohost*—and I soon learned that it would be a different ball game. It would require developing a near-instant rapport and chemistry with the other person. As I explained it to Sarah, there were no writers and no studio audience and we would have to be the sole audience for each other, all while making the viewers feel like they were right there with us. We would have to listen intently and respond right off the cuff to whatever the other was saying. There would be no meetings to discuss what we would talk about. In fact, we wouldn't even speak to each other—and some mornings, not even see each other—until we went on the air. Which continued to be my unchangeable and quite essential preshow policy with every other cohost to come. In other words, I was hoping to keep it entirely spontaneous. Whatever we wanted to say to each other needed to be said first in front of the cameras. (My motto sort of became "Don't leave it out in the hallway!" That means no small talk at all prior to setting foot in the studio at that moment of airtime.) I could do that by myself because I knew where I was going with each story I told; however, doing that with a cohost would be a new kind of challenge, demanding a lot of on-the-spot guesswork while navigating the course of our bantering. But, you know, it all worked out. Sarah learned quickly. And mastered it so well that, two and a half years later, NBC offered her a job on a prime-time show and she was gone.

One day near the end of her run, we had as our guests Steve Garvey, the popular first baseman of the Los Angeles Dodgers, and his pretty wife, Cyndy. A few hours after the broadcast, Severino called me into a meeting. Sarah, we knew, would have to be replaced the following week, and based on what he'd seen that morning, he suggested that we ask Cyndy. True, he said, she had very little TV experience, but she was also married to a Dodger great and was a beautiful blonde with charisma, so who cared about experience? "You'll make it happen," he told me—actually, more like ordered me—and that was that. Cyndy stepped in, caught on quickly, and became quite good at this almost indescribable Host Chat thing we were well on our way to perfecting.

Truthfully, only one thing threw me about having a cohost: It meant that I could never again conduct an interview alone, a direct and focused one-on-one with a guest. I missed having that opportunity to lean in and try to create an intimate, memorable conversation. Now it would always have to be two of us talking with the guest at the same time, during which we would inevitably go our separate ways in the interview. We were never really able to build naturally from one question to the next. But that's the way it would be for the next thirty-five years. It was a necessary and unavoidable compromise we had to make. And in the end, it wouldn't be all that bad. But sometimes, with certain guests, I can't help but think that a one-on-one interview could have been so much better.

Still, the ratings on that local show went through the roof and it became one of those must-watch Los Angeles TV mainstays. Nobody in our 9 A.M. time slot came close. Once, the heavy-hitting syndicated Phil Donahue show turned up against us on a competing station . . . and then slowly, quietly went away. Years later, Donahue would jokingly complain to me that he never got a break in Los Angeles until they moved him to the afternoons. Meanwhile, Cyndy and I rolled merrily on into the start of the eighties until I got that ultimately regrettable call from NBC in 1981 and then proceeded to let them destroy a show that could easily have still been running on their NBC affiliates thirty years later.

NBC president Grant Tinker, as I've noted, had personally reached out to offer me that job and suggested I keep everything exactly the way I was doing it on my *A.M. Los Angeles* show, and that included having a cohost. I thought about the possibilities. There was one young lady I'd noticed doing a local show on Channel 11 called *PM West*. Her name was Mary Hart. She had all the solid credentials along with her looks, her voice, and a keen interviewing technique. Also, there was, and still is, a genuine niceness about her and, of course, that relentlessly great smile. Yes, she was the one. But before we even started our nine o'clock run on NBC that last morning of November 1981, the New York–based network programming guys decided to cut the show to thirty minutes. That made success impossible. We really didn't have the time or the chance to get established as a team, to get that give-and-take rapport cooking in the opening segment—or for that matter to have an opening segment at all! It was a predestined heartbreak, but Mary was a champ about it. Then again, tell me the truth: Have you ever seen Mary Hart *without* that beaming smile on her face? So we knew the end was inevitable, and one day in early April 1982, it came. The show was over.

The very next day I got a phone call from John Goldhammer, my old program director at KABC, who'd become involved in developing a syndicated half-hour all-entertainment news show, the first of its kind. He wanted to know about Mary and whether she'd be a good fit for the format. "Are you kidding?" I told him. "She'd be a natural for that show." Well, Mary got the job and you know the rest. She's been the queen of *Entertainment Tonight* since it launched thirty years ago and is one of the main reasons for its enduring success. She gave the show a touch of elegance, friendliness, and sincerity that made it a hit. Her male cohosts have come and gone, but Mary Hart stayed and became one of the most famous names in the television landscape. I wish she could have done it with me on the national NBC network show that never had a fair shot.

In any event, by 1983, it was back to local television thanks to my mercurial old boss John Severino, who'd become ABC's network president. I was basically restarting my original L.A. show, except this time from New York City, where my cohost, very conveniently, would be Cyndy Garvey, who had recently moved east to be near her postdivorce love interest, the fine composer Marvin Hamlisch. Ratings for our brand-new WABC-TV *Morning Show* again started climbing pretty swiftly. Of course, the viewership couldn't have sunk any lower than the minuscule numbers we'd inherited from the station's previous morning regime. But in fact we were off to a truly great start, and at the end of that first year, I invoked the Misery Clause (remember that ploy?) and, just like in the old KABC days, signed a four-year deal (taken to the cleaners again) as executed by Sev, that ever-smooth contract negotiator. When Cyndy learned that I'd been given such a unique—and frankly, uncommonly considerate—option clause, she couldn't understand why she hadn't been offered one upon her hiring as well. I tried to explain to her about my especially nerve-wracking circumstances, having to uproot my family and such. But the issue escalated into a standoff between her and ABC management, then into a bitter feud, and before long it was over.

Time for another cohost.

This one came direct from Oklahoma, of all places, full of energy, moxie, and eager to make her mark on this hot show in the Big City. She was Ann Abernathy. We had already met in L.A. at an ABC affiliate preview of new season shows. She had a great engaging personality, and I knew she had all the right experience and qualities for her next big step. It occurred to me even then: *This* is our next cohost. She came here, fit right in, was quickly embraced by our viewers, and then, like something out of the movies, she soon after fell in love with someone actually from the movies—quite literally, the Columbia Pictures chairman Gary Lieberthal. Right before our eyes, those of us at the show witnessed their romance blossom at an accelerated pace and knew she would inevitably have to make one of the biggest decisions of her life, because she was also in love with her New York–based TV job. In the end, Gary swept her off her feet and took her away to a new, exciting life in Hollywood.

They bought the lovely old Richard Brooks–Jean Simmons home in Holmby Hills. Joy and I visited them there a year later, and she gave us a tour of her truly grand new lifestyle. And what a dazzling whirlwind ride it had been for her—from Oklahoma to New York City to the privileged enclave of Holmby Hills, all inside a couple of years. It should happen to all of us.

What did happen to me next, however, would be the beginning of fifteen years in the spotlight with the One Who Changed Everything. Well, actually, nothing about the format of our morning program changed, then or ever really, except that my new cohost would quickly enough establish herself to be something of a human tsunami—unpredictable, unrestrained, uncompromising, unstoppable, and most of all, impossible to ignore. She arrived on that last Monday of June 1985, flushed and slightly breathless, with a song in her heart and a pair of running shoes on her feet. That was because she had just raced up Sixty-seventh Street from the set of *Good Morning America*, where she'd then been working for a couple of years as a special correspondent and occasional fill-in host for Joan Lunden. In fact, she'd just pinch-hit for Joan again that very morning when, mere moments later, she made her debut beside me as Ann Abernathy's full-time replacement. She burst into our little WABC studio a few seconds after we'd gone on the air. "My new cohost can't even get here on time!" I hollered, teasing her from the start, which she would reciprocate in kind (believe me!) for the rest of our long ride together. In fact, I think it took her all of about one show before she first called me a jerk on live local television. That, of course, continued throughout all our years of live national broadcasts as well. But it was her special way, I think, of showing me affection and respect, as only she could. I think.

Yes, Kathie Lee Johnson had landed on the stool to my left and, from day one, the wattage level in that studio of ours would only get hotter, as she got better and better, month by month. She instinctively knew just how to go out there and really let it rip between us. During and beyond those years she'd spent in Hollywood—where she frequently watched my old show with its original zinging give-and-take Host Chat segments—Kathie had gone on to work all kinds of TV jobs, including one quick season on the mostly unseen sitcom spinoff series *Hee Haw Honeys*. She eventually made her way to New York, but in addition to her *Good Morning America* duties (which nicely showed off, in glimpses, her larger-than-life personality and no-holds-barred opinions), she'd also just begun turning up in national commercial spots everywhere, singing about the joys of taking those Carnival Cruises. Her signature big-energy shipboard beltings of song pitches like *"Ain't we got fun . . ."* and *"If my friends could see me now . . ."* would continue to run throughout most of our years together, making that cheerful disposition of hers all the more inescapable—not to mention that voice (but I'll get back to that in a moment). She could do it all, as naturally and as unself-consciously as they come—the best assets any broadcast personality can have, honestly.

Anyway, I'm sure it was that winning realness of hers that had captured the heart of Frank Gifford, the former NFL New York Giant great and ABC *Monday Night Football* commentator, with whom she'd worked a bit on *GMA* before joining our show. Somewhere not long into our second year of cohosting *The Morning Show*, they were married, and we eventually learned that her nickname for him was "The Love Machine"—which she knew would set off fits of exaggerated groaning from me. But that was key to what we were doing. We always found a way to stay edgy and needle each other, either gently or without much mercy. Each of us did our share of eye rolling when the other one revealed some story from our personal lives, whether about that infamous dark cloud of mishaps that follows me around (*which, by the way, it does*) or about the blinding sunshine and rainbows that lit up her world as a doting mother and adoring wife, etcetera. I used to always say, "I had to shield my eyes the first time I met her!" We kind of came across as diametric opposites, which seemed to give the audience as much of a kick as we got from our silly ribbings of each other. But we clicked. Gelman—as in our considerably younger, longtime executive producer, Michael Gelman, *who insists on always being right*—decided that the key to our success came from the "subliminal sexual tension" between the two of us. I told him he was crazy, that there was no sexual tension at all. At least on my part, anyway. But I'm pretty sure that that held true for her as well.

Besides her natural knack for cohosting, there was something else she could do, too: sing beautifully. Both of her parents had musical backgrounds, so her genes were primed for it, and she started singing as a kid in Maryland and never stopped. To this day, she's always ready to burst into song, which still happens now and then during that entertaining fourth hour of the *Today* show she does with Hoda Kotb. But in our years, she already had her own nightclub concert act down pat and drawing increasingly good crowds. Somewhere along the way, as I mentioned before, I'd started doing a club act myself and had been opening in Atlantic City for headliners like Tony Bennett, Steve and Eydie, and of course Don Rickles. It had been great training for me. Then she came up with the idea for us to work together on a nightclub act of our own, which actually turned out to be pretty good. Our agent, Lee Solomon, one of the William Morris stalwarts, booked us into all the best show places around the country, which in those years were booming, especially in Atlantic City. (Those days are sadly over now in Atlantic City and in so many other major venues.) But we made quite a team out there, taking our alternate turns onstage and also doing a lot of fun material together. In fact, we got so hot we used to do two shows a night on Fridays and Saturdays before packed houses.

But it was all part of the momentum that our syndicated *Live!* show had been picking up as we rolled into the nineties. We were flying high, and the ratings kept flying even higher. Gelman would put us through the paces and had us do a lot of physical business on the show, which usually wound up going haywire. Every time some new trend came along, we tried it. I remember one New Age healer-type guest who would place hot rocks on your body to release aches and pains. Naturally, I was on the table, shirtless, waiting for my pains to go away when Kathie Lee took advantage of the situation and dropped some rocks on a very sensitive, delicate area of my anatomy, which brought only more pain to another part of my body that was doing okay up till then. I also believe we were the first show to introduce those bulky fat suits that made us look like Japanese sumo wrestlers. We'd go at it, and our awkward sort of roly-poly tussles on the mat made for some very funny segments. Not to mention all the laughs we got when she won every match.

Then again, her competitive athletic streak was never to be taken lightly. She'd show her stuff whenever we'd mix it up with the many sports stars that came on the show. I forget who was first, but he was one of the great basketball shooters in the game. He and I were tossing ball after ball at a hoop we'd set up, all to no avail. Nothing would drop for either of us. Exasperated by this miserable scene, Kathie Lee scooped up one of the balls and just flung it recklessly at the basket and . . . *swish.* Even Kelly Ripa, who would later follow in Kathie Lee's footsteps so perfectly, has consistently done the same thing over the years. *Yes, it gets embarrassing!* But the audience loves that stuff—because it's not *them* looking so inept!

In any case, throughout our tenure together, Kathie Lee and I got into some memorable Host Chats of every stripe and color, which of course is the unpredictable nature of that opening segment. I would always find some new little irritant or major crisis to bring up at that table where we perched, and she would attempt to sort through whatever my stupid mess of the moment happened to be. Even as our popularity rose to greater heights, for instance, I would talk of having doubts about how I was spending my life—not that I had any real alternative in mind. But she would usually shake her head at my grousing and try in vain to talk me down off one ledge after another. Here's just a taste of one of those special exchanges. . . .

ME: What have I done with my life? I spent it in front of this stupid camera! For what?! It drives me crazy when I think of the way I squandered my life.

KL: The sad thing is, he really means that. You said that to me privately the other day and I got very upset.

ME: An unremarkable life!

KL: You're so wrong.

ME: Doing a little show in the morning?! Please! It means nothing in the grand scheme of things! Unremarkable! I've got a better word: insignificant! You think I'm kidding? I mean it from the bottom of my insignificant heart. I don't want to talk about it anymore.

KL: You need therapy.

ME: I came to the wrong place for it, I'll tell you that much.

You'd probably imagine that working together nearly every weekday for fifteen years could bring some bumpy moments along the way. Not between us, though. Toward the end of our run, I heard her tell Larry King the same thing: "Once in a while, we get on each other's nerves," she said—yes, please note that *she* said that! "But," she continued, "we've never had an unkind word between us in fifteen years. Never." Then, with great comic timing and a smile, she added, "Our *lawyers* have spoken. . . . No, I'm just kidding. We never have." Which is the absolute truth. For that matter, I hope you don't think I'm bragging here, but in all thirty-five years of working with cohosts, I can't remember a backstage squabble with any of them. I always knew how important it was for the show and for our on-camera chemistry to stay on friendly terms. True, once in a great while, something might be inadvertently said that stung the other's feelings. But that was very rare. Nevertheless, some obstacles came up along the way for Kathie Lee. Some bad moments that the twists of life had thrown at her and which I thought she handled so well. They were tough times to get through, but she was a stand-up fighter. Like she also told Larry King: "You know what? I am, if nothing else—even if you hate my guts, you've got to give me credit for being one hell of a survivor in this world." I happen to give her all of the credit there is to be had in this world for it and was very proud of the way she so gracefully navigated through those difficult situations. In fact, I learned that all these ladies, each and every one of my cohosts, were a lot tougher than many of the TV guys I knew.

The latest and last one, who I'll tell you more about soon, is no exception in that department. So, naturally, everyone likes to ask how did Kathie and Kelly get along when they met after the eventual changing of the guard in the cohost seat? Well, I'd like to tell you that there was always that underlying tension between them—especially over me!—and that it was just a matter of time before there would be screams and slaps and calls to the police to break it up. I'm only kidding, of course—but, you know, I really would have loved to have seen that. No such luck. Nope, Kathie Lee sent Kelly flowers on her first day, and it's always remained a very warm and cordial dynamic between them. In fact, a few seasons later, Kathie Lee even guested on Kelly's ABC sitcom *Hope & Faith*, in a winking inside-joke kind of episode where Kelly's character (ironically, a former soap opera star who'd fallen on hard times) got a waitress job in a diner where she was angling to replace a certain longtime waitress, at least momentarily, so as to take over serving the table of a big-shot Hollywood director who'd come in for a meal. That longtime waitress she wanted to bump was played, of course, by Kathie Lee, who later came on our *Live!* show to talk about the very funny premise of that episode, among other things. . . .

> **ME:** We were just reminiscing here about *Hope and Faith*, and Kathie Lee did a bit on Kelly's show. She played a waitress—
>
> **KR:** And I played a new waitress that comes in and tries to replace her.
>
> **KL:** Yeah, that was hysterical. I said something that was so defiant to you—
>
> **KR:** You said, "You think you could do *my* job?!"
>
> **KL:** *"You think you could just waltz in after I've worked here fifteen years and do my job?!"* And you said something that was funny, too. You said, "Well, I'm hip, blond, and buff . . ." or something like that.
>
> **KR:** I think I said, "I'm buff, I'm funny, I'm smiley. How hard can it be?"
>
> **KL:** *"How hard can it be?"* Yeah, right. Yeah, I hated you.

Fortunately, everybody laughed—the three of us most of all, I think. I happened to take another look at that particular *Hope & Faith* episode not long ago, since it was on my mind while writing this, and I thought you'd enjoy seeing how that sitcom dialogue exchange between them actually played out. Kathie Lee's character told Kelly: "Over my dead body. Listen, missy, I've been doing this for fifteen years. The people love me. You really think you can just step in and do *my* job?" (This got screams and big applause from their studio audience.) And Kelly's character, Faith, replied: "I don't see why not. I got a great face, a hot bod, and a big mouth. How hard can it be?"

Well, as they both knew well by then, the cohosting job is harder than it looks, but nevertheless it's also a terrific thrill when things are really clicking. And in the course of that fifteen-year run that Kathie Lee and I rode out together, we had clicked plenty and it really changed our lives in such enormous ways. We were lucky enough to pile up so many great memories and unforgettable television moments. Then one day—which was February 29, 2000 (oddly enough, the official Leap Day in that Leap Year)— Kathie Lee announced she was going to be leaving the show later that summer. It was a move that she'd been toying with for quite some time. And during that time she had grown into so many more things than just a cohost: She was, in fact, a one-woman conglomerate, who already had, among other projects in the works, her own clothing line at Wal-Mart and also a cosmetics line, while having continued on as the big-voiced face of Carnival Cruises and, maybe most important of all to her, she was becoming a prolific songwriter and even more polished stage performer with a bunch of CD albums on the market. I caught her one day reeling off dictation letters to her assistant down in her office and I realized, *This woman has become a mogul in her own right.* Then it further dawned on me that our show gave her the one hour a day when she wasn't making executive decisions. On *Live!*, as I've said before, she didn't have to conquer the world, so she just conquered *me* instead! Besides which, she had done a few big musical turns on Broadway that gave her truly great pleasure. And once you've had a taste of that kind of magic out on the Great White Way, the lure of those footlights can be overpowering. She was ready to spread her wings and soar on to new adventures.

Good-byes, especially after all those years of inseparable morning teamwork, are always tough. Her departure day was July 28, and naturally, the buildup to her grand on-air finale with me had been intense and emotional. As she would say, "Over a third of my life has been here. This is family. It's been an amazing journey." Gelman had all sorts of surprises to spring on her during the farewell broadcast, including taped testimonials from Dave Letterman, Rosie O'Donnell, and Susan Lucci. Mayor Rudy Giuliani sent over an official proclamation declaring it "Kathie Lee Gifford Day" throughout the city. Her whole family, including Frank and their kids, Cody and Cassidy, were there—as was our big boss, Disney CEO Michael Eisner, who presented her with a trophy and said, "The ratings have been so unbelievable this week, can't you do it again?" All through the weeks beforehand, she swore she wasn't going to cry, but of course there was no chance of her sticking to that promise. There were waterworks in the end—and not just from her. In the last few minutes of that last show, I sang a special version of "Thanks for the Memory" to her, some of which went like this:

> *Thanks for the memory,*
> *Your smile was always sunny,*
> *You've made a lot of money.*
> *You've come a long way since you were just a*

Hee Haw Honey—
And met Mr. Football. . . .

Now comes a time when we're partin'.
After fifteen years, that's an option.
We'll put Gelman up for adoption.
But don't lose heart—
There's still Wal-Mart.

And thanks for the memory.
They said it wouldn't last.
Sure has been a blast.
We never won the Emmy, but we never were
outclassed—
To the voters, kiss my —.

The next day the New York *Daily News* would report: "And in a week in which the star steadfastly refused to cry, it was Regis Philbin who finally brought Kathie Lee to tears, with his version of 'Thanks for the Memory.'" After summing up some of those personalized lyrics, the story then stated: "And he left her weeping when he crooned, 'Please recall, I love you so much.'" Yes, that was the last line of the song that I'd sung to her. And I meant it. It had been a great run. The broadcast ended. There were good-byes all around, although she and I have never lost touch because, well, how could we?

But once the misty eyes finally dried up a bit, the reality began to sink in. Which meant that it was time again to look for another cohost. And yet who could've guessed what a terrific new thrill ride next awaited me?

WHAT I TOOK AWAY FROM IT ALL

Developing a strong dynamic or chemistry
with a colleague takes time—but more
importantly it also takes, from the very start,
a mutual respect and the ability to listen
carefully to each other.

Good-byes are never fun, but certain people
don't necessarily have to leave your life
altogether. Nor should they.

Chapter Eighteen
KELLY RIPA

I ncidentally . . .

Yes, I'm starting this chapter with that word—*incidentally*—
because you-know-who thought it might've made a good title
for this book. She knew that I was writing about people who've
had an impact on me, by way of some personal shared history, feelings, or particular incidents that I've experienced with them along
the way. But mainly she thought it would be a great choice since she
insists that I've (*incidentally*) used that word on a constant daily basis
during nearly eleven years together of making our own special mix of
morning television chemistry. Well, incidentally, I disagree with her;
I'm fairly sure I don't use it *that* much. Just like I don't think I've ever
really said, "*I'm out of control!*" That one I blame on Dana Carvey,
who blurted it out so often when playing me in sketch after sketch on
Saturday Night Live back in the nineties that it got pounded into everyone's head as being "my" classic catchphrase. A catchphrase that *I
had no control over* . . . since I doubt I ever said it to begin with! Still,
I have to admit that Dana did channel a very funny "me" in those old
routines. But, you see, that just shows you that I'm not the one who's

out of control. Instead, it's the world I live in that's out of control. Believe me, those waves of day-to-day chaos or stupid little affronts I've regularly talked about over the years—all thanks, as you know, to that unshakable dark cloud over my head—do manage to keep me from having control of much of anything in this life!

But when it came to looking for Kathie Lee's replacement, Gelman and I very deliberately decided to take sure-handed control of the selection process. Honestly, we just took our time finding the right fit. What was the hurry at that point, anyway? In fact, I'd even gone so far as to utter the near unthinkable on that Leap Day 2000 when Kathie Lee dropped the bombshell and announced her upcoming departure from our show. At first, of course, I articulated half-joking disbelief: "She's kidding," I told the viewers in knee-jerk reaction, even though I already half knew this moment had been coming. "She ain't going anywhere. . . . She'll be back, crawling in here saying, *please.* . . ." Until I quickly saw that she meant it. Especially when she next offered, very sincerely, to stay on until we could "find the right lady . . . *if* it's a lady" to fill her seat. Then she added, "Hey, it's the new millennium! Why not a *guy?*" And that's when I shot off my mouth and said, *"Why does it have to be anybody?"* Naturally, she rolled her eyes and told me, "Oh, you're *really* out of control now. . . ." Thanks again, Dana.

Nevertheless, we had some fun over the next six months bringing in an array of different people to try on the cohost role for size. Some of them had no desire to take the job, but we knew they'd produce a day or two of laughs for the show anyway. Jon Stewart—yes, *a guy*—was one that I recall kidding around with quite enjoyably. Even Don Rickles got out of bed early one morning during a trip through New York and joined me at the desk. He wasn't thrilled about it, but that only made him *more* Don Rickles—feistier than ever, of course—and we loved it. As another novelty, I think we even managed to have the entire cast of that season's reality series *Survivor*, one by one, come give it a shot. None of them survived, however. There was pretty much a constant march of possible or improbable candidates—comediennes, actresses, musicians, newswomen, sports stars, you name it—and most dependably, my Joy, who has always been terrific at Host Chats and the guest interviews, even though she wanted absolutely no part of the full-time job. She gets more than her fair share of me off camera, as I'm sure she would happily tell you herself.

And it so happened that during those months, not only was the name of our show temporarily changed to simply *Live! With Regis* but also, at long last, I actually won a Daytime Emmy for best talk-show host, my first ever in the very category that my whole career was built on. In the years following that totally unexpected victory, and even up until very recently, I had a lot of fun shouting out to no one in particular: *"The only time Regis ever won an Emmy was when he was out there all by himself!"* And then I'd repeat this kind of general noisy blustering until everyone was fed up with it or just very, very annoyed. Frankly, it was thoroughly enjoyable being so obnoxious, although some people who don't know me better actually took it seriously. But those days are over now—with my solo Emmy outbursts, anyway—because just this year Kelly and I won the Daytime Emmy Outstanding Talk Show Host award together. Truthfully, it more than surprised us both. But what still bugs us most of all and remains an ongoing mystery is why the show itself, after twenty-three years of consistently strong production, has never once won the Best Talk Show award.

But not to get too far ahead of myself: So there I was eleven years ago with somebody new sitting beside me every week, each one of them hoping to eventually get that full-time cohost job. As we got increasingly serious about our search, there did emerge a promising handful who we brought back in earnest several times for yet another look. The process actually turned quite competitive: Many beautiful ladies realized it was a choice, high-profile role on a long-running hit show, which would ultimately mean for them the start of both a new career and an altogether new life. We carefully analyzed and weighed all the possibilities. When you've interviewed as many people as I have through the years—which was really what I'd been doing with each and every prospective candidate on live television during those interim months—they inevitably all seem to blend in with one another. Unless, that is, they somehow stand out and leave a certain sparkle lingering in the air afterward. That sparkle is very important, and it's obvious when it truly shines. There was one guest we'd had on with us a few years before who had done just that. Hers was a natural, quick-witted, unaffected, confident, fun-loving kind of sparkle that both Gelman and I remembered very well. Especially because it came from, frankly, such an unexpected source—I mean, *a young soap opera actress?* (Usually that kind of easy conversational spunk is innate only in a special breed of broadcaster types.) We decided to invite her back, this time to consider her as a possible cohost.

So that was when this smiling, petite ball of fire named Kelly Ripa made her return to *Live!* for a test run at the rotating, up-for-grabs hot seat to my left. And my God, who knew what spontaneous combustion we'd make together? By then she was in her tenth year as an *All My Children* fixture, having started on the classic ABC soap at age twenty as a bright-eyed ingenue. But now we learned that along with her great sparkle, attractive looks, and ebullient personality—the word *ebullient*, by the way, drives her nuts, which I love—she also excelled at telling a good story. And that, of course, was so crucial to the opening Host Chat segment. In pulling up her memories of things that happened last night, last week, or even many years earlier, she could instinctively zero in on the funniest details, which came out of nowhere and somehow hit a comic bull's-eye. That knack of hers pretty instantly struck a chord with the audience.

Not only was she something of a revelation to us, but early on she was actually blindsided by a real-life revelation of her own, live on our show. It was one of those astonishing, unforgettable, true-life TV moments that you couldn't have scripted even if you tried. We relived it, in fact, not long ago, during our tenth anniversary week, when Gelman sprang on us, as a surprise guest, my old Los Angeles psychic pal Char Margolis, who had also been our guest back on November 1, 2000—the morning of Kelly's initial tryout, believe it or not. "I don't mind telling you that Char, of course, is the reason I got my job here," Pippa said, as Char walked onstage this time. "I am convinced." For sure, Char had been the chief catalyst in creating what turned out to be an unforeseeable jaw-dropper of an introduction for any cohost, potential or otherwise. On that long-ago November day, she had spoken of how Kelly's dear deceased grandmother was always watching over her. But then Char continued to reveal that her grandmother's spirit also knew of other private developments on the horizon. . . .

CHAR: I heard you say earlier that you're married and you have a husband and a son. She watches over your son, and she's also showing me another baby. And I don't—

KELLY: [*gasping in shock here*]

CHAR: And she's saying that she's going to watch over you when this new baby comes. And it's soon. It's not far away. You're not pregnant yet, are you?

ME: Are you expecting?

KELLY: [*still gasping in shock*]

ME: Is that a yes?

KELLY: I haven't told my bosses [at *All My Children*] yet!
Oh my God . . . oh my God!

Well, right then and there, we all found out what she had shared with only a handful of intimates at that point—that she was a month or so into her second pregnancy. Sort of a broadcast minispectacular, which made a huge impact on the audience and also showed us what that most unguarded, spontaneous side of herself looked like. We had, up until then and even afterward for a couple more months, spent time working with other serious potential candidates, some of whom were quite good—but in the end it could only be Kelly. We kind of knew that from her memorable debut onward. She was the right choice and really the only choice. Like Kathie Lee, she knew exactly how to stir things up with me during the Host Chats. And also, just like Kathie Lee, who'd famously given birth twice during our years together, when Cody and Cassidy became household names, Kelly brought the promise of sharing further adventures in the Land of New Motherhood with us, too.

"Yes, we're talking babies again—get used to it!" I shouted, full of teasing exasperation on the morning of February 5, 2001, when we announced to our viewers that Kelly had gotten the job. And if you're wondering how we unveiled her as our final selection, I remember starting that show by just cutting to the quick, figuring that everybody out there, me included, had had enough of the half-year talent search experiment: *"Let's get it over with!"* I said, more relieved than anybody else, I promise you. "Say hello to my new cohost: Kelly Ripa. . . ." We all knew she had just the right equipment. Standing on the sidelines that day was her husband and *All My Children* costar, Mark Consuelos, with whom she'd already had a son, Michael, a few years earlier. During the broadcast, Mark hinted about various personality quirks I could expect from his wife (pregnant or not) on a regular basis, and I leapt at the chance to get the full rundown in order to arm myself: "Mark," I pleaded, "let's have coffee after the show!"

Of course, their daughter, Lola, would arrive that June, right after Kelly had made it through the all-important May "sweeps" ratings period before taking her first maternity leave from the show. Then, two Februarys later, their second son, Joaquin, was born—yes, the little guy that "Uncle Regis" accidentally dropped on the floor (*he was fine, and it wasn't my fault, I swear!*) when Gelman later cooked up a taped bit where I actually babysat for all three of the Consuelos children one evening so their parents could go out for dinner. Anyway, while I'm on this subject, it was mid-November 2001 when Kelly—and a bunch of our *Live!* staffers—went on the Letterman show to deliver a list of the Top Ten Things You Hear in a Typical Working Day with Regis. And it was Kelly who gave the Number One payoff entry: "Have you noticed how his cohosts keep getting pregnant?" Like I had anything to do with it! What, am I supposed to be some sort of fertility god? Then again, she *did* start referring to me on air in the very early going as Big Daddy, which I kind of liked. But that, I think, had more to do with a kidding sweet respect . . . I think? Meanwhile, I'd nicknamed her "Pippa" pretty quickly, which I still call her to this day. Besides the fact that the word suited her to a tee, another reason for it is that her real name begins with *K*, and it tricked me a little too often into mistakenly calling her "Kathie Lee"—and David Letterman has never stopped jokingly referring to her as "Kelly Lee" just to keep me all the more off-kilter.

(By the way, because you're probably wondering, I might as well tell you that among other entries on that Letterman Top Ten List were Numbers Seven and Six, "Regis, stop annoying people!" and "Does he ever shut up?" from our producers Mariann Sabol and Elyssa Shapiro—thank you, ladies—as well as Number Three, "Regis, put on your pants!" which came from Gelman, who you should know has never let me dress in privacy before the show throughout all our years together! He says it's part of his job as executive producer, since he's prepping me for the hour ahead with random last-minute details while I get myself suited up. But sometimes I wonder. . . .)

Anyway, from the start, Kelly's work ethic was strong—and it always stayed that way. At *All My Children*, where she continued in her long-running role of Hayley Vaughan until the end of 2002, she was used to putting in twelve-hour-a-day shifts. Even now, after ten years and counting, she still can't get over the fact that her primary job as cohost at *Live!* is finished, more or less, after only one hour each morning. By strange coincidence, though, back when she was maintaining double duties on our show and on the daily megahit soap series, I also happened to be hosting four prime-time hour-long episodes of *Who Wants to Be a Millionaire* every week. That added up to nineteen weekly broadcast hours the two of us were filling for the network. She joked on her first day, "I think it's an ABC policy—you must work two jobs!" I said, "Between the two of us, we've got forty percent of the schedule covered. If we go down, ABC is over." (For a while there, it wasn't far from true that the *Millionaire* quiz show had given the ABC evening lineup such enormous ratings that it returned from the near dead to become a powerhouse reborn—which, of course, prompted me to remind everyone who crossed my path that Regis had single-handedly saved the network! How could I resist?)

But back to that work ethic of South Jersey's very own Kelly Maria Ripa: Yes, she would develop into a terrific talk-show host, but she always kept her skills sharp as an actress. I believe in my heart that she has all the comic ability and range to become the Lucille Ball of her generation. She's just that good. So it only made sense that less than a year after leaving *All My Children*, she launched into a three-season run in her own ABC prime-time sitcom called

Hope & Faith, in which she starred as a wild and scheming former soap opera actress forced to move back to Ohio to live with her decent and practical sister Hope (played by Kelly's real-life close pal Faith Ford), a small-town wife and mother of three kids. To maybe heighten all the fine silliness of the series, she even coaxed me into my own recurring guest role—as the town's slick, sleazy used-car dealer and local TV pitchman, Handsome Hal Halverson. How she and her sitcom gang imagined me as *him,* I'll never know. But during the rehearsals and shoots for those episodes I watched her transform herself effortlessly from Kelly Ripa into the unrestrained Faith Fairfield, whose antics, I should add, tended to be very reminiscent of Lucy Ricardo at her most madcap. The show also gave us a chance to playfully blend our true-life daily *Live!* show bits into these two characters who were endlessly at odds—as Faith continued to try wheedling new cars from the unscrupulous Handsome Hal. I liked the way she set the tone for one of my appearances just before I came on-screen. . . .

FAITH: He's near. I can smell his cologne. It smells like—

HAL: [*emerging*] Dollar bills, baby!

At one point, Hal tried talking her into costarring with him in one of his cheesy TV ad spots: "You need a fancy car," Hal told her. "I need a fancy star for my new commercial. This is kismet!" Faith reluctantly agreed, then said in a comic aside to her sister, "But I seriously doubt that being on TV with *that* guy will do much for my career!" We even had some fun in another episode when Gelman came on to play my son, Hal, Jr., just so I could dress him down in the guise of our fictional characters. He'd walked up to hand me some sales reports (just like the way he's been plying me for years with daily Nielsen ratings printouts) and I barked, "Can't you see I'm with people? Now, you sit on this stool over here and wait for *me* to speak to *you!*" And I'd also constantly reject his pleas for affection: "Why haven't you ever said you love me?" he'd beg of Handsome Hal. "*Say it! Say it!*" That's when Kelly's Faith character looked on with disgust and said, "Could you imagine having to work with *those two?*"

But it was in my third and final episode where the lines blurred more than ever between real and sitcom life. Suddenly down on his luck, Hal decided that he and Faith would be shoo-ins to take over the local morning show, *Wake Up, Glen Falls,* whose longtime cohosts had left for a bigger TV market. And so there we were, pretending to be morning cohosts, doing a clumsy, exaggerated version of our real Host Chat, with me flipping through the small-town newspaper looking for various topics. Honest to God, though, the script had me eventually landing on one ridiculous item that led her into some familiar ad-libbing straight from our own usual repartee on *Live!. . . .*

HAL: Now, let's move on to this new phenomenon in town. There's a guy with a very long toe, right?

FAITH: A long toe?

HAL: A long toenail, I mean.

FAITH: Long toenail? Longer than *yours?* [*Here we actually started cracking up—since she'd gone off-script on a tangent we both knew a little too well, thank you.*] Because I happened to have seen your naked foot and I know you buy your shoes a whole size bigger to accommodate those toenails.

HAL: Oh boy. She knows me like a book.

My line there was extemporaneous, too, because she really does know me like a book. Maybe a little too much so. But that knowledge, of course, would only continue to make our own show's opening segment such a strong must-watch element throughout our years of teamwork. She's never been afraid to call me on my random peccadilloes: *"You need some moisturizer on your leg!"* she told me right on her first official day as my permanent cohost, in fact. (I think I'd been showing off a baseball scar received in Yankee spring training a few years before, always looking for some pity that never came.) Likewise, she'd pounce on whatever aggravations or oddities I've ever groused about—from my misadventures in finding the cure for snoring to my fondness for drawing elaborate diagrams to explain some new mix-up or other. ("Oh," she'd say, shaking with sarcastic delight, "this is exciting! It's been a long time since we've had a Philbin diagram! Come on, everybody, applaud!") Once she gave me a pedicure on the air—a terrifying experience! ("I lost a bet!" was how she explained it one night on the Letterman show, even though I was the one being tortured.) But she wielded that pair of nail clippers like a weapon and went to work as I squirmed: "Don't hurt me! Not too close!" I yelled. And she yelled back, "Stop it! You're making me nervous!"

Equally scary was the day she removed a splinter deeply embedded in my thumb. I know that this may sound like an everyday occurrence to you, but the magic of that opening Chat segment has always been to bring up our personal afflictions as they occurred and try to solve them right there. Regarding my splinter—needless to say, she probably does that sort of thing every day with her kids, which is maybe why she constantly refers to me as her oldest child. But this splinter, the darned thing just was burrowed so many layers beneath the surface. I tried to conceal my horror as she sliced and probed her way in there—"Look at the *size* of it!" I yelled, wincing like crazy, "I'm breaking out in a *sweat!*"—until she finally got it out and triumphantly displayed it to the cameras. Where else, I ask you, has splinter tweezing made for entertaining television?

But unpredictable escapades—even those (I truly hate to admit) that occasionally involved my more serious health issues—have led to quite a range of memorable moments in the course of our great ride together. I remember, once again during her first real day on the job, that I bellowed (purely as a joke): *"Angioplasty!* That's what Kathie Lee gave me!" Then I looked over at her a little fearfully and said, "What are *you* gonna give me?" Well, it was true that a few years before Pippa arrived I'd successfully received the blocked heart valve ballooning angioplasty procedure and all had remained fine for a long while. But out of the blue, in the spring of 2007, I had to necessarily undergo a triple-bypass heart operation, which as you may know is no fun at all, to put it mildly. Nevertheless, I managed to rally myself back to work six weeks and one day after that difficult major surgery. But in the interim, I was proud of the way Kelly held down the fort with such finesse—and all kidding aside, I was more than touched by her concern throughout my recuperation. A couple weeks before I returned, I saw her one night go on with Dave Letterman (with whom I'd already formed quite the heart-problem support system). She knocked me out in talking about how she'd dealt with my absence: "I'm kind of exhausted," she confessed very sweetly. "I never thought of a talk show as hard work. I thought that I was just supposed to sit there and, like, dust him off a little bit, and throw my head back and laugh at his jokes. Now, suddenly, I'm taking time cues. I'm trying to read off a cue card that I can't see. It's very difficult. The whole thing is, you go, 'Look—I didn't sign up for *this*. . . .' Regis really *is* the show, and he does the majority of the work."

Well, she was being beyond overly generous, especially with her last sentence there. But I confess that work has always been my lifeblood and my pleasure, so I was thrilled to get back to our studio and start mixing it up with her again—and to very quickly diffuse any chance of things getting all sentimental and maudlin. I'm not too good at that stuff. After the audience kindly embarrassed me with a beautiful ovation, Pippa and I did agree that it had felt more like six months to six years since I'd last been sitting there. But then it was time to find our old rhythm of teasing byplay, which, as I'd expected, picked up pretty close to where we'd left off a month and a half before. . . .

KELLY: I've gotta tell you. You look remarkable. I mean, it's incredible.

ME: Well, I lost eight pounds but I aged twelve years.

KELLY: No, you did not age. Be honest. Did you have a face-lift? His heart surgery was just a ruse, wasn't it?

ME: No, I didn't have a face-lift. I had a heart lift. . . . Anyway, I would regularly watch you in the mornings, and I've got to tell you something. When you're not with me, you actually *shine*! Little glistenings of light come radiating off your face, you're never happier, you're never more—

KELLY: [*rolls her eyes*] Ebullient?

ME: Exactly right! You really are. What *is* it? What do I do to you to dim the light? [*Here, despite my best effort, was where I saw the Big Emotion coming . . . uh-oh. . . .*]

KELLY: Let me tell you right now: I felt that, for six weeks, my light *was* dimmed. Completely.

ME: [*now fighting for my life to bring back a little humor—please!*] Awww . . . Isn't she something? That's a line she used on *All My Children*, 1988. I was watching that day! "My light has been dimmed!"

KELLY: You can laugh about it all you want, but I personally missed you. . . . There were all these moments that I'd go, "Gosh. I am the luckiest person alive. I get to sit here with *you* every day. . . ."

ME: Now you're talking, baby! Now *I'm* beginning to see the light!

Anyway, we were off and running and back on track with our regular routine that I've come to know so well. Every morning it begins like this: She comes out of her dressing room with about thirty seconds to go before airtime. We walk down the hall toward our studio to make that entrance and to begin that next show. And because she happens to be such a stunning-looking lady, I take great delight in stopping briefly at the occasional dressing room on the way down that hall and announcing to our male guests sitting there—in my most obnoxious way, "Take a look at what Regis gets every morning at nine o'clock, whether he wants it or not!" And then we're out through the door to the stage, where the fun begins.

That's the way it's been for just over a decade, as of this writing. Last February, we celebrated the tenth anniversary of *Live! With Regis & Kelly*, during which John Ogle—our associate producer, whose expertise at archiving and splicing together classic moments from the show is uncanny—produced a week full of terrific montages that brought back lots of great memories. Naturally, he included many bits from our incredibly elaborate Halloween shows, the ones in which Gelman has insisted that Kelly and I (along with himself and the always game Art Moore, our executive in charge of production) climb into the guises of various famous personas for each segment of that annual hour. And as arduous and annoying as the process of pretaping so many of these dress-up bits has been, they do always magnificently showcase Kelly's great versatility in truly becoming any character thrown at her. Each year, she somehow has made everyone she imitated look better and come across funnier than the real versions could hope to be. During the course of our 2010 Halloween show (which producer Elyssa Shapiro meticulously oversaw), for instance, Pippa's pageant of transformations included *Jersey Shore*'s Snooki (with me as her tough guy pal "The Situation"), Cher, Lady Gaga, *all three* Kardashian sisters, Katy Perry, Jennifer Lopez, and other assorted players. In some of those segments, I was turned into the likes of Justin Bieber, Elmo from *Sesame Street*, Steven Tyler, and *also* maybe a less convincing version of Lady Gaga, to name a few.

I mention that particular Halloween show for a reason—a reason that neither Kelly nor I fully understood back on the recent June evening when we found out we had won the Emmy for Outstanding Talk Show Hosts during the Daytime Emmy Awards ceremony, which was being televised live from Las Vegas. I probably don't have to tell you that neither of us were in Las Vegas at that moment: Kelly was off attending a music festival in Colorado, and I was half watching the festivities with Joy in our Greenwich weekend house. You see—despite my fluke solo victory back in 2001—it gets to the point that, when your show keeps going down in flames after contending so long for these awards, you just can't help but lose interest. Kelly's pal Anderson Cooper opened the envelope onstage that night and took a stymied look at the card revealing the recipients' names before announcing that there had been a *tie* in the hosting category— between Oprah's favorite medical guru, Dr. Oz (whose new syndicated series had already just won for Outstanding Informative Talk Show), and . . . *us* . . . Regis and Kelly. "Did you see the look on

Anderson Cooper's face when he saw our names?" I asked when we returned to our show a week later clutching our shocker Emmys. "The look said, *'Why them?'*"

Kelly defended him by postulating, "We *all* know he *just said our names*—we probably didn't even win these things!" And then she announced: "Now that we've won the glorious Daytime Emmy Award for Outstanding Talk Show Hosts, we have decided to take ourselves out of the competition! So everyone else can experience Emmy gold. . . ." I added, "Yes, let the little people win!"

But back to that 2010 Halloween show, which—we learned, further into the Host Chat on that postaward summer morning—turned out to have been the only hour from our entire year of work that Gelman submitted for Emmy consideration, representing not just our hosting skills but the *Live!* series as a whole. Strange but true—every Emmy nomination, whether for prime time or daytime, is always based on a single episode and never on the full season's offerings. Which seems utterly ridiculous to me. I mean, we won our Emmys for playing dress-up? *Please!*

"But that wasn't a talk show at all!" I dismally complained on the air. "It was just an *impersonation* show. . . ."

"Right," Kelly piped in, "but the reality is—as long as we are not ourselves, we can win!"

I had to laugh. There was that spark again. Between the two of us, we'd found that one detail that could help us all laugh at the absurdity of the situation.

Back in January, of course, I had announced that I was moving on from our show after fifty years since it all started for me talking into the camera on Saturday nights in San Diego and then having spent the last thirty-five of those years cohosting—on both coasts, no less. I spoke of all the fun I've had with each of the talented ladies I've worked with, and put my arm around Kelly, noting how

I'd gotten to "look at this one over here every morning" during the last ten-plus years. Frankly, she had known of my decision for only a very short while and seemed to be terribly upset by it. At one point, she said, "I wish I could do something to make you change your mind." At last, a straight line! And one that I didn't let go by. I made like I was reconsidering everything I'd just said: "Well, now wait a minute . . . *waaaaaiiiiitttttt a minnnnnnnutttte* . . . maybe we can reach an agreement here—" It got a big laugh, but her sweet sentiment did mean a lot to me.

Of course, we still had many more months ahead to keep having our usual fun, including one morning when we were marveling over all of the major departures by television mainstays that had been taking place during the last handful of months. Everyone, all at once, seemed to be moving on from their long-standing programs—Larry King, Katie Couric, Keith Olbermann, Meredith Vieira, Mary Hart, Jim Lehrer, and, of course, the queen of them all, Oprah Winfrey, who'd departed from her megahit program some days earlier. . . .

> **ME:** Wait, did Oprah go, too? We're *allllllll* going—we're making a run for it! *You're* the only one left, you know what I mean?
>
> **Kelly:** Listen, somebody's got to hold down this ship.
>
> **ME:** [*teasing*] Yeah, well, you'll hold it down all right! To say the least!

Which prompted the audience to applaud and cheer her on, not that she'll need it. And to think that on her very first day as the full-time occupant of that seat to my left, I ended the show with the words: "I don't know if it worked out. But if you don't see her tomorrow, don't blame me!"

Well, believe me, you'll be seeing her for all the tomorrows she ever wants. Her ride is only just beginning all over again. And incidentally, I'm so grateful to have helped launch the first leg of it.

Wait a minute, did I just say "incidentally"?

See what I mean?

WHAT I TOOK AWAY FROM IT ALL

People who sparkle tend to make you sparkle, too, when they're near.

Awards are nice. But giving people a reason to smile is a reward you'll value and experience far longer.

Chapter Nineteen

DONALD TRUMP

There used to be so many famous, oversize characters in New York—I mean, you couldn't miss them! Must have been a dozen of them in Toots Shor's great old saloon every hour of every day and night, back in those colorful years so long ago. Their names were always in the papers. They were millionaires, athletes, show business people, and just regular hard-striving folks who were funny and lively and trying to take their place in the biggest big city anywhere.

Nowadays, the wealthy are more or less in hiding. The athletes keep to themselves. Everybody is pretty private about where they go and what they are doing and what they may have to say. Once in a while, a young movie star will come through town stirring things up and the paparazzi and tabloids will go nuts—but it's nothing like the boldfaced exploits of New York's golden era. (I can't help but wonder how gruff old Toots Shor himself would've dealt with this new breed of "reality show" stars—I mean, what would Toots think of Snooki? Or of those screaming Real Housewives of New Jersey and all these other places where women are shown screaming at each other? No question—and kind of sadly—we sure do live in a whole new world of "celebrities," don't we?)

There is, however, one legitimately large-scale guy who will not go undercover, who certainly will not be quieted. He is one of the few great New York characters we have left: Donald Trump. Or as I like to call him: *the Trumpster!*

Yes, he is flamboyant. He is colorful, and he is unafraid to take chances. His private plane is bigger than most. His Palm Beach home, Mar-a-Lago, is enormous, too. His golf courses are among the very best in the country. He literally lives higher—and also probably more luxuriously—than anyone else inside that tower he built . . . that tower which rejuvenated Fifth Avenue and brought New York real estate back to life in the early eighties. He is seen at movie premieres, Broadway show openings, and galas everywhere. Even at Lady Gaga's Radio City Music Hall debut—which was filled with curious New Yorkers—she actually sent an aide into the audience to find Trump and bring him backstage. She desperately wanted to have her picture taken with him. And he was quite flattered. Also, Trump never misses a big fight—especially if he's the one putting on the fight (or taking part in it!). He goes to all the key Yankee games. He once owned a pro football team, an airline, and, when Atlantic City was jumping, Trump built the biggest casino of them all, the Trump Taj Mahal; it ruled the town for years. He seems to be everywhere, and he doesn't mind a camera taking his picture or a reporter quoting his latest provocative statements. In other words, he loves publicity. It's part of his life and part of his business. He thrives on it. It works for him.

When I came back home to New York in 1983 and was looking for a colorful character to interview for my show, I was told to go get Donald Trump. I took a camera crew over to his Trump Tower, which you couldn't miss. Not only was it the most spectacular, most blinding, and most beautiful building on Fifth Avenue, but Trump had the most wildly dressed doormen in New York standing at its entrances, too. It was all a part of the show that is his life. And whether the crowds on Fifth Avenue loved it (as most did) or hated it—what passion that gleaming structure inspired!

The doorman swung open the portals for me that day, and there he was—thirty-five years old, the hottest young guy in the hottest town. We met in his building's overwhelming lobby, which features an eighty-five-foot waterfall spilling down over one of the walls. I had never seen anything like it—*now this was a lobby!* And I was truly just as impressed with him. I wanted to know about this guy—where he came from, how he built this monument to his own dreams, where he was going from here. I thought I'd get a good five minutes out of him. Forget about it. He was on fire. We must have stood there for a half hour, with Trump doing most of the talking, until the camera ran out of tape. . . .

Maybe it takes one to know one—but this is a guy with the most amazing ability to talk extemporaneously when he's "on." And he never stops! So while the city's rousing, old-time, larger-than-life days were quieting down, this young guy was practically yelling at the top of his lungs: *"I'm here, New York! And I'm not leaving till I'm on top!"* And once he got on top, he even enjoyed seeing how the press followed his personal-life adventures, some of which were kind of sticky if not pretty darned unpleasant. But he's just that fearless.

Many years ago, for instance, I happened to be having lunch with an old friend at an Italian restaurant in the lobby of the Trump Tower. And while sitting there, who do you think I caught sight of picking through the magazine racks just outside the restaurant? That's right—it was none other than the Trumpster! After pulling down a few publications for purchase, he instantly rolled them up in his hand, making it impossible to see what he'd bought. At which point he spotted me and, without missing a beat, came over smiling, cheerful as ever. (Even way back when the tabloid papers were constantly beating his brains out with headlines about his divorce from his first wife, Ivana—the *New York Post* had designated it a front-page story for twelve straight days!—I wondered how he could take such a daily bombardment. It must have hurt, but he never showed it. He simply lived with it, got over it, and kept on going—which is no small feat, really.) But I was intrigued by these magazines that he was hiding from view. So I told him I wanted to know! "Okay, you got me," he confessed with a shrug. And then he unrolled the latest editions of the *National Enquirer*, the *Star*, and *People* magazine. Back then—same as now—he might not have liked what the media was saying about him, but as long as they were saying it, he wanted to know what it was. Anyway, I recall him walking off afterward still smiling. He also quietly picked up our lunch tab.

It wasn't too long after our very first meeting that I saw Trump again at Yankee Stadium for one of those celebrity exhibition baseball games designed to fill seats before the regularly scheduled ball game began. Trump played first base, and I was crouched nearby as his second baseman, but I could see pretty quickly that he could handle himself nicely with a bat and a glove. I don't know exactly when we started becoming good friends, but it happened right around that time when we'd been teammates for a day. In the years since, I can't tell you how many times we've driven up to Yankee Stadium together and sat in what was, and will somehow always be, George Steinbrenner's suite. We loved George. He was the Man, the Boss, always happy to see us and always hungry for another championship. And as usual, there'd be a gang of New York notables on hand up in that suite. Everybody from the late Elaine Kaufman (whose Upper East Side restaurant, Elaine's, was until its recent closing a famous literary hangout) to newsman supreme Mike Wallace and even His Honor, Mayor Mike Bloomberg—to any number of those aging eternal Yankee greats like Yogi Berra (with his fingers all weighed down by so many championship rings) or the "Scooter" himself, Phil Rizzuto, or the heroic slugger Reggie "Mr. October" Jackson.

Once, we drove up to Yankee Stadium with Eddie Malloy, the top boss of all the construction unions in New York—and what a crazy experience that turned out to be. First of all: Do you have any idea what it takes to build anything in New York? It's an incredible ordeal—and not too pretty to endure. You've got to get past city officials, cutthroat lawyers, neighborhood opposition groups, smart guys, wiseguys, and union guys—just to mention a few. Anyway, on this night—for an actual World Series game—we were joined by Eddie. He was a tough old Irishman with piercing blue eyes, and he'd had plenty of face-to-face time with Trump in the course of their many business dealings. But now we were all friends going to a ball game. Except on that night Trump—who secretly delights in having more fun than you'd think at the expense of people he likes (and sometimes dislikes, too)—decided that he would dig in and playfully tease Eddie. He told Eddie, a powerhouse guy in his own right, that if he had any trouble getting into the stadium he should just stand near him, because no one would dare turn Eddie away if they thought the two of them were there together. Eddie answered quickly; he said he had a ticket waiting for him and wouldn't need the Donald's help! Wouldn't need it *at all*.

A few minutes later, Trump went at him again, playfully reassuring him that just in case the ticket wasn't there, he'd make sure Eddie got in. He was baiting old Eddie—and it was working. Eddie's face was getting red, and he made it *absolutely* clear that he wouldn't need Trump's help—EVER! I was getting a kick out of it, but thought that the razzing had gone far enough. Not Trump, though—he wasn't finished. As we pulled up to the stadium, Trump did it again: "Let's just go in together, Eddie. I don't want to leave you stranded out here on the sidewalk. . . ."

That's when Eddie blew up. The Irishman bellowed out for all to hear: "If I don't get in there, all the f— lights in this stadium will go dark in five minutes!" He wasn't kidding. Naturally, they let him right in without pause. But Trump and I laughed about it all night.

Given his unrelenting notoriety, it would only be a matter of time, I guess, before television would find fascination with the Trumpster and come calling. And boy, was he ready. Business-oriented shows don't usually make it to prime time, but Mark Burnett, a young producer with a great idea, zeroed in on Trump and laid it out for him. It would be sort of a contest between Trump "apprentices," who would compete at running various minibusinesses, trying all along to avoid getting fired and to ultimately win the big guy's respect. Some people didn't think it would fly, but Trump loved the idea as soon as he heard it. His own show on prime-time TV! *Of course he loved it.* And so *The Apprentice* was born, and it was an enormous hit (with equally successful variations that would later follow, such as his *Celebrity Apprentice* series in recent years).

From the start, I would call Trump first thing in the morning after the previous night's show and give him the ratings, which were big and getting bigger. And then we would talk about his TV persona and, more importantly, about his attitude on camera. He shouldn't be a tough boss all the time, I told him. He had to be understanding, warm but firm, and decisive when it came to the firing scenes. And he did it just like that—and all of America started loving him just a little bit more! But it came easy to him. The audience was transfixed by his thoughtful demeanor at that boardroom table. The ratings shot up all the more, and damned if Trump didn't become a full-fledged national TV celebrity—constantly in the public eye and hotter than ever. And I don't have to tell you how much he enjoyed it.

Trumpster later recounted to me that on one subsequent warm summer night, he and his lovely wife, Melania, were headed out to dinner at the famous restaurant 21—just a few blocks down Fifth Avenue from where they lived. He most always moves around town by car, but this was such a beautiful evening that they decided to make the brief pleasant stroll. Walking down Fifth Avenue, in the same direction of the traffic flow, with all the cars cruising along beside them, they got to the restaurant unnoticed. But walking home after dinner, it was a different story. With traffic now headed straight toward them, how could this tall, striking couple be missed? Well, they couldn't. Drivers blared their horns at them, while strangers were yelling, "We love you, Trump! Please, can you just say, *'You're fired!'* for us?" That Trump catchphrase had by then taken on a life of its own. And Trump reveled in it. He had never received this kind of recognition for all the great buildings he had put up. But these were the *real* people—and now they were *his* people. Then it happened: As one car rolled toward them, a gruff voice yelled out in, let's say, a rather uncomplimentary manner: "Hey, Trump, you're f— fired!" Don't forget—New Yorkers are never too shy with their opinions. Now, somebody else taking that kind of shot might be offended, but not him. To Trump, it was like someone serenading him with a love song! He talked about it for weeks. Proud as could be.

And to me, that's the beautiful thing about Donald Trump. They can't get him down. In the early nineties, when New York was going through its almost dependable once-a-decade financial crisis and bankruptcies were being declared everywhere, Trump was no exception to the economic disaster. His empire was on the verge of collapse. He privately told me about standing out on Fifth Avenue one evening with his daughter Ivanka. He pointed across the street at a homeless man huddled down in a doorway and Trump informed his daughter, "See that man over there? He's got more money than we have right now." And he was only half kidding.

He's been through it all, this guy. Not every one of his projects has worked out, but he's always in the papers, always good for a story, and sometimes it's not so pleasant. Yes, he has detractors and rivals in his assorted business ventures—those who resent him, don't like him, think he exaggerates too much. Then there are those who just can't get past his unique hairstyle. I happened to weigh in on the subject on our show several months ago and, for the record, I'm sticking to it: "What's wrong with Trump's hair? What do they want the Trump to do? Once in a while the wind blows it around a little, and that's about it. No, I like his hair." Even though the studio audience might have laughed—*which they did*—I think I made my point! But you should also know that the people who work for him, and who know him best, talk endlessly about his energy and his confidence and, most important, his optimism. It even works on me. Sometimes I'm down or in a bad mood, but with one phone call to Trump, I'm up again. Just like that. He never fails me.

Recently, however, there was a new development in Trump's life—when he created a national furor by contemplating a run for president. Everyone in New York, of course, had a take on the issue. Frankly, in this heavily liberal town, the notion of Trump running as a Republican, or maybe as an Independent, stirred great storms of derision. I talked to him often over the course of the whole dramatic scenario, and at the time of this writing he seemed to be thinking that he could still do a lot more good from where he stands in the private sector. But there's no telling what he'll attempt in the future. Whether Donald Trump ever wins or loses a bid for the presidency— or anything else, for that matter—he will always be the one-of-a-kind New York guy who keeps this town talking.

It would be very quiet around here without him.

WHAT I TOOK AWAY FROM IT ALL

To become big, you cannot be afraid to play big—and to dream even bigger.

Always keep self-doubt to yourself—as best you can. And never buy into it for very long.

Chapter Twenty

CLAUDIA COHEN

I like to think I'm a New Yorker. I mean, I was born about eight blocks from the studio where we've been doing our morning show for nearly three decades now. But my boyhood years here seemed to speed by so quickly, and then, after my high school graduation from Cardinal Hayes in the Bronx, I was *gone*! By now you know that I spent the next four years at Notre Dame in South Bend, Indiana; then, immediately afterward, enlisted in the navy for two years and was stationed out near San Diego, California, when not at sea. I did briefly come back to the city for the summer of 1955 to work as an NBC page—which was exciting, to be sure—but then I got that call from Hollywood, which could not be ignored. Yes, it was only a job in a prop house for a local TV station, but at least it was a hands-on start in a new medium that I very much wanted to be part of. So, for me, it all really began out west. And then it just stayed out there—a twenty-eight-year run in California, where I had my share of terrific ups and gut-twisting downs, which is life in a nutshell, I guess.

So despite my Big Apple roots, when New York tempted me back, offering an exciting chance to start all over again, the transition wasn't all that smooth. I used to make jokes on the show that I felt like an old elephant who had come home to die. But the fact was that I really *had* come home, and in time it would feel great again. I just had to get used to things. It helped that the new live morning show I was doing was more or less the same as my *A.M. Los Angeles* show. I wanted to hold on to that friendly "local TV feel," and we did. In fact, we even held on to it after we went national five years later—on WABC-TV. (The irony of my remembering all this now is that we debuted on the first Monday in April 1983, and I'm writing these words on the Sunday before the first Monday in April 2011, marking another twenty-eight-year run, but this time in the town where I'd been born, so this difficult move had to have been worth the effort after all!) What also eased the transition was being reunited with Cyndy Garvey, who had been my morning cohost during the last few years at KABC-TV in L.A. As it turned out, she, too, happened to be a newly transplanted Manhattan resident, so in many ways it was easy to pick up where we'd left off—except that instead of our old routine of chatting each day about Hollywood (what else do they talk about out there?), we were now able to talk about a whole new world.

To put it mildly, New York was as different as could be: The city continually bursts with major events and daily manic complexities that make great lively morning-after stories to share during the show's opening Host Chat segment. I wanted the city to become—*or at least feel like*—the third cohost of the show. I know that so many tourists come and go just to get a taste of its wild pace, wondering if they could actually ever live here. It's a tough town, no question, and maybe most go home after their visit more grateful that they don't stay. And then there are all those who never get here, but can't help seeing it in the movies or on TV, and certainly reading about its nonstop action in the papers or on their computer screens. It's pretty much the capital of the country, and to be honest, in many ways it's also the capital of the world. Millions of people are here, always in such a hurry—it can be overwhelming for a newcomer and sometimes even for those who've lived here forever.

But from the time I hit town onward, there was one person who made all the difference for me. Quite simply, she unlocked the doors to the city, introduced me to the people and places I needed to know about. And it helped our show's opening segments so much—to be able to talk about where I'd been the night before and who I'd met and what glittering adventures had taken place, never mind all the peculiar little things that can also happen when you're just out wandering about or even when you stay behind the closed doors of your apartment. I wanted to capture the color and craziness of New York. And it worked, all because she helped get us started.

Of course, I'm talking about Claudia Cohen.

She was pure glamour, charm, wisdom, and warmth, all rolled into one remarkable lady. As the *New York Times* once characterized her, Claudia was "a crucial person to know if anybody who was somebody wanted to become even more of a somebody." And was that ever the truth! She not only became our show's "gossip girl," but she was also the absolute best friend I had in those early days of my New York homecoming. She knew everybody and everything—including the good and bad about each one of them. She was a walking encyclopedia on who was who around town and all the specific ways they mattered most. She'd had a gossip column in the New York *Daily News* before running the famous (or sometimes infamous) Page Six celebrity column in the *New York Post*. Believe me, she had her eye on everyone.

And it was such a great luxury having her shepherd me around the city. Naturally, she made sure to introduce me to the storied Elaine's restaurant on the Upper East Side—whose illustrious namesake owner, Elaine Kaufman, passed on not too long ago. But I still remember that first time Claudia escorted me into that now-shuttered place. There was Woody Allen entertaining a party of four at his usual table—or was he just staring at them? (The brilliant Wood-Man is, you know, a pretty quiet guy.) There, at another table in a remote corner, was Francis Ford Coppola sitting behind a typewriter, thoughtfully working on his next script. There were writers all over the place. I knew only their names—men and women whose work filled various newspapers and magazines and books, those who reported and interpreted all the things that made New York jump. And Claudia, like the instinctive super press agent she really was, would pull me toward each of them and give me a terrific over-the-top introduction like I was the next big star they simply had to know! Most of them would look at me for a moment and then continue talking amongst, or about, themselves. To them, I was just another TV guy trying to get one more talk show up and running in New York. Their disinterest practically screamed, *So what! Who cares?* (if I may borrow Joy Behar's great catchphrase from *The View*). But Claudia's zealous introductions made me sound like the new savior of morning television. *Which was embarrassing,* I don't mind telling you. So many times I'd ask her, actually *plead* with her, to tone it down. I mean, I appreciated all she was trying to do, but it felt a little heavy-handed for this sophisticated crowd. And how could I ever live up to these accolades she was doling out, anyway?

But to be sure, there were many *very* exclusive parties and dinners I would have never been invited to if it weren't for her. Same goes for so many impressive people I would've never gotten to know. She was a certifiable whirlwind who enjoyed covering those splashy star-studded events for our show, and she was a great asset to all of us there. Beyond that, I so admired a couple of Claudia's personal traits that most of our viewers probably never knew about. Her loyalty to close friends, for instance, was unmatchable. One such friend was Steve Rubell, co-owner of the famous Studio 54 disco/nightclub, who went to prison for tax evasion—and every day during the thirteen months he spent behind bars, she wrote him cheerful notes and letters. Yes: *I said every day.*

Also, she was unafraid of a good fight. Like the time, in the early days of our show, when she and my old Hollywood friend Zsa Zsa Gabor locked horns in our tiny guest makeup room, which was equipped with *only one chair*—meaning that all the guests had to wait their turn, one at a time, to get their faces prepared for those bright TV studio lights. Zsa Zsa, well known for her temper, walked in while Claudia was in the chair and ordered her not only out of that chair but also out of the room! Claudia wasn't about to budge and said so. As you can imagine, all hell broke loose. The shouting match made the front-page headline story of the *Daily News* and had everyone in town talking about it for weeks.

Anyway, at the end of my first summer in town, Joy and our girls—who'd initially stayed behind in L.A. to enjoy the summer and rent our home while I got the new show rolling—finally joined me around Labor Day and we stuffed ourselves into a two-bedroom apartment on the Upper East Side, all of us hanging on as best we could while adjusting to that dramatic cross-country move. Joanna and J.J. had their troubles getting accustomed to the city. They missed their house in Los Angeles, their street with the palm trees and the backyard with the swimming pool. Hey, so did Joy and I! But now, forget it, those days were over. Joy and I would go out for an evening, and believe it or not, Gelman (then in his early twenties) would babysit for us. Afterward, when we got back, the girls would be asleep, but we would inevitably find notes they'd left on our pillows, scribbled with things like "Please, please, Mom and Dad, take us home!" The notes were so heart-wrenching and sad—and frankly, the change of location was plenty tough on all four of us. But in the second year we did move into a bigger apartment; the girls now had their own bedrooms and more space to move around—and bit by bit we started letting a little more New York magic come into our lives.

Joy, meanwhile, had finally met Claudia at her fabulous apartment overlooking Central Park. That particular day, we all watched from her terrace as the runners in the New York Marathon trotted along down below. The three of us instantly formed a great friendship. Soon enough, Claudia would be telling us about a special gentleman she'd met at the original Le Cirque restaurant, then located on Sixty-fifth Street. He was Ronald Perelman from Philadelphia, the incredibly successful business magnate who happened to own Revlon, among other companies—and he came on like gangbusters: flowers, cards, gifts, romantic dinners, you name it. Claudia loved the chase. She had never married, never really had the time for it, so this was something new and very important. Joy and I met and liked him very much; all of us who saw them together soon waited for the inevitable wedding.

And once Claudia and Ronald married, they bought the grandest house, I think, on the oceanfront of East Hampton. Those Hamptons on Long Island are a great place to be in the summer months. Practically every big shot in New York has a getaway house there. But no one loved to throw Hamptons parties more than Claudia. Over the years, Joy and I were lucky enough to be invited to those events and to spend glorious weekends there so many times. And Claudia was simply the best hostess in the world. She filled those weekends with aerobic training, tennis lessons, massages, wonderful food—anything you could imagine, and then some. And even after Claudia and Ron divorced, she remained in that big beautiful house, and her parties continued unabated.

There was always a great collection of New York characters on the guest list, and she took such great pains to dazzle them all.

At dinners, every place setting had to be perfect. Each of those Saturday-night bashes was memorable—but equally fascinating were the Sunday-morning postparty wrap-ups. That was when those of us who had stayed over as her houseguests would gather around the breakfast table and review the events of the previous night, dissecting who said what to whom and who had too much to drink and so on. It was gossip, pure and simple—the very thing she did so well in the New York papers and on our show for years. But the laughs we had during those breakfasts were priceless!

Then later, as the years passed, Claudia became quite ill. You could see it developing over time, starting maybe around 2005. No one was sure what was happening to her, but it was increasingly noticeable, serious, and heartbreaking. Eventually we learned that she'd been stricken with ovarian cancer. She spent a lot of time in Germany looking for a cure. Her ex-husband, Ron Perelman, who always adored her, spared no expense in searching out new experimental treatments—but none worked. It was beyond sad. Here was this dynamic woman in the prime of her years, in love with her life, her family, and her friends—and unable to conquer this beast.

Joy and I saw her for the last time in the hospital. She was wearing a Yankee baseball cap and a robe, and even though she was in certain pain, she still had the courage to pretend everything was just fine, that it was just another Sunday in New York. Claudia died a short time after that visit, on June 15, 2007. It was a blow to everyone who knew her—and practically everyone did. At her funeral, the synagogue was packed with family and friends, numbering nearly one thousand mourners. Naturally, countless New York boldfaced names were there, too—Calvin Klein, Barbara Walters, Senator Al D'Amato, Matt Lauer, Jon Bon Jovi, Diane von Furstenberg, Bryant Gumbel, Rudy and Judith Giuliani, Penny Marshall, Lorraine Bracco, Graydon Carter, Liz Smith, Donald and Melania Trump—

the list was overwhelming. And of course, most all of our show's staffers—past and present—had also come to pay their respects, including Kelly with her husband, Mark Consuelos, Kathie Lee and Frank Gifford, the Gelmans, and the battalion of people behind the scenes who keep us going every day. Claudia had been part of the fabric of our lives in such a special way.

I was privileged to be asked to speak among the eulogists, who were quite eloquent and spoke beautifully about her. I followed them and talked about the quality of friendship Claudia displayed, the way she introduced me to New York, the way she wanted me to succeed—but above all, how she loved all the people there and always, if they were in her company or at her parties, wanted them to have the best time. She really cared about them. "She had a terrific zest for life," I said. "And she made you enjoy your life more." Then I told the story of how she once called me every night for two straight weeks before one of her parties, only to talk about who should sit next to Calvin Klein. *"Two weeks! Calvin Klein!"* I marveled. For the first time on that sad, solemn day, the mourners laughed long and loud. Claudia would have loved it.

I miss her.

WHAT I TOOK AWAY FROM IT ALL

New York is a breeze as long as you're lucky enough to know the somebody who knows all the other right somebodies.

A generous spirit is an unforgettable spirit— and also irreplaceable.

Chapter Twenty-one

GEORGE STEINBRENNER

H ere is how the Boss entered my life: Surprisingly, it didn't happen in the Bronx, where his Yankees were based and my own boyhood was spent. No, instead we came together in Indianapolis, of all places, where we both wound up one Memorial Day weekend in the early nineties to enjoy the hoopla and excitement surrounding that greatest of great auto races, the Indy 500. As part of the race day festivities, I'd been given the honorary and truly incomparable thrill of being paraded around that famous two-and-a-half-mile track in an open car with four hundred thousand people letting out a roaring cheer I'll never forget.

But on the night before that overwhelming experience, I had the unexpected pleasure of meeting this unforgettable man who knew a thing or two about roaring. And also about cheering. That night, I was invited to dinner by my old TV executive friend Chris Kelly, whom I'd known in both St. Louis and Chicago, and who was now running a major Indianapolis station. Chris's other guest that evening turned out to be none other than the colorful and controversial

New York Yankees owner, George Steinbrenner, who was then somewhere in the midst of riding out his second baseball suspension for a stupid mistake he regretted very much. It was not a good moment in his life, to say the least. He missed his Yankees terribly—"Owning the Yankees," he once said, so proudly, "is like owning the *Mona Lisa*"—but he was happy to be at the 500 that weekend, which probably made for a perfect distraction from his troubles. We hit it off almost immediately and had a great, lively dinner.

The next day we toured those Speedway spaces beside the track that housed the cars and driver crews, all prepping themselves for the race. As we wandered around together, we started playing a made-up baseball trivia game along the lines of "Do you remember this guy?" That is, we would quiz each other about who played what position during whatever year from long ago. I remember being impressed when I threw a real tough one at him: "First base, Cleveland Indians, 1949?" And George smiled confidently before he shot back: "Hal Trotsky." I didn't think *anyone* remembered Hal Trotsky anymore, but I always loved that name when I was a kid, and sure enough, George did, too. I was amazed that he got it—until I later realized that George grew up in Cleveland, so of course he knew Hal Trotsky! But still, you've got to love the sound of that name. Anyway, we shared a terrific day at the big race and didn't lose touch afterward.

Once George's ban had finally been lifted and he returned to his beloved team, he invited me to come watch ball games from his private suite at Yankee Stadium, which was always such a pleasure. And he also made sure to let me know that I'd be a welcome guest during spring training in Tampa if I ever happened to be in Florida when the Yankees were getting ready for the season ahead. Well, one springtime during the height of my big *Who Wants to Be a Millionaire* prime-time quiz-show-hosting heyday, I came through Tampa to perform my concert act. George not only gave me the royal treatment at the beautiful Legends Field complex that he'd built for his minor-league franchise and also for the Yankees to use as a workout facility, but he instructed me to go to manager Joe Torre's office and put on a uniform—*yes, those immortal pinstripes!*—and then join in a practice session. He wanted to get me into the mix with Joe's current crop of players, as well as with the former Yankee greats who'd regularly turn up down there to help stoke the team during the preseason. What a thrill it was to hang around the batting cage with those formidable Bronx Bomber heroes of years gone by, like Reggie Jackson and Chris Chambliss, along with all the new younger guys. Soon enough, they insisted that I get into that cage and take some swings. Willie Randolph was on the mound doing the practice pitching, and of course everyone stopped whatever they were doing to see what this TV guy had to show for himself with a bat in his hands.

I can't tell you how nervous it made me. I mean, talk about pressure! Keep in mind, I'd done plenty of silly batting contests out on Columbus Avenue in New York with all kinds of big-league hitters who'd guested on our show. But now I felt so awkward, like some out-of-place interloper in their exclusive world. Every time I swung and missed, or hit a little harmless ground ball, I was totally humiliated and devastated. Here I was, right in the heart of Yankees spring camp—*actually wearing the sacred pinstripes!*—surrounded by all the players who'd won all those pennants and World Series rings and made baseball history, and I could barely dribble a ball out of the infield. Some of the guys on the field and fans in the stands kidded around, hollering out my *Millionaire* show catchphrase, *"Hey, Regis! Is that your final answer?"* I can't tell you how often I was asked that question wherever I went during those years—but for some reason, hearing it now as I took my not too impressive cuts at Willie Randolph's pitches was not helping me feel all that confident.

Then Coach Bill Robinson had me shift my stance at the plate, and suddenly I began lifting some balls with more distance into the outfield, at least. I got a little cockier with each swing, hoping to crush a couple and shut everybody up. Like an idiot, I'd loudly announce: *"Okay, watch this, guys! This one's going all the way!"* I swung at the next pitch and fouled the ball down with a hard slam, right onto my shin. We've all seen this sort of thing hundreds of times in games, and the batters just shake it off and get ready for the next pitch. But I'm here to tell you that it *hurts*. Like crazy, it hurts! And stings. *And keeps on stinging.* I almost crawled out of the batter's box. It was actually bad enough that someone decided I should let the Yankees medical staff take a look at it. So I wound up in the first-aid room under the stadium on a table next to right fielder Paul O'Neill, who was there with a *real* injury, I'm sure.

Needless to say, I didn't get immediate attention, but I did have a lot of fun showing off my wound—a swelling black-and-blue bump on that shinbone—especially to Boss Steinbrenner. "George," I joked, "I love you, but if this welt is still here tomorrow . . . *I'm getting a piece of the Yankees!"* He just laughed. Naturally. And back in New York on our *Live!* show, I proudly displayed that welt every chance I got, day after day, both at the time and also over the years to come—*because it didn't go away anytime soon!*—while receiving no sympathy at all from Kathie Lee or Kelly. All they did was call me a wimp. But to tell you the truth, it became my badge of honor. No, I didn't get any big hits wearing my Yankee pinstripes, but that mark on my shin became my favorite new claim to fame—an authentic major league injury!

Meanwhile, my friendship with George continued. He honored me at one of the Yankees' spring training games, and I even threw out the first pitch that night. Another time, when Don Rickles and I did our show in Tampa, George was in the audience cheering us on. He was as generous in spirit as he was in rewarding his players those astronomical salaries. Everything was a class act with Steinbrenner. He took such tremendous pride in all things related to the Yankees, especially winning. "Winning is the most important thing in my life, after breathing," he once said. "Breathing first, winning next." And did he ever make sure that winning remained not only a tradition in the Bronx but an absolute requirement! So many times over the years, I'd be up in his suite at Yankee Stadium, with the team nearly always thick in a pennant chase. Steinbrenner watched every game with a life-or-death intensity, and if the Yankees fell behind and lost, many of his friends would disappear very quickly to let him get over it privately.

I remember one year, as World Series fever again swept New York, I was there for a play-off game against the Minnesota Twins. The Twins had taken a 2–0 lead very early on. But play-off games are difficult to predict; any team can get hot without warning. In postseason action, you can never be sure of anything. Somewhere around the third inning, nature called and I decided to quickly dash off to the men's room. I'd been watching the game from the special mezzanine box seats just outside of George's suite, which I'd have to pass through in order to get to where I suddenly needed to go. At that particular moment, the suite—a beautifully spacious room equipped with a large-screen TV—was empty. Empty, that is, except for George, who sat there all by himself, intently studying the game. He looked lonely, and I thought I'd stop to briefly cheer him up with some light banter about his assistant football coaching days at Northwestern University. George loved his early football experiences, so we reminisced a bit and also compared notes on all the great Notre Dame coaches we'd known over the years—frankly, anything to take his mind off this potential loss the Yankees looked like they might suffer that night.

Suddenly, though, the Yankees pushed across a run, which I thought would give me an opportunity to finally make it to the men's room. But as I got up to quickly exit, George said, "No, wait! You can't go now. Your sitting here just brought us luck. We need more runs. You've got to stay." I thought he was kidding, but I could tell by the tone of his voice and the determined look in his eyes that he really meant it. And God forbid if I did leave and the Yankees lost any momentum toward taking the lead, I would never hear the end of it. So I sucked it up and stayed put beside him, shifting this way and that to offset the need for my bathroom break, while the game droned on.

Around the seventh inning, the Yankees scored a second run to tie the game, and I thought maybe I could slip away. I promised that I'd be fast about it! But that burning look in his eyes was still there. "No," George said firmly. "Now more than ever the Yankees need you to stay right where you are. You can't move." Okay, maybe I'll admit that this was kind of flattering—that the entire fortunes of the Yankees suddenly rode on the strength of my bladder—but now I felt in real danger. I mean, let's be honest, the men's room was really just a few feet away. I could slip in and out before the commercial break ended. But it was unthinkable. I had helped the Yankees tie the game, and now I was responsible for helping them win it. And then, to my absolute horror, the game actually went into extra innings! I thought I might explode, but there was no escape. I think it must have been in the eleventh inning when the Yankees scored the game-winning run. What a relief! And I do mean *relief*. George and I congratulated each other, and that's when he asked me, "Can you come back tomorrow night?"

George Steinbrenner was one of the greatest characters New York City has ever known. Certainly there's never been another baseball owner like him—in any city. Yes, he made mistakes and paid heavily for them. And the sports press was relentless about taking shots at him, always finding some new reason to criticize the larger-than-life way he ran his legendary ball club. But his players, believe it or not, understood him better than anyone outside of the franchise. He just wanted to win. He wanted his team to always score one more for New York City. His motto: "The way New Yorkers back us, we have to produce for them." That mission simply became his life.

I can't tell you how deeply I miss seeing him at the stadium now. He made the place that much more special—both at the venerable old House That Ruth Built structure, as well as at the new Yankee Stadium that Steinbrenner built on the adjacent parkland, which opened a few years ago. There's no ballpark like it; George not only lovingly incorporated many of the iconic features of the old place, but made sure it also kept the original facade that once flanked the now demolished Bronx baseball shrine. Inside, it's both fascinating and a great thrill to walk down hallways lined with huge pictures of players that New York will never forget. The stadium's Monument Park, which so beautifully commemorates all those magical Yankee heroes long gone, has been relocated just beyond the center field fences. It's always quite moving to go out there and spend time studying those plaques.

During the 2010 season, they added George to the group. He had died suddenly on the morning of that year's All-Star Game, which seemed kind of poetic, I suppose. He once said, as only he could, "I will never have a heart attack—I give them." But sadly, that's what took him. Donald Trump and I went up to the stadium on the night of his tribute to pay our respects.

As would be expected, the ceremony was done with great class and showmanship, just before the game. Yankees captain Derek Jeter led the team out of the dugout and onto the outfield Monument grounds to watch the unveiling of George's plaque. Yes, it was bigger than the rest, and the engraved image of him captured his classically stern expression. But that, in fact, was the way it was with him all those years at Yankee Stadium. That was George's look. He dominated all of us, and everybody understood that's the way it had to be.

At the end of the ceremony, the players solemnly filed back to the dugout—all of them but one. He remained out there for a long, long time, just looking at the image of his old Boss. He might have been saying a prayer, but he was too far away to tell. You could see the heartfelt affection, though, and it was quite touching. That player was the great reliever Mariano Rivera, who one day will have his own plaque there with George and all the other greats. It was a marvelous and unforgettable moment, which fifty-four thousand people quietly and lovingly watched unfold. They understood the player's reverence. George must have loved it, too.

WHAT I TOOK AWAY FROM IT ALL

Most superstitions in sports are, of course, crazy. But guess what? Strangely enough, they often work.

The bigger you build your dreams, the more likely you are to take heat from detractors. Forget about the heat and just keep building.

Tough guys have more heart than you know.

Next time you see a baseball player
get hit by a pitch, just know it hurts.
Believe me, it hurts a lot.

Chapter Twenty-two

JOE DIMAGGIO

The New York Yankees, as you've probably figured out by now, have always been my favorite baseball team. Raised in the Bronx, not too far from the great stadium, I went to more than quite a few of their games as a kid. At one of them, my father said to me, "Watch how Joe DiMaggio runs out to center field. He's different from the rest of them." I watched intently and saw exactly what he meant. DiMaggio had a graceful gait to him. An almost elegant lope combined with a proud, confident look. You could tell he knew how good he was and what he meant to his team. The New York press noticed him, too, right from his rookie days onward: His greatness was just that evident from the start. They loved him. They helped make him into even more of a national hero than he was already when he set the record for hits in consecutive games. He did it in fifty-six straight games during the 1941 season—a streak nobody has broken in seventy years. In that same year, Les Brown's band had a big novelty hit record called "Joltin' Joe DiMaggio"—I remember it started out with the lyric "Hello Joe, whatta you know? / We need a hit, so here I go. . . ." Twenty-seven years later, the unforgettable impact he'd made came up once again in the Simon and Garfunkel hit song "Mrs. Robinson": "Where have you gone, Joe DiMaggio? / Our nation turns its lonely eyes to you. . . ." Joe, by then long retired, was reportedly upset by that line at first—he hadn't gone anywhere, he complained—until Paul Simon personally explained that Joe represented a great continuity the world yearned for more than ever. Really, it was a very poignant reference in a terrific song that will play on forever.

I don't need to tell you that Joe had a tremendous career, even though military service took him away for three seasons while he was at the height of his powers. But even after he returned, his amazing skills picked up right where they'd left off. Then, in the early fifties, his successor came along just as Joe entered retirement at the end of the 1951 season. Young and swift and powerful, Mickey Mantle took Joe's place—as much as anyone ever could—and the next generation fell in love with the Mick the way the prior one had fallen in love with Joe. Rarely has one team had two great center fielders like those two immortals, back-to-back. For more than thirty years the Yankees were covered in center field like no other team in history. Mantle, who was my age, was simply great in his own right, a star in every category. But DiMaggio was my first idol. And when you're a young kid and you fall in love with your first ballplayer, you always remember him best.

For a while, DiMaggio's private life got almost as much attention as his professional life had. Everyone remembers Joe's marriage to Marilyn Monroe, the most beautiful and iconic movie star ever. What a match they made—on paper, at least. But the sheer combined star power of that union probably meant that it could've never lasted, which it didn't. DiMaggio was simply not cut out for Hollywood. And she was the most publicized woman in the world—her movies, her personal appearances, her every move hounded by the press. Once, when she went over to Korea to appear before the troops, DiMaggio decided to stay home. The troops loved her, of course—how could they not?—and gave her thunderous ovations. When she got home, she was still so overcome by that reception that she said to her husband, "Joe, you should have heard the cheers." And Joe answered quietly, "I have." That very famous little exchange alone tells you why it just didn't work out between them; even though he loved her and always would, divorce was inevitable. When she died in 1962, DiMaggio flew to Hollywood, took over her funeral service, banned many people he thought had brought harm to her, and had her body placed in a marble crypt at the well-known little Westwood Village Memorial Park Cemetery. For decades afterward, someone sent a half-dozen fresh red roses to Marilyn's crypt three times a week. There was never any indication as to who the mysterious sender was. Many thought the flowers came from Joe, which indeed was probably the truth.

By the time I returned to New York in the early eighties, Mickey Mantle had left the game many years earlier and the Yankees were floundering. But DiMaggio remained the city's premier legendary baseball idol. One night, while walking on Seventh Avenue, I watched a limo pull up to the Sheraton Hotel and out stepped Joe, tanned and silver haired. The crowd spotted him and immediately began a commotion. They formed two lines to flank his walk toward the hotel and started chanting, "Joe! Joe! Joe!" He smiled, waved, and kept going. Even after he entered the building, they ran after him, up the stairs and into the lobby. It was quite a demonstration of pure awe and respect, and it truly warmed my heart. They still remembered and revered him.

On a warm sunny day in July 1997, the Yankees were playing an afternoon game at the stadium. My devotion to the team had been renewed all the more after befriending George Steinbrenner a handful of years earlier at the Indianapolis 500. And as I've said, I was regularly invited out to watch the games from his box at the stadium. Hideki Irabu was pitching that day. The press was very high on him. Reports from Japan said that Hideki was sensational on the mound. They said he would ignite the Yankees again. I wanted to take a look for myself, so I went up to the stadium with one of my agents, Kenny DiCamillo, via the subway, which always makes that trek to the Bronx so much less complicated. Turned out, we got out there so early that Steinbrenner's suite was empty; everybody was still at work. Then Kenny and I peeked through the windows at the Boss's private box of about forty seats attached immediately outside of the suite. We saw only one person sitting there. He had silver hair and wore a suit. We looked at each other and we both knew it was Joe. All alone. No one else was there or anywhere near, for that matter.

Kenny suggested I go down to a seat across the aisle from him and maybe he'd say hello. DiMaggio was very private, very reserved. He had been bothered by fans all his life, besieging him for autographs, pictures, whatever. I didn't want to be one of those people. But I walked down the stairs anyway and sat across the aisle from him. Like I said, the afternoon was an increasingly warm one, but he was dressed in a dark suit, a starched white shirt, and a dark tie. He looked great—cool and comfortable. A few seconds later, he looked over and said, "Hey, how did you get here so soon?"

Joe DiMaggio had recognized me.

That alone knocked me out.

I told him I took the subway, and almost before I finished the sentence, I'd crossed the aisle and was sitting next to him. Apparently he was waiting for a friend to join him and didn't mind striking up a conversation. What luck! To be able to sit with him at the stadium he had owned, symbolically at least, back when I was a kid. . . . Did I tell him I was a big fan? Yes, you bet I did. I wished I'd had more time to prepare for this conversation, but as soon as I told him that, I backed it up by reciting his old Yankee lineup for him: Charlie "King Kong" Keller and Tommy Henrich flanked him in the outfield. The infield had Red Rolfe at third, Phil Rizzuto at short, Joe Gordon at second, Babe Dahlgren at first (Lou Gehrig had passed several years earlier), and either Bill Dickey or Yogi Berra alternated behind the plate. DiMaggio smiled and warmed to the names. It wasn't long before we got to talking about those players and about the old stadium as it looked in his day. He reminded me of how, back then, the left center field wall was 430 feet away from the plate, but it had since been moved in considerably closer for today's hitters. Also, there'd been a high black wall out in left field that would have turned present-day home runs into doubles. Now it was gone. He told me he could have hit at least seventy-five more homers if he'd had this modern field reconfiguration to play on. We really got into so many of those differences between the game of yesteryear versus the way it's played today. Batters now have gloves to support their hands and tighten the grip on their swings. Joe used his bare hands. And when he played, the old center field bleachers weren't blacked out in the middle to make it easier for hitters to spot a fastball, which otherwise could blend into the crowd of fans. Joe had to eyeball all those pitches coming at him, with perfect precision, through that blur of white shirts in the stands.

I couldn't believe it. Here I was, carrying on an impromptu and spontaneous conversation with the Yankee Clipper himself. He even told me he had watched my show lots of mornings down in Florida, where he now resided. Anyway, the Clipper and I went at it for an uninterrupted twenty-five unforgettable minutes before his friend showed up. I went back to sit with Kenny in another area of the Steinbrenner section. We were both thrilled at my luck.

After twenty-eight years in L.A., it was off to the Big Apple and
Kathie Lee . . .

My great friend and the entertainment reporter, Claudia Cohen,
opened up New York City for me when I first arrived.

Fifteen fun-filled years later I would sing "Thanks for the Memories"
to Kathie Lee on the day she left the show.

And then, in 2001, the exuberant Kelly Ripa came on and the laughs continued.

In the time between co-hosts, I won my first Emmy! Later, Kelly and I managed to get one together.

But awards aside, the real thrills have been in meeting and getting to know some truly amazing people.

Jack Paar was the one who showed me what my true talent was—it was what he did so well to open his own show: *just talk about your daily adventures.*

The very wise, droll, and somewhat mysterious Charles
Grodin always kept me on my toes. I never knew what he'd
say—or what he meant after he'd said it.

Jerry Seinfeld,
of course, stole
our show's
philosophy of
talking about
"nothing"
and became a
billionaire. But
I still think
his is the best
sitcom ever!

Then there's Dave Letterman, making a rare guest appearance on our show. We've had some memorable moments together on his show as well. . . .

Dave asked me
to wish you
the Happiest of Holidays.

Season's Greetings
from Regis
and the
Entire Staff
of
Late Night with David Letterman

MR. PHILBIN PROVIDED HIS OWN SWEATER

How could I ever forget the Christmas I became the good cheer guy on Dave's *Late Night* holiday card . . .

or the time Dave desperately tried to figure out who the
surprise guest was under that Shrek costume? (Me, of course!)

I know I've asked *Who wants to be me?*, and I've meant it, too, but every guy wants to be George Clooney. Me, too. That's us at George's villa on Lake Como. You should have been there.

Hey, it's just me and Jack getting together again. This time at a Lakers game with coach Bryan Scott. Jack never had so much fun.

Then there was the time I made that infomercial for *The Dean Martin Variety Show*. Even though Dean wasn't there, we closed with a song together (thanks to computer graphics technology). It was the biggest TV thrill I ever had.

Can't believe I was in the Steinbrenner box with the Yankee Clipper at Yankee Stadium. Me and Joltin' Joe DiMaggio, just the two of us talking about the old Yankees days.

What great times I had hanging out with Yankees owner George
Steinbrenner. There will never be another like him.

And here I am at beautiful Mar-a-Lago with Joy and the Trumpster.

Trump is a pretty good athlete. He should buy the Mets, play first base, and talk them into a championship.

Radio villain Howard Stern turned out to be one of the best neighbors I've got. Here he is with his wife, Beth Ostrosky, and the love of their lives, Bianca.

Every now and then I get the urge to do this to Gelman, but then I realize, *What would I do without him?*

Yes, the years roll by, but Joy just gets more beautiful. She's still the greatest joy of my life.

Near the end of his life, which was just a couple years later, Joe was admitted to the Memorial Regional Hospital in Hollywood, Florida, for lung cancer surgery, along with other complications. He had helped build a children's wing at that same hospital and he was among friends there. But the medical reports were ominous. I called the hospital and spoke to his nurses. It didn't look good; yet he hung on for a while and was able to spend his last several weeks at home. Some mornings on the show, I would give him a shout-out: "Joe, New York loves you! Stay strong and don't lose this one. We're counting on you!" But Joe didn't make it this time. He died March 8, 1999. As terrible as I felt, I knew how fortunate I'd been to spend time having that easygoing chat with him and the chance to tell him what he meant to me as a kid. And on through the rest of my life, for that matter.

Now, when I watch the YES baseball cable network in New York and see those old clips of the Yankee greats, I know exactly what's coming: The Babe is first, and then Lou Gehrig, and then there's Joe making an incredible catch in the outfield—and making it look ridiculously easy, too. Or I see him smacking a line drive and turning on the gas around first base, stretching a single into a double with a beautiful slide. And then I remember so well how he used to trot out to center field with that gait, that class, that pride. Nobody ever ran out there like Joe did. Nobody ever will either.

WHAT I TOOK AWAY FROM IT ALL

The most talented people will make their
work look much easier than it really is.

Marriages that look much too glamorous
to be true usually are.

Our quietest heroes, more often than you
think, make the loudest impact of all.

Chapter Twenty-three

JERRY SEINFELD

People who know me—maybe the one who married me, most of all—understand that there's one thing in life that aggravates me to no end: *I hate being late*. I'm sure it's the lifelong broadcaster inside of me that's hung so watchfully on to every ticking minute of locked-down airtime day after day. But I'm the same way off the air—probably a little too much so, to tell you the truth. Nevertheless, I do get upset, for instance, whenever we turn up late to a party. And this is why I'm slightly embarrassed to confess that I came *ridiculously late* to the party that happened to be the popular and brilliant *Seinfeld* television series, which thrived on NBC prime time for nine great seasons through the nineties. In fact, I only began watching that phenomenal Jerry Seinfeld sitcom when it started running in syndication every night of the week at 11 P.M. in New York. By then I'd gotten to the point where I could no longer take watching the grim local newscasts at the end of my day anymore. I couldn't possibly fall asleep after learning about all the ongoing murders, robberies, political backstabbings, and troubles without solutions. So one night I finally just started flipping around the dial to the other stations in search of relief and escape—and there I discovered Jerry and Elaine and George and Kramer on this show that was so well written and perfectly cast that I knew pretty quickly that it would stand as this generation's *I Love Lucy*. I became obsessed with it, in fact.

So almost every morning on our own show, I began talking about the previous night's episode: the terrific fast-paced, triple-layered plotlines, those awkward situations that crept up on each character, the mundane annoyances they all endured as everyday New Yorkers—it was a masterpiece. And also timeless. Except, of course, that—timeless or not—most of those episodes had originally aired years earlier, which, as I recall, prompted a little bit of eye rolling from both Kathie Lee and our audience. *Okay, I'd come late to the* Seinfeld *party—I admit it!* Nevertheless, I was crazy about the show, which was famously described by Seinfeld and his series cocreator, Larry David, as being "about nothing." Jerry, of course, had guested with us a few times during the show's prime-time heyday and had once even congratulated Kathie Lee and me by declaring that we did "nothing" better than anyone else on television. At the time, I sensed it was a compliment, even though I wouldn't fully appreciate what he meant until those *Seinfeld* reruns overtook my bedtime television viewing routine. I remember responding to his comment sometime later, saying, "We have a lot of fun talking about nothing all that important and nothing in particular. We just cover the little incidents and minutiae of life. To Jerry, that's nothing. If he thinks we've elevated it into an art form, what am I going to do? Argue with him?"

Well, I would never argue with Jerry's great observational comedic genius. But back in early 1994—which was still before my *Seinfeld* fever had fully gripped me—I found myself in a minor (but everlasting!) quibble with him and his writing team. Let me explain: Turned out a call came from his Los Angeles production office. They wanted to know whether a scene set on our morning *Live!* show could be filmed and incorporated into what would become a very famous episode entitled "The Opposite." One of the plotlines involved the irrepressible Kramer character coming on our show to promote a stupid coffee-table book he'd dreamt up that could also convert into an actual miniature coffee table. Kathie Lee and I would play ourselves and conduct a crazy interview with Kramer (as played by the fine, unpredictable actor Michael Richards), who'd end up wreaking his usual havoc with us during our chat. Soon enough the script arrived and it was very funny, of course. Except the *Seinfeld* writers had, for some reason, decided to have me react to Kramer's antics by repeatedly declaring, "This guy is *bonkos!*"

Now I had never said the word *bonkos* before in my life. I'd never even heard of the word! I thought what they meant was *bonkers*—which wasn't funny either, but at least it was recognizable. Right away, it began eating at me: *bonkos?!* Finally I called the *Seinfeld* headquarters out in Hollywood. I wanted to talk to someone on the writing staff to make sure it wasn't just some typographical error. And if it wasn't, could I *please* get the word changed! I mean, it just wasn't funny—and why should I become the only *Seinfeld* guest in history who never got a laugh? Whichever writer I wound up with on the phone listened to me and probably decided that I was in fact bonkos. After patiently hearing me out, he then quickly assured me that *bonkos* would definitely get a laugh. He said, I swear to you, "Don't worry about it, Regis. We think it'll be very funny! This is what we do for a living—get laughs." Well, how could I—a mere TV morning-show host—argue with one of those award-winning top-notch comedy writers?

So I hedgingly accepted his promise, and before you knew it, the day arrived when we would shoot our big scene with Kramer—

immediately after one of our actual *Live!* broadcasts. I was impressed to see Jerry Seinfeld on the studio floor with us, off to the side, making sure the scene captured exactly what they wanted. But even then, at the very last minute, I appealed to Jerry about *bonkos*. And Jerry, too, thought *bonkos* was hilarious.

For the record, I will now share with you just how hilarious *bonkos* actually was. *Three times* they had me blurt it out during the course of our brief scene with Kramer, who was dressed as this suave and distinguished coffee-table-book author. First, before I introduced him: "This guy could be a little *bonkos*, really." (Confused silence from the audience on that one.) Second, while he clumsily demonstrated how the book transformed into a little table: "Did I tell you this guy was *bonkos*?" (Here, Kramer got screams; Regis and his *bonkos* got nothing.) And third, before the interview ended with Kramer gulping some water that he then deposited in a spit-take all over Kathie Lee: "I'm telling you, this guy's *bonkos*! He really is!" (Kramer had now brought down the house, while Regis had instantly wanted to leave the house and never come back.)

Yes, our studio audience loved the whole thing, and Kramer was, naturally, a hilarious smash with everybody. Me and *bonkos*, on the other hand—we got nothing, not even one laugh. Only silence. I mean, *deafening silence*. I'd known it from the beginning. I had died a horrible death on that otherwise great episode. It was so bad, in fact, that I'm certain I'll go down in the annals of television history as the only guy who never even got so much as a chuckle on the classic *Seinfeld* series, whose reruns I continue to love, in spite of that nightmare. Still, I will never forget that silence, nor will I ever get over it. It remains embarrassing to this day, okay?

I guess I've never let Jerry forget it either—but more importantly, I've also never stopped reminding him that his series will always stand the test of time and never stop being funny. I recall being out one night for dinner several years ago with Joy and some friends when who should suddenly approach the table but none other than the man himself, Jerry Seinfeld, with his then future wife, Jessica Sklar. I not only crowed to him about what wonderful work he'd done with that show, but I also confessed that we were about to rush right home to watch that night's syndicated repeat. "I've gotta get my *Seinfeld* fix or I can't sleep," I told him, which he took in the right way (I'm fairly sure). Fate, however, had conspired against me this time because when we got home and turned on the TV, there it was . . . again: the dreaded *bonkos* episode. Sleep came a little harder to me on that particular night.

In the years after the show ended, Jerry moved back to New York and still lives on the Upper West Side of Manhattan, exactly where his series was set (although the show was primarily filmed in Los Angeles). He's become quite the devoted family man, thrilled to be home with his beautiful wife, Jessica, and three kids, when not out on the road doing his terrific stand-up act. I see him from time to time around the city—in Central Park biking with Jessica, at various functions around town, and sometimes as a guest on our show. Earlier this year, he walked out as a surprise, dressed in black tie no less, to present Kelly and me with an enormous cupcake commemorating the ten years Pippa and I have been working together. Who else but Jerry could pull off black tie first thing in the morning? There was even one night a while back when the Seinfelds invited us out to dinner and he patiently answered my endless stream of silly questions about the series, probably boring poor Jessica to death. But I think he enjoyed all the reminiscing, anyway. He never stopped smiling.

And that's the one thing I continue to notice about Jerry Seinfeld in every situation where our paths have crossed: It's his smile. It's always there. The man is genuinely happy. You can't get Jerry down with any bad news. He doesn't allow it. If he's not smiling, it's only because he is too busy laughing. What a wonderful quality—and one that we should all be lucky enough to possess. Frankly, because I happen to envy that specific quality of his, I was all the more shocked and touched one day when I read a terribly generous quote he gave after I announced that I was leaving our morning show: "Every place he goes is much better for having him, and everyone he's with is much happier when he's around."

Really, I still can't believe he was referring to me. Because that's exactly how I feel about him—and also about the ongoing effect of that wonderful show he gave us. It's still running every night. It's still hot, even in syndicated repeats around the world. And it's still the best sitcom I've ever seen. In fact, the only time I don't laugh while watching is when one certain episode turns up again and I hear that word—*bonkos*. I don't care what anyone says: It's just not funny. But that is my *Seinfeld* legacy, and there's nothing I can do about it now. Still, I was proud to be a part of it. *Bonkos* and all.

WHAT I TOOK AWAY FROM IT ALL

Guess what? Watching bad news at the end of the day will never help you sleep restfully. Not these days.

It's better to arrive late at a great party than never to arrive at all. The best parties always last longer and keep getting better anyway. Just show up!

The funniest things that happen
in life are usually to be found in the
tiniest aggravations.

Chapter Twenty-four

STEVEN SPIELBERG

One night during my L.A. sidekick years on ABC's *The Joey Bishop Show*, Joey sent me into the studio audience to ask young people about their future dreams. As in what did they want to do with their lives? (Sometimes, even on big network shows, you have to fill time any way you can!) So down into the audience I went. Immediately, I zeroed in on one kid, a typical teenager, who caught my eye for some reason. He looked a bit shy, but I put the microphone right in front of him and asked the question anyway: "What do you want to do with your life?" He didn't answer. I got a little uncomfortable. Did I pick the wrong kid? Maybe he didn't know. Maybe the mic in front of him on a live TV show was spooking him. Gently, I repeated, "Joey just wants to know what the young people are thinking about doing with their future lives." He still didn't speak. I could tell he truly wanted to say something. But the words just wouldn't spill out. I tried one more time: "You know, something you dreamt about your whole life. . . ." He looked like a good kid and I could tell he was trying hard—but the camera and the studio lights and the attention had frozen him stiff. Finally I said, "Well, keep thinking about your answer and good luck to you. I hope you get whatever it is you want one day." And then I moved on to another young person.

Who knows why, but I never forgot that moment.

I felt for the young guy and wished him well. Most probably, I think he reminded me of myself as a teenager and how difficult it was for me to tell anyone what my own dreams were.

So flash forward to one night about forty years later: Joy and I were attending a movie premiere courtesy of one irrepressible New York showbiz publicist who was in charge of that event. She is a ball of fire, this woman, and also a good friend, and that night she wanted me to meet the great film director Steven Spielberg after the screening. When I approached Spielberg for our introduction, he was surrounded by five people. I waited for a few moments, then felt foolish and finally decided to quietly take my leave. Steven Spielberg probably had no idea who I was anyway, I figured.

But as I edged away, I heard him say, "Regis, wait a minute." He pulled me over toward him and continued, "You know, there's something I always wanted to tell you. Anytime I see you on TV, it reminds me of a night that has haunted me my whole life. Once when I was about eighteen, I went to see *The Joey Bishop Show* in Hollywood, and you came out into the audience to ask a tongue-tied young person about future dreams. Well, that was me. I froze. I couldn't answer you, couldn't tell you and the whole world that I wanted to be a movie director. I stood there and wouldn't say it. It was embarrassing and humiliating. Finally you had to move on to someone else, and I sat down stunned and a little angry with myself. And that's what I invariably find myself remembering every time I see you on TV."

Well, as I've said, I've always kept that same awkward moment wedged somewhere deep in my memory bank. And for this man—who went on to create and direct some of the most important blockbuster films ever made—to remember it too . . . it simply amazed me. He quite obviously had gone on to realize that "embarrassing" dream of his and in the process became revered for his many great visionary achievements. Yet there we were—maybe the only two people alive who vividly recalled that night, and that question, and that moment of sheer panic. Now, at least I know this much: I actually did pick the exact right young person in that studio audience, after all.

He didn't tell me his dream then, but he's shown the world evidence of that dream ever since.

WHAT I TOOK AWAY FROM IT ALL

Never underestimate a shy teenager.
Particularly if you happen to be one.

When starting out, it's probably best to first demonstrate your prospective talent than to try talking about it—especially before that talent has had its chance to develop.

Chapter Twenty-five
GEORGE CLOONEY

Believe it or not, there once was a time in America when many cities and even medium-size towns had their own locally produced hit television shows. It was a new and exciting world in those days, and the TV stations took great pride in creating programs of all sorts—their own local newscasts, of course, but also hour-long variety and talk shows as well as entertaining daily after-school series for the kids. More often than not, those who fronted the kids' shows became the most popular characters in their regions, but the men and women who hosted those daytime and late-night programs were also well-loved personalities—*stars*, even—in their areas. I knew what it was like, just from having my own local Saturday-night shows in San Diego and later in St. Louis. But most of that great local action would change forever once the likes of Oprah and Phil Donahue—and yes, even the rest of us who started as "hometown sensations"— became syndicated forces around the country. These prepackaged daily series, complete with built-in national sponsors, made it easier and cheaper for each individual station to simply buy programs and forget about the expense and headaches of producing its own shows.

Anyway, for the longest time in Cincinnati, one of the hottest personalities on the scene was a guy named Nick Clooney, whose midday show on the CBS affiliate WCPO-TV became a local staple. Sometime in the early seventies, not too long after *The Joey Bishop Show* had ended, I was invited to pinch-hit for Nick while he took a weeklong vacation. Happily, I jumped at the chance, since I always loved going back to the Midwest—especially to someplace within driving distance of Notre Dame, so I could make a visit to the campus and feel that old glow again. So one Sunday morning, Joy and I boarded a plane at LAX for a flight to Cincinnati and a week of fun doing Clooney's show, followed by a drive across the Ohio-Indiana state line and up to South Bend.

Now, if you have seen Joy Philbin over the years on my various TV shows, you must know that she is a meticulous dresser. She cares *deeply* about the way she looks, whether on camera or off, and especially when traveling. Keep in mind, too, that this was still the era when people actually got dressed up for their plane trips. And I'll always remember how beautiful she looked that day as we took our first-class seats on that Cincinnati-bound American Airlines jet. She wore a very pretty orange dress with white polka dots. We both felt excited about the week ahead, so we ordered some drinks after take-off and sat back to enjoy the flight. But somehow, even before she had taken a sip of her Bloody Mary, the drink slipped from her hand and splashed all over that lovely outfit. This was not good. She was furious. Trapped on a plane . . . with no chance to change into something else . . . no, not good at all. She could only just sit there and let that Bloody Mary sink into her beautiful dress and ruin my—excuse me, I mean, *our*—flight across the country. Not the greatest way to start our weeklong adventure: with the seething furies of an immaculate woman drenched in tomato juice mixed with vodka. It's the kind of thing you remember for the rest of your life, to tell you the truth. I mean, it still gives me chills.

Meanwhile, *The Nick Clooney Show* was a live daily noontime full-scale variety show anchored, as the name suggests, by the dashing Nick Clooney himself. It regularly featured an array of talented, well-known Ohioans, as well as celebrities passing through town, and often welcomed Nick's own singing sisters. Rosemary Clooney, of course, was already a major music star who'd occasionally return from Hollywood and visit on camera with her brother. But Nick's other sister, Betty, also had a great voice and would, in fact, be my cohost during my fill-in week. Immediately, I was surprised to see a full band on the set, keeping the atmosphere always lively. The audience was even treated to lunch before each broadcast, and everybody was in a good mood, welcoming me in their gracious midwestern way. This wasn't the rat race I experienced in Hollywood or later on in New York—it was absolutely smooth, easygoing fun.

And oh yes, there was somebody else who would regularly hang around on the set, especially during the summertime when school was out. He was a sweet little guy, I was told, that everybody liked as much as his father. His name was George. I never saw him—he was away with his family for the week—but everybody who talked about Nick inevitably also mentioned George and what a nice-looking young boy he was. Yes, it was the same little George who would later, more than once, be named *People* magazine's "Sexiest Man Alive." Let's face it: Those Clooneys had a great gene pool.

As it was, we had a terrific week of shows, and every night, Joy and I ventured out on the town: One night we went across the river to Kentucky to see Woody Herman's big band in concert; the next night we had dinner at the city's top French restaurant, Maisonette; the following evening we headed to the new Riverfront Stadium to watch the Cincinnati Reds in action with their superstars Pete Rose, Johnny Bench, Tony Perez, and the rest of that legendary Big Red Machine team; and on still another night we enjoyed the famous city zoo where the Cincinnati Opera gave one of its special summer performances, a favorite seasonal event in that town. And yes, that weekend we did return to Notre Dame, where my old classmate Jim Gibbons, who by then was the school's vice president of protocol, showed us around—and of course I simply inhaled it, loving every moment. The campus was even more beautiful than I remembered, and through the years it has just continued to expand and improve in every way, a place everyone really ought to see and experience before they leave this earth. Or have I mentioned that already?

Then it was back to Hollywood, where over the years Rosemary Clooney had become a regular repeat guest on my morning show and also a dear friend. I liked to remind her that the first time I saw her perform was, in fact, back at Notre Dame where she sang one Saturday night with the old Vaughn Monroe band. In those days, there were no girls on campus—but suddenly here was this gorgeous twentysomething blonde in a yellow dress walking so sprightly into the old fieldhouse to give us that big swinging show. We saw a lot of her from the seventies onward—both in interview situations and off camera as well. She spoke of her ups and downs, of her deep depression after divorcing Jose Ferrer, of how her old friend and *White Christmas* costar Bing Crosby swooped in and took her on tour with him, giving her a huge boost and fresh outlook on life again. In later years, every time she appeared here in New York, Joy and I would be there on opening night and then always visit with her backstage afterward. She was one of our truly great singers, a wonderful woman whom we miss terribly.

What we didn't know until much later was this: When her handsome young nephew George had first decided to leave Ohio and try his fortunes in Hollywood, he moved into his aunt Rosie's house in Toluca Lake, helping her out as an assistant and chauffeur while looking around for acting jobs. Obviously, he found his acting jobs. Did he ever! There was, all of a sudden, now another Clooney in town. He picked up early work on some sitcoms and then became that heartthrob doctor on the NBC smash medical drama *ER*. But next he did something that doesn't happen very often. He walked away from a hit TV show to take a whack at the movies. Most often, a change like that doesn't work out so well for television actors, but it didn't stop George. There was lots of speculation—much of it rather doubtful—about whether he could pull it off. Hollywood, of course, is rampant with that sort of jealousy and envy. But George proved them all wrong, and then some. He even got better looking while growing into a finer actor with each new film he made. And soon enough he was right up there, a bona fide major star with a suave persona as close to Cary Grant as his generation will likely ever produce.

But now, cut to one special summer, just a few years ago:

Joy and I and our friends Barry and Susan Glazer were invited to spend a week in an Italian villa formerly owned by the late designer Gianni Versace, located on Lake Como, outside of Milan. Our pal Ed Walson, a cable TV big shot, had won this exclusive stay at the villa at a charity auction in New York. And I'll tell you, this was quite the grand home, complete with statues and paintings and exotic chandeliers. You get the idea. While there, I received a phone call from Stan Rosenfeld, a longtime friend and a publicity agent for some of the biggest big stars, including George Clooney. We'd heard that Clooney owned one of the great villas that ringed the lake, and that's what Stan was calling about. "George would like you and your gang to come to his villa for dinner and wine some night while you're here," Stan informed me. "He even lives fairly close to where you are, and believe me, you'll have a good time."

A private dinner at George Clooney's Lake Como villa? How do you turn that down? And why would you? Absolutely, we all looked forward to this night—with Joy and Susan seeming maybe even a little *too excited* about it, if you know what I mean. *He's George Clooney, after all, isn't he?* George met us at the door. He couldn't have been more charming, showing us around the house and telling us how it came to be that he found and then bought this gorgeous place. It was, he said, practically fate: He'd been on one of his many motorcycle trips through Italy when one day his bike broke down right smack in front of that house. He knocked on the door to ask if he could use the phone to call for help. The family welcomed him in and gave him a tour. He fell in love with it immediately—on the spot. And bought it. Just like that. Ever since, his summers there in Lake Como have become what he loves most about his life. He showed us the improvements he had made, the plans for future adjustments— he was a man who enjoyed every aspect of his house, especially on those perfect Italian summer nights.

And why not? We all looked around and couldn't believe that we were there—on this gorgeous starry night in the spectacular home of one of Hollywood's top leading men, living it up right on the banks of gleaming Lake Como. George had invited some of his friends there for what became a big lavish dinner, and we all began drink- ing wine and eating all that great Italian food. And then more wine. And then even more wine. It was an exuberant kind of night, and we began swapping stories.

I told him about that terrific week years ago in Cincinnati when I filled in for his dad. He talked about coming to Hollywood and how he finally broke into the business, first on TV, then the movies. And of how he had first lived with his aunt Rosie and how she once banished him from her house for a little bad behavior and how they of course made up later. One story led to another, each one funnier than the last.

I told him all the backstage Joey Bishop stories and started recalling all the crazy guests I'd encountered over the years. And the laughs became howls. George himself was a scream. He could tell a great story and he had plenty of them to tell. We laughed through the night and finally somehow got ourselves home to our own villa on the lake.

The next morning I woke up with a serious hangover and was feeling the fog. I had to ask Joy if we'd truly just had one of the best nights of our lives or were we just imagining we did? You know, the old morning-after game of second-guessing everything that happened the night before, especially following wonderful parties like that one. George had been such a gracious host, but then you start wondering: Did we stay too long? Did we bore him with those silly stories? Did we completely empty out his wine cellar? Did we leave him any wine *at all*? Sometimes you're never sure. I must tell you that I wondered about it for a long time.

And then two summers later, at a New York movie screening, I took a seat next to a woman I had never met but whose name—Amy Sacco—was familiar from getting frequent mentions in the *Post*'s Page Six column. Her popular nightclub, Bungalow 8, was a site where all sorts of celebrity goings-on made for a steady flow of boldfaced gossip items. We shared some small talk, and it turned out that she'd just returned from Italy, where she had spent time at Lake Como. I told her about our unforgettable trip there, and to my amazement, she said she'd just heard all about it—*directly from George Clooney*. She, too, had visited that beautiful house of his. In fact, she reported, George had said that ours had been "the most fun night he'd ever had there."

I didn't let on that I had often worried about what George had thought about that night and whether he'd had as wonderful a time as we all did. But I couldn't help asking her, "Did he really say that?" And she replied, "That's *exactly* what he said."

I can't tell you how relieved I was. Just one more doubt erased from the corners of my mind, thank God. By the way, she also reported that George still seemed to have had plenty of wine left over to keep his future guests happy. Never mind his success in the movies—that kid from Cincinnati really knows how to throw a party.

WHAT I TOOK AWAY FROM IT ALL

Almost without exception, midwestern
people are a uniquely open and friendly
breed apart. (Don't ask me why,
but they just are.)

Sometimes, when you hear that old
phrase "it's all in the genes," it really *is*
all in the genes.

Chapter Twenty-six
JACK NICHOLSON

Everybody loves Jack Nicholson. In fact, most guys *want to be* Jack Nicholson. He's as good an actor as there is anywhere currently breathing, of course. He can play any kind of role—charming guy, crazy guy, serious guy, bad guy, funny guy. You name it—Jack's done it. And done it so well. Then there's his personal life—which has always fascinated everyone in and out of Hollywood. But did you ever wonder why you've never seen Jack in anything but a movie? Well, the reason is simple: He doesn't give interviews on camera. He would rather die than do a talk show. That's the way it is. And everybody knows it and accepts it. The man is a great actor, a true legendary star, and we love him up there on the screen, showing us how life ought to be lived. So I always let it go at that.

But it seemed like our paths were bound to cross eventually—and then they did. It was after the New York preview of his film *Something's Gotta Give*, in which we see Jack as the roaming bachelor who's caught up with a much younger girl before he begins falling in love with her mother, played by Diane Keaton. It was a fun comedy and Jack played this rogue guy to the hilt. Anyway, the New York press and TV people were invited on a Sunday night to preview the film and then attend a small dinner afterward on the Upper West Side. So once the final credits rolled, we were led down Columbus Avenue to a new apartment house under construction, and then upstairs into a near-completed loft. Frankly, going someplace different for one of these postpremiere dinner schmoozathons was far better than going to what the bigger budget movies usually seem to demand. Tables and chairs were set up around the multilevel rooms—right next to ladders, sawhorses, and all the construction stuff that was still in place. I took my daughter Joanna to the film and we were joined by my producer Michael Gelman and his lovely wife, Laurie. Like always, we began exchanging opinions about the film—until somebody said, *"There's Jack Nicholson."* I looked over, and sure enough, there he was, sitting at a table a few steps higher than us with the famed New York artist and director Julian Schnabel. It was a thrill to look over at Jack in the flesh right after we'd seen his movie. He looked great. What did you expect? *I mean, he's Jack, isn't he?* Then I felt a hand on my shoulder. It was Peggy Siegel, the glamorous, bulldozing New York go-to girl Hollywood calls on to set up screenings and premieres and to get the New York media buzz churning.

She said, "I want you to meet Jack Nicholson."

"Why?" I said. "Let's leave him alone."

"No, I think you'll enjoy meeting him."

"Peggy, he looks busy. I really don't want to bother him."

But Peggy Siegel is one of those indomitable women. So full of ideas and someone who never takes no for an answer. (She was the one who had also insisted that Steven Spielberg and I meet under similar crowded party–like circumstances.) Gelman and Joanna and everybody at the table were all for it. I said no again, but Peggy was unmoved by my protests. Finally, reluctantly, I said, "I give up, let's go and get it over with."

We walked over to a stairway where she took two steps up, putting her at eye level with Jack. Because those steps were so narrow, I had to stand behind her. I couldn't see Jack and he couldn't see me, but I could hear everything that followed. All my instincts told me we were doing the wrong thing: *Don't interrupt him now . . . he's still talking to Schnabel . . . please leave him alone.* But this woman is a *force*—she will not be deterred! I'm sure Jack knew her and knew she was looming right there in front of him. But when she said, "Jack, I—," Jack simply said, "No." Without even looking up! That's all I had to hear. I tugged at her back, hoping she would take that for a *"Please-let's-just-go"*—but no, she was determined to get this introduction made. Jack continued talking to Schnabel. I said to myself, "Please, God, make Peggy stop. Don't interrupt him now! Regis doesn't need Jack thinking of him as some nuisance. . . ."

But now she said even louder, "Jack, JACK, I want you—"

And Jack said gruffly and loudly: *"Not now."*

He was really getting annoyed—and there I was caught behind this hurricane-force woman who I'm sure wasn't going to budge and would only keep asking him over and over again. I had to make a move quickly—just to end this nightmare. God knows I didn't plan this, but I pushed in beside her, got my face in full view of Jack, and told him how much I enjoyed the movie and thought he was great and good luck with it. Bang. Zoom. Over. And OUT!

I didn't wait for an answer—*because there was no question!*—and I left as quickly as I could. I was angry that I'd let my group talk me into it, and I didn't think it was especially funny when Gelman said, *"So, did you ask him to come on the show?"*

But frankly, these are the kinds of train-wreck stories that always provide great material for our show—which it did the next morning. When I brought up Jack's name, the audience leaned in—*naturally.* You don't hear many firsthand stories about bumping into Jack. I told the story slowly and agonizingly, just as it had happened, and built to its sad but funny conclusion. Did Regis meet him? Did Jack recognize him? Did Jack get angry? Did Regis chicken out? (Answers, in order: Not exactly. Who knows? Seemed angry. And absolutely Regis chickened out!) Well, it was excruciating but entertaining—a good story. And the crowd seemed to feel every bit of my anguish. And laughed riotously—*because it didn't happen to them!*

Next day, another show: Kelly and I take our seats, and suddenly Gelman is holding up a card: GO TO THE PHONES.

I ask, "Who is it, Gelman? Who would be calling us on the air right at the top of the show?"

Gelman gives me one of his inimitable know-everything Gelman looks and says, "It's a surprise."

I don't normally like surprises, but the show is live and it's too late to quibble with Gelman.

"Hello," I say.

"Regis," says the voice, huskily, definitively.

"Yes."

"It's Jack."

Ohhhhhh God . . .

I mean, nobody else sounds like that. *It has to be Jack Nicholson.* I mean—how nice . . . but why is he calling us live on the air? Is he still upset about being interrupted the other night? *It wasn't my idea*, I keep reminding myself.

I start in: "Jack, it's two minutes after nine in the morning! You got up early to make this call?"

Jack said, "No, no, Regis, I just got home."

Big laugh—Jack understands his high-living legend! Then he went on to apologize for our Sunday-night miscue. "I didn't see you until you peeked out from behind that woman."

Another big laugh. Jack is scoring!

I said, "Jack, I didn't want to bother you but—"

He took over: "Look, if you're ever here in L.A., let's go to a Lakers game together. You'll enjoy it."

Of course I would. Who wouldn't?

"Call me if you can make it sometime," he said in that silky smooth voice, totally irresistible. "It'll be just us—the Reege and me!" He couldn't have been more pleasant. And more importantly, Jack had just laid on me his own personally coined nickname: That's right! To Jack Nicholson, I was now THE REEGE!

I liked it. A lot.

Well, it didn't take long to figure this one out. Next chance I had, I would fly to L.A. and go out on the town—or at least to a Lakers game—with Jack. The idea would even be to film some of it for the show—*but not all of it!* Because men like Jack and me (the Reege, remember?) need some private time to bond, maybe even talk about women and art collecting and why I've never been in one of his movies. You know, stuff like that.

My producers called Jack's people to confirm the date, and suddenly, there I was arriving at Jack's famous compound high up on twisting Mulholland Drive in the Hollywood Hills, right beside Marlon Brando's property. Warren Beatty's place was just a few doors down as well. It was Superstar Row! My driver let me out at the impressive gate that sealed Jack's premises from the rest of the world, all of it behind a sprawling fence. I rang the bell and sent the driver away. The gate swung open and I walked down the driveway. Jack had lived up there for many years—even acquiring neighboring lots, including the Brando home, and it all felt very big and secluded. Next thing I knew, Jack came rushing out of the house to greet me—"It's the Reege!" he announced loudly to the world. He was very gracious. We went inside his main home—one of a few he keeps on the property—and we shared a couple of Diet Cokes and some laughs. I peered down at the beautiful canyon that lay below his home—with Jack pointing out various geographical details. Also, everywhere in sight there was his art collection—or I should say one small part of it, lining the walls and looking beautiful, expensive, and intimidating. He is, it turns out, a very passionate collector. Who knew?

Before long, he signaled to his personal driver that it was time to get us to the Staples Center. We climbed into the backseat of his black town car together. And now it was time to *really* talk to Jack—guy-to-guy, once and for all. We covered his early New Jersey years right on through to his landing in Hollywood and the famous low-budget director Roger Corman who helped give starts to so many future stars in those days. Then we touched on his *Easy Rider* breakthrough, *The Last Detail, The Postman Always Rings Twice, The Shining*—frankly, you can barely scratch the whole scope of his work in any single conversation. But it was fascinating.

And then, of course—well, you know how it is when two guys get finished talking about things like business and sports. To start out, I tried to make it delicate: "You know, Jack, you've starred with so many beautiful women in your films. Did you ever fall in love with any of them?" Jack gave me one of those trademark grinning looks of his and then said it all in just one word. With mock astonishment, he simply replied, *"Regis."* And honest to God, the way he spoke my name told me everything. And then some! I mean, this was Jack—who could ever resist him?

We arrived at the Staples Center as the usual huge crowd was filing in. I wondered how Jack would maneuver his entrance. Well, he was like a stealth commando, undeterred, going in for the kill. We got through the turnstile and then slipped into a side door that nobody noticed. That took us down a long, vacant hallway to another door that more or less opened at a special entrance inside the arena—and just a few steps away were Jack's seats. Of course, we've all seen him at televised Lakers games sitting in his front-row seats. He's a fixture. People know he's going to be there—they know exactly where to look for him. He's had those seats for years—there in Section 102, right on the floor courtside. Naturally, he is a consummate fan: *Loves* the Lakers. Actually argues with the refs over bad calls. Takes it hard when a Laker misses a shot. Gets a little nuts when they lose. To put it mildly, he is totally involved with every aspect of every game.

But let me tell you: It's a different feeling to walk into that place with Jack and then be planted right next to him all night. If a game gets a little dull for fans, there's always Jack to stare at, and then check out whoever he's with. Well, that night it was me! I would've felt more comfortable if I was with Gelman at Madison Square Garden. *But not as important.* I'm sure many of the fans wondered out loud, "What the hell is Jack doing with Regis?!" It was kind of intimidating. The next day I was told there were constant shots of us on TV during the game broadcast. People probably wondered how we were getting along. Once, I slapped Jack on his knee after a great shot, which gave the play-by-play guys in the booth a big laugh. *Why don't they mind their own business up in the booth and leave us alone,* I thought. *Jack and I are trying to enjoy the game!*

Finally, the Lakers win. Or as they like to scream out there, "THE LAKERS WINNNNNN!" And thank God they won that night. I didn't know how I'd handle Jack after a loss! Anyway, game over, we made our escape. Back down that empty hallway. Then out through the crowds for a moment. Which, by the way, was quite a moment: People are trying to give Jack their own movie scripts and to take his picture or shake his hand. He declines, but always graciously with no hard feelings in his wake. Meanwhile, the car is idling outside, waiting for us. Driver at the wheel. Off we go. Jack's got it down cold. And he does it just like that for every home game.

Final stop: We went to dinner at Morton's Steakhouse near Beverly Hills. It was a complete night. A tour of his home, the drive to Staples, the game, a dinner, and then back to my hotel where he dropped me off . . . while the doorman simply gaped at him. In that moment, my stock at the hotel went up 100 percent.

And to just think that if Jack at that New York party hadn't said, "Not now!" none of this would have ever happened. It was one of the greatest Guys' Nights Out ever. Actually, it was even better than that. It was a great night out with Jack Nicholson.

Top that! How can I?

WHAT I TOOK AWAY FROM IT ALL

Once you've perfected a mystique for yourself you can have fun doing wildly unpredictable things (like get through to Regis on live television if you happen to be Jack Nicholson!).

A man who doles out nicknames is a man who pays more attention than you think. (It happens to be one of my own favorite things to do—I like noticing people and their quirks. . . .) And, believe it or not, they really like their nicknames. Makes them feel special.

Chapter Twenty-seven

HOWARD STERN

W hen I came back to New York in 1983, Howard Stern was at the top of his radio game, as he remains today. Because Howard is Howard, he's regularly had field days blasting me and berating me, practically from the minute I started our local morning show and onward after we went national. Funny thing is, I never heard him. I was so busy every morning—waking up, showering, shaving, grabbing breakfast and taking the kids to school, and then getting over to our West Side studio to go on the air—that there was no time to get an earful of Howard's show. But practically every other day, people would stop me in the street, in a restaurant, wherever, and give me a word-for-word account of what Howard had said about me earlier that morning. I must admit some of it was laugh-out-loud funny. And of course, I knew what he was up to. I was the new guy in town and fresh meat for him—another TV guy to pick on. I understood. I also knew that Howard's occasional attacks were prompting people to tune in to watch our show for themselves, just to see what Howard was talking about. I held no grudges. It's all part of this business.

One day, about thirteen years later, after Joy and I had moved to a new West Side high-rise apartment, I walked through our lobby and into the elevator and was startled when the only other person inside that elevator was . . . a very, very tall man, with the longest curls, which covered most of his rather handsome face.

Yes, for the first time ever, I was meeting Howard Stern. Alone. Trapped together in an otherwise empty elevator. Sometimes fate does funny things! Then again, I'd heard that he'd recently gotten an apartment in the building—and so here we were. Now you've probably experienced that sort of queasy feeling—when you've had a lot of fun putting down someone you don't know and then you meet him or her in person and suddenly feel a little guilty? Maybe I was wrong, but the minute our eyes met I sensed that Howard had a little rush of that feeling.

We looked at each other for a moment and he said, "Go ahead: Hit me. Punch me. Kick me." And I said, "Howard, welcome to the building." And by the time we reached the fiftieth floor we were good friends. He wanted to see my apartment. I wanted to see his. Remember that old line—"I'll show you mine if you show me yours"? Well, that's exactly what we did, giving each other private house tours. And we had a few laughs, too. (How can you not, with that guy?)

Pretty much beginning that day, I learned that Howard is not exactly what he sounds like on the radio. That's show business Howard—a professional persona he's managed to perfect, as his mega-deal contracts have kept on proving. What you get in our apartment house, on the other hand, is a good neighbor, always gracious and pleasant in every exchange, and funny, too. And I mean that.

One night recently I couldn't sleep, got up, and flipped on the Letterman show, and there was Howard on a tirade about my moving on from our morning show. Howard was exaggerating the situation a bit, getting big laughs, talking Dave to death like nobody else alive can. And then he said something I thought was both flattering and touching, if not profound. He said, "Yeah, Regis is leaving—but he could walk across the street tomorrow, get a new show, and take his old show off in two weeks."

Well, I don't think it's going to happen, Howard, but it was nice hearing you say it.

WHAT I TOOK AWAY FROM IT ALL

People who outwardly seem the most intimidating are usually quite the opposite— once you get to know them a little better.

Nice and unpredictable things can happen during elevator rides. So try to tolerate all the "ups and downs" in between.

Chapter Twenty-eight
CHARLES GRODIN

harles Grodin is one of the most unique characters I know. And one of the most versatile. Certainly I've never met anyone like him. Probably because there couldn't possibly be another who could even come close. For instance, Chuck began his writing career at the age of nine (smarter than the average kid stuff, I'm sure), has authored a handful of great memoirs over the years, and now, in his mid-seventies, he writes and delivers a fresh commentary every day about the world at large for the CBS radio network. As an actor, which is how we all first got to know of him, he studied with masters like Lee Strasberg and Uta Hagen, then starred in some big Broadway hits, and even directed the smash stage production of *Lovers and Other Strangers* in 1970. His first taste of movie stardom came a couple years later in Elaine May's terrific dark comedy and everybody's favorite, *The Heartbreak Kid*.

Not too long before that, he'd been cast to star as Benjamin Braddock in *The Graduate*, but the deal fell apart over a salary dispute and Dustin Hoffman went on to make movie history in the classic role. That didn't stop Chuck. His résumé is stacked with so many memorable film performances, always brilliant and subtly hilarious, including playing the conniving villain to Warren Beatty in *Heaven Can Wait* and the neurotic mob accountant under the protective custody of no-nonsense bounty hunter Robert DeNiro in the great *Midnight Run* picture. The younger generation may know him best on-screen as the helpless dad in those two box-office sensations about that dog named Beethoven.

I remind you of all this so you can share my own shock and disbelief that for the last fifteen years he has simply turned down one movie role after another. Unlike so many other veteran actors who continually yearn for just one more job, Chuck says no over and over again, and he means it. Since we're pretty close in age, I'm not only surprised by his unbendable position, I'm actually impressed. I mean, where does this guy come off saying no, when so many other actors in his age bracket, and beyond, are saying, "Please, think of me—I'd love to get an offer for . . . *anything.*"

But really, there's so much more to Charles Grodin than many people know. Truth is, he's deeply involved in matters far more important to him than making just another movie. First and foremost, he's a relentless advocate for those who, to put it mildly, haven't been as lucky as he's been. I refer especially to those people locked away in prison who, maybe, shouldn't be there. Immersing himself in the dark circumstances of such desperate cases is quite a jump from the world of his show business friends. But Chuck loves battling against injustices of all kinds. Always doggedly and in complete earnest, too. You would never expect it from that guy with the defensive sarcastic persona he perfected as a regular guest on Johnny Carson's *Tonight Show* years ago. Johnny actually happened to love playing with that "character" of Chuck's—this angry, bitter guy firing verbal bullets at the great host and getting zinged right back in return. It's an act that he's continued on Dave Letterman's show—and on mine as well—ever since. And yet some people have still never figured out that it's always been a put-on, just a way for Chuck to keep things lively and different.

Over the years I've introduced Chuck to some friends of mine like Jack Paar and TV exec Henry Schleiff who were, of course, instantly delighted by his company. Henry happens to be one of the funniest behind-the-scenes guys in the business. And when he gets going with Chuck over dinner, it's like seeing *Midnight Run* all over again, with the two of them happily quibbling away and Chuck always wanting to get to the bottom of things. That, by the way, is Chuck's specialty, no matter what the topic—*he needs answers*. Meanwhile, I brought Jack and Chuck together about a year before Chuck launched himself into the nightly talk-show business with his own, yes, *lively and different* CNBC interview program back in 1995. He loved Jack, and Jack took quite a fancy to him, especially when probing Chuck's unusual mind, which always led to great rounds of laughter for all of us present.

Jack, in fact, had been extremely encouraging from the get-go when he heard Chuck was starting up that CNBC show, calling him regularly in the weeks and days before its debut, offering big boosts of support and pointers. Well, near the end of his first week on the air, I'll never forget, Grodin phoned me, barely containing his panic. He hadn't heard a word from Jack all week and it was driving him crazy. He wanted me to find out if there was a problem. Was Jack Paar, the forefather of all true talk shows, disappointed in his performance on the program? He needed answers! And I had to get them for him! I softly mentioned it to Jack, who as it turned out had been so pleased with Chuck's work that he'd actually spent time that week calling various critics and influential pals, urging them to watch. He simply hadn't gotten around to letting Chuck know how terrific he thought the show was.

But it was a wonderful kick whenever the three of us and our wives gathered for dinners—and maybe all the more so after Chuck had gotten his show up and running. I remember the first time we all went to my favorite Greenwich restaurant, Valbella, and at the end of the evening, Tony, the maitre d', insisted that he was so thrilled to have three talk-show hosts at one table that there would be no check. Chuck was very proud to be recognized as a member of the host fraternity but also just as elated that there'd be no charge for the great meal. That was when Jack devilishly leaned over to remind Chuck: "It's still going to cost you at least a buck to pay the parking attendant outside." And Chuck being Chuck instantly let his glee turn to gloominess. He shook his head in mock defeat and said, "There's always a catch."

Anyway, Jack and I guested together on Chuck's final CNBC show, which turned out to be Jack's last appearance on TV, and it was a great conversation. We still talk about it and, of course, about Jack and how much we miss him. But in retrospect, Chuck's passion for helping those who've been wronged by the system all began with that CNBC program of his. At first he wanted the show to be a true mix of guests from show business as well as from real life. Before too long he chose real life—not only as the main focus of his show but also for himself. He simply couldn't stand the way certain laws destroyed the lives of essentially innocent people, and he wanted to help correct that. I know there is skepticism about the good intentions of well-known people these days. You might think that maybe it just makes for good publicity—but there are no maybes about this guy. He means it. For instance, drug use and the legal penalties surrounding it were then as always a hot topic in the media, and Chuck pounced, in particular, on New York's notorious Rockefeller Drug Laws, considered by far the nation's toughest at the time. Someone caught selling two ounces or carrying four ounces of marijuana could be sent to prison for fifteen or twenty years to life. Chuck took cameras up to the Bedford Hills Correctional Facility for Women, a maximum security prison, and interviewed four women serving time for such minor offenses. He wanted to illustrate how these harsh laws were victimizing a lot of helpless poor people, not the drug lords and dealers. And despite those laws, he hammered home that the drug situation in New York had become more rampant than ever. Three of the women were granted clemency that year and the fourth the following year.

In 2004 the Rockefeller Drug Laws were finally reformed, long after Chuck's show had gone off the air. But Governor Pataki made a point of citing the work of Charles Grodin in prompting these reforms to be implemented (even though Chuck believes they're still too harsh). Anyway, Chuck's persistence helped make that happen, even without the continued benefit of a nightly television platform. He has studied and taken a personal interest in so many hard-luck cases over these years. One that sticks in my mind concerns a woman named June Benson, who was caught pawning some jewelry a few years ago while high on crack. She received a 27½- to 55-year sentence. It took Chuck and others two years to persuade New York's Governor Patterson that she had suffered enough to earn clemency. After her release, Chuck chose to take it upon himself to financially support her and her children until she could reestablish herself in our society, which tends to shun those with even the smallest criminal records, not to mention those who've been penalized with apparently unjust cause. Recently Chuck has also been quite enmeshed in the case of a young Florida man named Ryan Holle. Holle lent his car to his roommate, who, along with several others and unbeknownst to Ryan, committed burglary and murder while using the borrowed car. Ryan was at home asleep in his bed when those crimes took place, but he was nevertheless sentenced to life in prison with no chance of parole. He's a victim of the unintended consequences of the felony murder rule. But then again, with Chuck on the case, who knows what could happen?

And there's another young man in the Los Angeles area named Brandon Hein, who was involved in a drunken backyard brawl with other teenagers. In the fight, one boy stabbed another, who bled to death. Hein didn't stab anyone, nor did he steal anything, but he, too, was still sentenced to life with no parole. He's been imprisoned since he was eighteen, but through the efforts of Chuck and other legal eagles, his sentence has now at least been reduced to the point where he will be eligible for parole when he turns forty-six years of age. Of course, there is no guarantee of Hein's parole even then, but Chuck continues to fight the good fight for this young man. And he does this all completely under the radar, choosing not to have a press agent. These stories drive him crazy and he becomes obsessed with trying to do whatever he can to correct things. I hope he doesn't mind that I'm sharing them here with you, but I tell you these things because I stand in awe of his quiet conscientiousness on behalf of good people in trouble.

Anyway, after reading all that, you may think Chuck Grodin—that droll funny guy you know from the movies—is so consumed by nonstop outrage that he no longer smiles, much less laughs, anymore. Far from it. He still loves to play jokes on friends, still tells great funny showbiz stories, and keeps in regular touch with all his pals in our industry. But even with those who know and love him, he can also be very persistent about the damnedest things. He wants to know why even the smallest stuff goes wrong and who is responsible for it . . . and until he gets his answers, there is no rest.

So to demonstrate this, let me tell you one more Charles Grodin story. Among his pet charities is an organization called Help USA. Every now and then, if you're a show business friend, he will call on you to participate in events to benefit the cause, and you have no escape. Just like that, you're part of a charity show, which Chuck produces and micromanages down to the tiniest detail. On one such night a few years ago, he had commandeered a Broadway theater stage where Martin Short, Chuck, and I were each taking turns performing bits and entertaining a packed house. Suddenly, while Marty Short was in the midst of his very funny act, out of seemingly nowhere, the fine comedian and *Law & Order: SVU* actor Richard Belzer strolled out onto the stage, with his dog on a leash. This was not a planned surprise appearance, to say the least. As far as anyone could guess, he'd been wandering through the neighborhood walking the dog, happened to notice that the backstage door was open, and . . . he just walked in. It was all quite harmless, I thought. But nevertheless, Belzer and his cute little dog more or less stole the show.

I was sitting next to Chuck just offstage at the time and he asked me immediately, "Did you invite Belzer and the dog?" I said, "No, I didn't." Chuck was simply stunned. A few moments later he asked again, "Tell me the truth. Did you invite Belzer?" And *again*—after a few more minutes, *"Honest to God, Regis, tell me! Did you invite him?"* But he still couldn't comprehend it, so over and over again that night—and many more times during the months that followed—he brought it up. In fact, he still brings it up. His rigid old-school theater training couldn't accept that his perfectly orchestrated show had been upstaged, out of the blue, by Belzer's spontaneous walk-on. But boy oh boy, did we all pay for that. Chuck still suspects that Marty Short or I must've had a hand in it—and both of us laugh about it to this day. But no one, least of all Grodin, knows how or why it happened. And it drives Chuck nuts. But remember, he's persistent—*he needs answers!* He hasn't solved it yet, but that doesn't mean he'll stop trying. Not ever.

SPECIAL ADDENDUM

All right, are you ready for this? Exactly four days have passed since I finished writing the chapter above—and I swear to God, you won't believe what just happened. A few minutes ago Chuck Grodin called to discuss upcoming dinner plans, among other things. Then, without my even mentioning that I had shared the Belzer story with you, Chuck once again brought up the topic! The never-ending mystery of Belzer and the dog—which, I remind you, is now about three years old and counting! Like I said, he still hasn't let it go. I had to stifle a laugh.

"Wait," I said. "You're telling me you have new information about the Belz?"

"I ran into him a few weeks ago," he said. "He was sitting near me at a restaurant and I just had to get up and ask him: 'How did you and your dog ever wind up on the stage that night during our benefit show?'"

"A few weeks ago this happened?" I said. *"And you're telling me about it now?* Well, I can't wait to hear his answer. You've driven us all crazy about this for years! What did he say?"

"He didn't answer me."

"What do you mean he didn't answer you? I can't believe that he didn't answer you!" I practically screamed. Then I decided to just bait him one more time. After all, at this point it might as well just go on forever. So I instructed him, "You know you're just gonna have to be more persistent."

"Yeah, you're right," he said with a sigh. "One day I'm gonna find out who did it."

WHAT I TOOK AWAY FROM IT ALL

There's a difference between wanting
answers and desperately *needing answers.*
Especially if you ever hope to get any
sleep at night.

Helping others will, more often than not,
help you yourself find a greater sense
of fulfillment.

Chapter Twenty-nine
DAVID LETTERMAN

Not to jump too far ahead here, but let's just face this one head-on:

David Letterman and I have somehow established what is probably one of the more unique television talk-show relationships of all time. Hard to fathom, I know—but true. It's a strange, electric, and always feisty bond—but an important one, too—and it took a while for us to get to this point. Nevertheless, for years now, hardly a week or sometimes even a single night would pass without my name coming up in the course of his CBS *Late Show* broadcasts. Usually in some new giddily insulting way . . . usually during the monologue . . . and usually just as I'm trying to settle quietly down for bed. I hear it all stems from his affection for me—which, of course, is reciprocated—but there are moments when you'd never guess it. In fact, before I even begin to tell you of how our worlds came to meld so significantly, let me share a sampling from one evening a few years ago, when I arrived at his desk with a list of grievances I'd gathered up in the form of jokes he'd recently unloaded at my expense.

ME: [*overwrought*] I swear to God, *every night* there's another Regis put-down joke!

DAVE: [*earnestly, maybe*] I know. It's because I think the world of you, and I love you, and I know that, because you're the big man, you can take it.

ME: No, no, no. You've always been the Big Man! But the jokes are getting . . . Well, here [*pulling out a sheet of paper full of raw evidence*], here—listen to this: "The Austria Supreme Court ruled a chimpanzee is not a person. If the U.S. Supreme Court agrees, then Regis loses his show!" [*Dave and his audience laughed at that one . . . again.*] Or this: "Magician David Blaine postponed his stunt to stay up for thirteen days. He accidentally kept falling asleep while watching Regis!" [*More laughs all around, naturally.*] One more—then I'm done.

DAVE: Okay, good.

ME: [*reminding audience again*] I mean, these are things he has said in the last few days! Okay: "Two guys wheeled their dead pal"—now look at this! *Do you understand what the man here is saying?* The man is saying that two guys wheeled their *dead* pal . . .

DAVE: [*squirming just a little*] It may not have anything to do with you.

ME: We'll see. "They wheeled their dead pal through midtown on an office chair to cash his Social Security check."

DAVE: True story, by the way.

ME: "The last dead guy in New York to cash a check was Regis!"

DAVE: [*quickly changing the topic to butter me up*]
Regis–the word means "king," doesn't it?

ME: [*giving up on all hopes for an apology*] Yeah, it
means "king" . . . so what?

And that, my friends, is a small taste of how two grown men
have maintained a crazy dynamic that has somehow only brought
us closer. Or as close as we can be–intertwined in our mutual admiration society that defies any kind of interpretation. But with him
that's exactly how it ought to be. . . .

By now you should probably know that I've always been a fan
of the late-night talk shows. Clearly I was formed by them as
much as anything else. I started my own TV talk career by becoming the host of a popular local one that ran late on Saturday nights
in San Diego and, afterward, was involved with more than my share
of post-prime-time programs, whether syndicated, network, or local.
But even as a kid, I remember how we all eagerly watched NBC's
first venture into the form, *Broadway Open House*, starting in 1950.
That was the beginning of it all. Comedian Jerry Lester was the host,
but the real reason all the guys in the neighborhood watched was
his remarkable sidekick, Dagmar–a big, beautiful, buxom blonde
with one very exotic name, which was enough. Life and career detours being what they are, I found myself paired in the late sixties
with Dagmar in a summer-stock stage play in Houston, Texas. Now
please don't laugh, but my role was that of–yes–the virgin boy in
A Funny Thing Happened on the Way to the Forum. And Dagmar,
well, at that point in time, she actually played my mother. But those
many years later, she was still big and beautiful and buxom, thank

you very much. And I might as well just confess this now: I was never as happy when I was a naive, inexperienced kid as I was playing one onstage during the run of that show!

Later NBC reconceived *Open House* as *The Tonight Show*, and a trio of talented men each came and left his inimitable mark while hosting that television institution: Steve Allen, Jack Paar, and, of course, Johnny Carson. What a great triumvirate, each with his own set of strengths. Of course you know how I watched and observed and studied these guys in action all those years and admired every one of them. And you also know what Paar meant to me and to my broadcast style, in particular.

Now, of course, they are all gone and so are too many of their fans. They were in a class all their own—but in my opinion, the only one who can match them these days is my great sparring partner and friend Dave Letterman. Now don't get me wrong: Anyone who is chosen to host a network talk show late at night has to be uniquely talented, and all of the rest of them are. And the newer ones will only get better. But Dave just possesses so many of the qualities I remember in that *Tonight Show* holy trinity I mentioned. He has Steve Allen's imaginative spontaneity. He's learned to turn interviews with the biggest names into events—thoughtfully probing away like Jack Paar did—but regardless of what his guests do for a living, they tend to come off great. Or at least more memorably than anywhere else. And he has that midwestern flavor like Johnny; He can deliver a monologue, especially as he's grown through the years, with that Carsonesque command and sly dexterity. His show has it all—writing, directing, production values, really great lighting (which always made me envious)—it's all purely top-of-the-line.

During the early nineties when Dave was in his final days at NBC, having hoped in vain to replace Johnny Carson, my dear friend Peter Lassally (who had worked as one of Johnny's invaluable top producers for decades) joined Dave's brain trust to eventually help guide him to CBS and to a bright new future. You all remember the drama that followed. It's a very tough thing to walk across the street to set up shop at someone else's network, and I'm sure Peter helped tremendously to ease that transition. Dave wanted to be on his own so he could be himself and not have the network types hovering around analyzing him and throwing reams of audience research in his face. He actually locked the studio doors tight when it came to the network suits and nobody got in. Even on opening night, all the major execs from CBS, its president included, had to watch the show at the bar next door. Having been through a similar experience years ago—the too-many-chefs-in-the-broadcast-kitchen nightmare—I was proud of him. He did it his way, and it worked.

Peter was always after me to be a guest on Dave's show. I always resisted. I thought of myself as the interviewer, not the guest. I didn't think I had anything of interest to offer. If I had funny stuff to say, I would use it all up on my own show in the morning and wouldn't want to repeat it. But Peter persisted: "I think you would work well with Dave," he kept saying. They were doing some wacky Steve Allen–type things in the early years of the CBS *Late Show* (just as they had back at Dave's NBC *Late Night* program) and Peter would always think of me for these stunts. I liked the show so much that I wanted to be a part of it—even if it meant running up and down the aisles of the Ed Sullivan Theater like a maniac, interrupting Dave and throwing crazy items out into the audience. You name it, I'd do it: I would paint graffiti outside on the studio walls on Fifty-third Street late at night for a skit or get flattened by a giant runaway manhole cover. There would be lots of little clever vignettes all over New York, which were overseen by his associate producer Jill Leiderman, who later went on to become executive producer of Jimmy Kimmel's entertaining ABC late-night show. Most of these bits were very funny, well produced, and meticulously directed by Jerry Foley. I loved the exacting way they were plotted and thought out and the precise way they came off. I became such a staple and go-to guy for them, Dave's other big-shot producer, Rob Burnett, once told me in front of an *Esquire* writer: "You know what we call you around here? Two words: show saver." It had a nice ring to it, I admit.

But Peter wanted more than just these Stupid Regis Tricks: "You must sit down as a real guest and talk to him!" he told me. "You must."

Finally I gave up and gave in. I don't actually remember the very first desk-side interview, but Peter, who's famously a tough judge, gave me the big okay signal when it was over. Ever since, they've kept on calling for more and more Regis—and as it stands right now, I have appeared more times on Dave's *Late Show* than anyone else. The truth is, I have a great time with him; I think, from the start, we created a uniquely warm but jabbing rapport. Whenever we're together, I try to keep it a little edgy, a little playfully confrontational, so he has a chance to be edgy with me. Sometimes that edge of his comes on like a steamroller—but a toy steamroller, for the most part. What I'm saying is that I think he enjoys it. People always ask me about him, but very much like his hero Johnny Carson, Dave keeps it very private and even a bit mysterious. His staff doesn't know him all that well. I probably know him best when he's seated behind that desk—unless we're privately comparing medical notes, which I'll get to shortly. Anyway, I'm always a little thrown off by the introductions he gives me when I'm about to come out—frankly, they're quite effusive and very generous. Some nights I stand backstage there with his stage manager, Biff Henderson, and the audio man, Bobby Savene, listening to what he's saying, and these intros are just so warm and complimentary that—honest to God, how can I say this?—sometimes I don't feel worthy enough to come out onstage. I mean, who can live up to that kind of glowing introduction? Fortunately, the minute I sit down with him, he starts taking shots at me, and then we're off to the races again as usual.

I know he's a private guy, pretty much unknown to everyone, especially the New York press, even when he masterfully navigated through some unpleasant public moments. But I always thought that elusive quality makes him even more interesting. I wish I could have been more private about my own life—but without writers to invent things for me to say on television each day, all I can do is recount what I did on the previous night and hope for a morning laugh. So when I became a regular guest, I decided very early on to exploit this intense privacy issue. I began telling him how I wanted to be his friend! I mean *a real friend*! And not just another guest on the show. Every time I'd go on the show, I made it a point to lay into him: "Why can't we be friends? You need a friend! We need more time together. Why can't we go to the movies together?" Once, I said to him, "Let's go see *Hidalgo* together!" Even he had to laugh at that one.

Then I started taking a different tack. I starting asking, "Why don't you invite me to your top-secret Montana ranch where we can sit by a fire and maybe sing cowboy songs, where we can go riding—a horse for you, a pony for me? Why can't we be together? Why can't we be friends?" He brushes me off every time, but the audience loves it.

Once I'd gotten to be a dependable presence in that guest chair, calls for yet another appearance would come at times when I least expected them. One such call came at perhaps the grimmest moment our country had ever seen—in the immediate aftermath of September 11, 2001. Those were the never-to-be-forgotten horrible days in New York after we lost the Twin Towers. The city was in shock like we've never known it. The toll was enormous. Some three thousand people lost. All the late-night talk shows were silenced.

Paralyzed, in fact, because there was nothing they could do. It was all news, all the time. Finally, Dave made a decision to return on the night of September 17, just six days later. He would be the first. The other late-night hosts later admitted they had waited for Dave to be the first, just to show them the way back again. But around two in the afternoon of that day, he called and told me he was going back on the air and that he would like me to join him. I was flattered—but what a spot to be in.

When I got to the studio late that afternoon, I learned that long-time CBS News anchor and esteemed managing editor Dan Rather would be the first guest. Dave was quite eloquent in his opening remarks, especially describing the effect on that little town in Montana where he also resides, where people actually had passed the hat to gather money to help our stricken city. Dan Rather was quite somber as Dave interviewed him about the whys and hows of what had happened. I remember that Rather, who'd covered more than his share of major crisis stories in the span of his great career, began to display an emotional crack in his steady composure. And then he sobbed. It was more than a little traumatic to watch, but who didn't feel like crying over this tragedy? Dave quickly went to a commercial, and when they came back Dan seemed to be regathered, but suddenly, as he talked further about the terrible events, he again broke down. That's how emotional the situation was.

Finally it was my turn. It seemed to be dark and gloomy out there on the set. The audience was silent. There hadn't been a laugh on TV since this disaster. Dave wanted to know my thoughts, my reaction. I was as distraught as anyone, and when I finally ended my comments, I said, "Look, let me tell you how we can end this quickly. Send Kathie Lee over there. She'll straighten them out in a hurry!" Kathie Lee was, of course, quite vocal and opinionated about things and everybody knew it—and they still do. But the most important thing was that the audience laughed. Like that, it was okay to laugh again, just a little, even though no one knew what other terrorism might follow. It was a night to remember.

And there were other times, more personal. Like the night twenty-one months earlier, in mid-January 2000, when I was sitting there in the guest chair and he confessed to me—and to his entire viewership—that he was worried about going in the next morning for an angiogram and possible heart procedure. Not even his staff knew about it until that moment. Suddenly he was telling me that I was his "role model" and began asking me all about the angioplasty I'd undergone years earlier. . . .

DAVE: Were you scared?

ME: I was scared, yeah.

DAVE: Because they take that thing and go right up inside your . . .

ME: They run it right up your groin muscle.

DAVE: Right. Very close to your deal!

ME: Well, in my case, it was *too* close to my deal. In fact, that was a big deal! It's not so funny when it's *your* deal!

DAVE: No, it's not funny. I don't know why you're laughing and kidding around here!

Understandably, the man was rattled, and rightly so. The next morning he received a very successful quintuple bypass at New York Hospital from the same surgeon who would do my own triple-bypass operation seven years later. (When that time came and I knew the bypass was inevitable, who else but Dave could I call, just to get his reassurance that everything was going to be okay? And guess what, he told me all the right things, which helped me more than he knows.) Anyway, five short weeks following David's procedure, there he was back on the air, and once again (at his insistence!) I was sitting right next to him, picking up right where we had left off. And as usual I was trying to pry loose some of the details of what he'd just gone through. . . .

> ME: Now let me ask you something—when they had you on the gurney and they were wheeling you down the hallway, what were your final thoughts before you went under? Did you think of me at all?
>
> DAVE: Actually, I was thinking about Joy. . . .

Anyway, as I told you at the top of this chapter, Letterman slips my name into practically any given monologue on any given night. His head writers, the Stangel brothers, and their writing team have made sure I remain a choice punch line, no matter what the setup. And frankly, I like it—even though I've protested onstage with regularity. Naturally, since I'd become his "role model" as a hospital patient, he has always pounced on my medical problems with glee. On the eve of my triple-bypass operation, I was sitting in my bed watching his show and he told the audience: "Well, Regis is going for his heart bypass operation tomorrow morning. They're going to take his clothes off, put him on a gurney, and crack him open like a lobster." And the audience screamed with laughter. Try to sleep after that one. He used that operation for material all through my hospital stay. "This wasn't Regis's first operation, you know," he said one night. "A few years ago, he had Kathie Lee Gifford removed." But on the day I came back to work six weeks following the procedure— even though he never, ever appears as a guest on any show—he was there for me that morning. He wanted to return the favor of my being his first guest after his bypass surgery seven years earlier. I was both thrilled and touched. And of course he was very funny, which couldn't have been more welcome after that trauma:

DAVE: You look tremendous. Unbelievable. Wow. Look, Regis, don't be a hero. If you need to lie down, Kelly and I can finish up here. This is good. A couple of heart patients. This isn't a TV show, this is a recovery room. [*big laughs*]

ME: [*to the audience*] You know that David, of course, went through a quintuple bypass . . .

DAVE: Actually, my first bypass was *The Tonight Show*. Thank you very much.

ME: Boy, some things we just can't forget. Let go of it, Dave!

DAVE: Let's start talking about the surgery! C'mon! For me, it was the most exciting thing in my life, ever. Even today.

ME: Listen to the man . . . you came on your show just as you are now, and you talked about the glory of having this surgery.

DAVE: Oh, it's the best. And it looks to me that when they put you out, they gave you a little rinse. Looks to me like your hair is a little lighter.

ME: It got a little grayer, I think! But, Dave, you didn't tell me how tough this procedure was.

DAVE: It's HELL! But now don't you feel like a hero? Don't you feel like nothing can stop you? Nothing can get in your way? [*Then he turned to Kelly and said in an aside, holding two fingers an inch apart*] You know, you came this close to having your own show. . . .

And of course, later that night on his *Late Show,* he talked about his visit with us earlier and said, "I saw Regis today. He's a changed man. Yeah, I saw a nurse change him backstage." There's no stopping him, you see, when it comes to me. I guess it's that bond I mentioned earlier, one that operates on some unspoken wavelength all its own, maybe just broadcaster to broadcaster—because Dave Letterman has always considered himself a broadcaster first and a comedian second. That could be why he took the news of my departure from the morning show much harder than I could've begun to imagine. But on that morning of January 18, 2011, when I made my announcement about moving on, I apparently didn't hammer away hard enough to clarify the "moving on" part of it. Which meant, in fact, that I was simply leaving behind the early-riser broadcast routine and *moving on to other ventures.* Suddenly the word spread like wildfire that I was retiring—which, in fact, was the one word I never said. I thought I'd been clear about that. But ever since, people everywhere have kept telling me they're so sorry that I'm retiring. They hope I enjoy my retirement; they tell me I deserve a nice retirement. Nobody remembers "moving on." I should have known this would happen when Dave called me twice that day: once right after the show, full of concern, and then later on at home, while he was on the air taping his show, so that he could talk me out of this "retirement" I'd never announced to begin with. . . .

> **ME:** [*overwrought, as usual*] Dave, this is one of the busiest days of my life! I've got reporters here. Barbara Walters is at my door, Katie Couric is down in the lobby crying! I mean, there's only so much I can do! What do you want?!

DAVE: Regis, when I spoke to you this morning I was crestfallen at the news that you were leaving television, but I think I misunderstood something. Is there something that needs to be cleared up about the announcement?

ME: Well, you know, I had a drink before I made the announcement.

DAVE: Well, like any other Tuesday.

ME: What'd I say? I'm leaving the show. I'm not retiring from show business!

DAVE: Right, but as I said to you, my concern was that once Johnny Carson left his show, we just never saw the man again. But you're telling me now that we *will*, in fact, be seeing you again?

ME: No, I didn't say that, Dave.

DAVE: Will you at least come on my show?

ME: Once in a while. But not too often, Dave. Really! . . . You know, it's twenty-eight years, Dave. Every day. Day after day. The same studio. The same desk. The same audience! Those same thirty-five people who came every morning to see me!

DAVE: [*visibly shaken*] Ohhh, Regis, don't say that. I don't want this to happen. I don't want you to leave.

ME: Really? You mean I should stay? No kidding?

DAVE: I don't want this to happen. This is too important. This is too meaningful. I don't want this to happen.

ME: Dave, it's too late. I mean, I made the announcement. I'm gonna have to go now. But you know,

I'm gonna have a lot of time on my hands. Can I come and hang out at your office?

DAVE: Maybe . . . I don't—no, not really. But we will be seeing you after you leave the show?

ME: Dave, you'd make me feel much better if you'd just sing a couple of lines of "There's No Business Like Show Business" with me. I mean, I'd really sleep well tonight. Okay, Dave, come on, just you and me!

TOGETHER: "There's no business like show business / Like no business I know. . . ." [*We got up to the lyric about "stealing that extra bow" and then he just hung up on me.*]

DAVE: [*to his audience*] Coulda gone on forever. But I'm tellin' ya, I'm just sick about this, ladies and gentlemen. Because he's one of a kind. Television will not be the same. And it's making me ill to think that no more will he be on the TV. But I hope to God he comes here. God bless, Regis Philbin. We'll be right back. . . .

Okay, I'm pretty sure nobody had ever asked God to bless me since my sainted mother did so many years ago. I do think Dave actually likes me, deeply! But who knows for sure? He is, as I've said, a man of mystery. Anyway, a couple months later, at the end of March, I made my first *Late Show* appearance with him since the day I'd delivered my misinterpreted Moving On announcement and received David Letterman's invocation of God's blessing. And he still wouldn't stop with the pleading and cajoling—until at least we hatched a plan together. . . .

DAVE: Now listen to me. I gotta talk to you about this seriously.

ME: What?!

DAVE: You can't leave the show. I know we were screwing around about it last time, but you really can't leave the show. First of all, we don't want you to leave. Second of all, you don't want to leave. So, three . . . *don't leave!*

ME: I don't know what to tell you, Dave. I mean, how much longer are you going to sit here?

DAVE: I'll stay as long as you stay, because I know the network would like me to go. I know they want me out.

ME: Really? Well, then maybe we should go together.

DAVE: No, no. You're not going anywhere—because you're an icon. You gotta stay. Don't go. You don't want to leave.

ME: Now why do you say that?

DAVE: Because I know you don't want to leave. You *are* TV.

ME: Why don't we leave together?

DAVE: All right.

ME: Honest to God. I'll tell you what. I'll leave in November. I'll walk down the street. I'll wait in the back here for you. Then you leave—we get out on Fifty-third Street, we walk into the sunset. You know how the sun sets? . . . And we sing! We gotta sing. Sing with me!

DAVE: Okay, what are we going to sing?

ME: [*starts singing "The Way We Were"*] "Memories, like the corners of your mind . . ."

DAVE: [*caving in once again, singing*] "Misty water-colored memories . . ."

TOGETHER: "Of the way we were . . ." [*huge applause*]

DAVE: I've got another idea. You do the same thing, except I come out and we get on horses. We re-create the ending of *Shane.*

ME: I remember *Shane.* [*Paul Shaffer and the band started playing a galloping cowboy rhythm complete with harmonica.*]

DAVE: You're on a horse. I'm on a horse. And we don't know whether Shane is coming back. But we know Shane has been shot. We just don't know whether he's alive or dead. So you and I are on the horses. We're slumped in the saddles, and we ride down Broadway. And then we get a kid to come out onto Broadway. And we have him saying, "Shane! Come back, Shane! Shane, come back!" And then we ride right out the door and right down to Times Square.

ME: Right out the door. I love it.

DAVE: That's something, huh?

ME: Will we be singing "Memories . . ."?

DAVE: *No. We're not singing "Memories . . ."!!*

Well, at least, we would've finally achieved something close to my Montana Letterman ranch dream scenario with the two of us in cowboy mode—out there roughing it and sitting round the fire, like real friends. Except, in our special way, I know we're just that already, and have been for a good long while now. I also know I've had great fun with him on his show. And great fun watching him most nights at home. He is a real broadcast comedy pro at work and a truly great original talk-show host. A perfect throwback to all those legendary guys I admired so much a long time ago. And that's why he's the late-night guy for me. Don't get me wrong. They're all good or they wouldn't be there. But for me Dave is the best for now and maybe for all time. I'm just happy to be a small part of his program and of his own remarkable legacy.

WHAT I TOOK AWAY FROM IT ALL

A joke at your own expense really costs you nothing, if it's delivered with affection. Or something close to it.

Those who've shared the same health scares as you and eagerly comfort you along the way are the realest friends you can find.

Laughter heals us all. So you might as well just laugh. A lot.

Chapter Thirty

JOY PHILBIN

This is the chapter I fear the most.

Yes, it's true: Right in that classic tradition of saving the best for last . . . without a doubt, that's what I'm doing now. But when you finally get to talk about the best, how do you even begin to put into words everything that this one remarkable person encompasses and means to you? You can write about all kinds of people, even about your friends who maybe never knew how you really felt about them . . . but writing about your wife?

Well, that's about as dangerous as it can get.

And as difficult.

Because, I promise you, there won't be room to say everything that could be said or should be said. I'm not so sure there are even enough words in the English language to do the full job, anyway. Others who have appeared in these pages certainly may have influenced or enhanced my life in various important ways.

But this one—well, to put it simply, she *is* my life.

How to start? She's really a beauty, inside out and vice versa and then some. Great face. Great figure. Wonderful personality. Charming conversationalist. All the things you desire in a woman. And it's really an understatement to say that she's been a great wife, a great mother, a great cook, and loyal as the day is long. She also happens to be as smart as a fox, loves the finer things in life, and isn't afraid to work hard for them. She wins all the arguments, returns your puny salvo with sheer dynamite, and asks you the most absolutely unanswerable questions you've ever heard. She sees right through all the baloney, wherever she may find it, from whomever it might come. It's uncanny. She is the complete package.

She came with the right name. Joy. You couldn't improve on that. Or on her, for that matter.

Her special presence in my world, of course, has been right on view practically forever. You all know her, even if you haven't met her. Back when I started hosting these morning shows and in the years since, Joy's been coming on TV with me. At first, in those *A.M. Los Angeles* days especially, she was apprehensive and would give herself negative reviews and swear that whatever show we'd just done was the last show she would ever do. We don't go through that anymore. She's over it. She even had her own series dedicated to home design and celebrity lifestyles for many years, and always came across with great flair and ease. But for sure, I think she's been a great asset to our *Live!* show. When you do a show like this for decades, your audience wants to know more and more about your life. Wants to meet your wife, know your family. They always enjoy some inside stuff, the simple day-to-day quirks and realities of your personal world. And I've always had plenty of stories to tell them about adventures with my one-of-a-kind wife.

And I do mean adventures. Or maybe I mean misadventures, all things considered. Sometimes I make the mistake of saying yes to going shopping with Joy, and that, a little more often than sometimes, can lead to a problem. I don't know anyone who can totally disappear in a department store or a grocery store or even a one-room hair salon like her. She just vanishes, while I trudge up and down the aisles or floors looking for her . . . in vain. The shopgirls dependably get a kick out of seeing this dopey husband trying to track down his wife. Sometimes they shout out to me, "She went that way!" I feel like a lost child trying to find his mommy—and I just know those girls behind the counter will be talking about this pathetic sight with everyone who crosses their path the minute I'm out of earshot. It's embarrassing.

Sometimes, up in Greenwich, further misadventures happen when we set a time to meet back at the car where we've just parked. She may take a different route. She may get lost. I can't help her. I'm trapped in the car waiting for her while she's walking north to Boston. It's almost unbelievable. (All right, I admit I could make matters easier by actually having my own cell phone handy, but as you may know I keep hoping cell phones and computer technology will turn out to be a passing fad—and to her infinite credit, Joy somehow puts up with it.) Sometimes when I've told stories on the show about things like this—how we got so mixed up and how it prompted our latest stupid argument about who was right and who was wrong—the finer details would get so complicated that I'd have to draw a map or make a sketch of the logistics so the audience could follow along. Every once in a while, those are the tales that later lead to a knock-down, drag-out war, after I blabbed about it on the air. A war that always seems to end abruptly with me, for some reason, apologizing profusely.

The only thing worse has been when, right after one of these crazy squabbles, Joy has ended up pinch-hitting in the cohost chair on the following morning. That's when I know I never had a prayer. I remember once, on the night prior to one such morning, I tried taking her in the middle of a blizzard to a certain film she wanted to see—and frankly, I guess I'd gotten so confused about which theater we had to get to that we never did make it there, or anywhere else for that matter. We just went home. In cold, stony silence. Because by that point, she had stopped speaking to me. For the rest of the night. Joy recounted the story in an interview a few years ago, which went like this: "We went to bed not speaking and the next day Kathie Lee called at six thirty in the morning and said she was snowed in. . . . So I went out there on the show with him and we had not spoken a word. It was very icy out there. We didn't look at each other until we finally had to tell the audience what was going on." (Let me just interject here and for the record note that I actually opened that particular show by telling the audience, "Just so you know, we're not speaking to each other right now. . . ." Hey, at least I got it out there right away. Anyway, back to Joy's all-too-correct version of the outcome of events that morning.) "We each told our side of the story and then we took an audience vote and I won. I was right."

That's right—everyone sided with her, and, naturally, I ate crow on live television.

I expected nothing less.

If you don't know how Joy landed in my life, it happened in the late sixties at *The Joey Bishop Show*. She was Joey's executive assistant—Joy Senese was her name, an effervescent young woman who'd come to Los Angeles from Chicago. And of course, she saw all the ongoing drama behind the scenes at the show with a bird's-eye view. She knew the ins and outs, the tantrums, the laughs, the works. She was extremely attractive and very efficient and more or less ran the office. Bishop had many friends dropping by to visit him during the day, most of them male. I used to watch them enter that office and stop dead in their tracks at the desk of this gorgeous redhead who was sweet and charming and always in charge. Often these guys found a way to loiter around her desk longer than the time they ever spent visiting with Joey. Let's just say she was very popular.

Somehow David Letterman led her into this topic a couple years ago during an appearance we made together to plug our duet album of standard tunes, *Just You, Just Me,* and perform a number from it. (Joy's singing voice had always been a revelation to me. Long before she and I ever decided, on a lark, to put together our own occasional nightclub act, I'd heard that beautiful voice trilling some song or other around the house. She did this whenever she happened to be especially happy—so it always made a big impact on me for that reason alone.) Dave, meanwhile, had always been *verrrry* complimentary about her during my frequent guest shots, usually making fun of how a guy like me could've ever gotten a magnificent woman like her. (*What a scream, right?*) Anyway, poor Joy had no idea Letterman would go probing into those old Bishop days on that particular night. Then again, neither did poor Regis, as you'll see here. . . .

> **DAVE:** Joy, I know you worked on *The Joey Bishop Show.* You had to meet all the big stars. [*then, as a sad afterthought, he gestured over to me*] Including you, Regis.
>
> **ME:** Okay, thanks for remembering me! I appreciate it.
>
> **JOY:** And also including Warren Beatty—he was a great-looking guy.
>
> **DAVE:** [*brightening*] Now Warren Beatty, he was a bachelor in those days?
>
> **JOY:** Yes, he was for a long time.
>
> **DAVE:** Was there any kind of . . . ?

JOY: I mean, he was just very flirtatious.

ME: [*perking up uncomfortably!*] I never heard this story! He was flirtatious, did you say?

JOY: Excuse me, can I finish?

DAVE: [*lecturing to me to butt out*] Have you ever been on a show before?

ME: Good heavens, I'm sorry! Go ahead, Joy—tell him.

JOY: Anyway, Marlon Brando came in one day.

DAVE: Marlon Brando! Wow.

ME: *I never heard about him, either!*

JOY: He came into the office and was very charming. This was when Marlon Brando was thin and handsome. He engaged me in conversation.

ME: [*leaning in, because how could I not?*] What did he say?

JOY: He was very smooth.

ME: How . . . *smooth* . . . was he?

JOY: And he invited me to have dinner with him. I said, "Where would we be going?" And he said, "To my house." I said, "Ohh," and thought—

ME: I think I'm gonna leave now. *I can't take it anymore!!!* [*then composing myself*] Okay, so tell us what happened.

JOY: He frightened me, so I turned him down. I thought it was just as much fun to be able to say, "Marlon Brando asked me out and I turned him down."

DAVE: [*clearly a little too happy about all these revelations*] Oh yeah, that's a great story! It's a wonderful story.

ME: [*clearly a little sick of this topic*] Big deal, big deal.

So how did she end up with me?

I still don't know. Lucky, I guess. We married on March 1, 1970—less than a handful of months after the Bishop show had shut down, leaving me not exactly knowing what I'd end up doing next, other than taking her as my bride. On March 1, 1995, I sat down to write a little essay about her (which, like this chapter, was far from easy to do), and I thought I'd share a little of it here again now:

> Our anniversary day. Twenty-five years. Silver. I remember her, and that day, like it was last week. She was the sweetest and the savviest and the sexiest. She had perfect posture, the greatest pair of legs I had ever seen, and a walk that instantly captured your imagination. She was charming, friendly, and always smiling. . . . She was independent and proud and had just enough of a temper to keep you on your toes. . . .
>
> We met in the middle of my life's low cycle. She was in her prime. She could have had anyone she wanted. Some of Hollywood's biggest stars were wooing her. She could have wound up with any of them. But it turned out to be me. I wasn't so sure about her choice. There were so many problems. The future looked bleak. Once I remember stopping the car and advising her to get out and run as far and as fast as she could. Luckily for me, it was in a rather shabby part of Hollywood and she wouldn't leave. I never knew for sure if it was because she was afraid, or too much

in love to get out and run. Then, March 1, 1970, we were
married. Of all places, we did it in Forest Lawn. One of
the most famous cemeteries in the world. I wondered if
that was an omen. But the wedding chapel was charming.
Despite a driving downpour of rain that lasted all day and
all night, we had a lovely wedding. It was held around four
in the afternoon. It was all ahead of us from there. The
next twenty-five years. And now, a quarter century later,
she remains exactly the same as I found her. Only sweeter.
And savvier. And sexier.

T hose early years of our marriage were especially tough ones for
me professionally. But at each new twist in the road, she has
always guided me with her terrific innate wisdom through the big
decisions we had to make. The job possibilities or impossibilities.
The homes we purchased. The moves we made. Moving can be a
terrible experience. We had just completed all the renovations in
our Los Angeles residence, culminating with a brand-new gourmet
kitchen she had so long yearned for. And along came an offer to
go to New York. She never blinked an eye about leaving when we
talked about it. She sensed bigger things in the big city, especially
once we'd set our minds to giving it a whirl. Still, that one was hard
to believe when the four of us finally uprooted to New York and
found ourselves initially cramped into twelve hundred square feet
of apartment space. Prior to that, I had been out of work for a year
and a half, but we did have a lovely large house out west, which we
would have to give up. The kids had been enjoying their lives and
friends at school. It wouldn't be easy for them to make this change,
and it wasn't. Years later, they would thank us for taking them to
New York, telling us that it had added so much enrichment to their
young lives. But eventually, in adulthood, they did wind up back in

Los Angeles. Their work was there. I will tell you, though, that Joy *did* blink an eye earlier this year when I decided it was time to move on from my morning show toward horizons yet known. It reminded me, just a little, of our crosstown move back in the mid-nineties from the ritzy Upper East Side, which she loved so much, over to the Upper West Side high-rise that happened to be located directly across the street from my studio and office. I had come to hate that traffic-clogged commute every morning and dreamt of the ease of walking to work within two minutes. Luckily, she took very quickly to what turned out to be our vibrant new neighborhood full of nice shops (of course) and great restaurants and the fabulous Lincoln Center. The only contingency was that she made me promise that I would never come home for lunch and hang around the rest of the day. That's when she decided I needed a second job to get me out of the apartment. Thankfully, the *Millionaire* show happened around that time and she got her personal space back.

After that period, I've still mostly kept myself occupied with other projects along the way. Then, of course, some rough health scares came out of nowhere, as they do—the biggest being the triple-bypass heart operation a handful of years back. And so now there I was, day in and day out, under her constant watchful care while I went through the recuperation paces. She was beyond terrific, then and always. After I had my hip replacement surgery a few years later, however, Letterman got me on the phone to have me recite my list of Top Ten Ways I Was Passing Time While Recovering. "Annoying the hell out of Joy" was, I believe, among the entries the writers had cooked up for me—and I suspect it might have been the truest one I delivered.

Anyway, once I made my big announcement to leave the morning-show grind this past January, the *Late Show*'s head writers, Justin and Eric Stangel, and their team were quick to jump on this startling development. No huge surprise there, of course.

Within a couple of weeks, they seized on the idea of how my decision might have struck Joy and assembled for her a Top Ten List all her own to go deliver onstage at the Ed Sullivan Theater, which she did quite triumphantly on the night of February 15, 2011. Some of the entries were clearly just in fun . . . and some were dead on the money. Here, for the record, is the full list that she shared with the world:

TOP TEN THOUGHTS THAT WENT THROUGH MY MIND WHEN REGIS ANNOUNCED HIS RETIREMENT

10. "He better be kidding."

9. "I don't remember giving him permission to quit."

8. "If he thinks he's going to be home all day, I'd better stock up on Advil and Kahlúa."

7. "Does this mean I have to play Travel Trivia with him every morning?"

6. "I heard they caught him stealing makeup."

5. "So much for my one hour a day of peace and quiet."

4. "Kelly gets paid to chat with him every morning. Not me."

3. "If I put him in a wig and a dress, maybe they'll hire him on *The View*."

2. "God, why are you punishing me?"

1. "Why can't he just keep phoning it in like Letterman?"

She may not be completely thrilled with my decision, but I'm sure she'll pull us through what promises to be this new adventure as well. She can handle just about anything. Years ago when our two daughters came along she gave up everything—all of her time and maybe hopes of launching a career of her own—for them. She was there at home every day when they returned from school. She was full of perfect womanly advice as they grew up. And she is responsible for the two smart and beautiful women they have become.

Back in our Los Angeles years, my friend and onetime stage manager Paul Brownstein began taping and saving shows we'd done, including some on which Joy had appeared with me. Nowadays, Paul has become quite the renowned television archivist, and not long ago, he sent us copies of a few of those particular shows. One of them happened to be the final broadcast ever of that ill-fated NBC morning show from the spring of 1982. Before we knew the plug had been pulled on the show, the producers had scheduled for that morning a special episode in which Joy and I would "renew" our wedding vows on-air, followed by a trumped-up reception party. They thought, hey, everybody loves a wedding, and, you know, it'll be great for the ratings. Of course, the ratings no longer mattered, as we learned just prior to that day. But we reluctantly agreed to go through with it, absurd as it sounds.

"Well, this is it," I told viewers in my opening segment with co-host Mary Hart, who would play Joy's maid of honor that morning. "Married and canceled on the same day. I mean, I've been married and I've been canceled. But never on the same day." The wedding part was all basically a gag anyway, since the ceremony was presided over by the star of NBC's popular *Father Murphy* prime-time series, Merlin Olsen, the huge former Los Angeles Rams tackle. My best man was Ed McMahon. Our flower girls were, naturally, our own girls, Joanna and J.J., being sweet little troupers on this strange day. Stranger still was the fact that it did turn out to be a lot of fun, despite the gruesome cancellation.

And as a bonus (or as the game shows call it, a fabulous parting gift), we were actually given a complimentary one-night honeymoon at the luxurious Hotel Bel-Air. I know, I know. You're waiting for our long-suppressed original honeymoon story. Well, my friends, that one may just have to come out as a book all on its own someday. Maybe. But let's just say we got through our second honeymoon just fine and have lived happily ever after—way more so than less so—for over forty years since we first took our real vows.

And she has always been the reason why.

She's still simply the greatest.

WHAT I TOOK AWAY FROM IT ALL

If you are lucky enough to find the right one, you'll know it. Then just hang on for dear life. Dearer life, really.

Acknowledgments

As with all big endeavors, there are many people who have my sincere appreciation for their support.

At Harper Collins/IT Books: Deepest gratitude to my always hopeful editor, Hope Innelli, for her great enthusiasm, unstoppable spirit, and wise insights throughout, as well as to the rest of the publishing team: Lisa Sharkey, Carrie Kania, Cal Morgan, Kevin Callahan, Joseph Papa, Michael Barrs, Amanda Kain, Lorie Young, Beth Silfin, and Lisa Thong.

At William Morris Endeavor: My patient and profound agent, Mel Berger.

At LIVE: My assistant, Monica Buccini, for her tireless typing and retyping of my longhand writings; Barbara Warren for her indefatigable and persistent help getting this book out there; Schully and Goldie for our daily preshow meetings; and to Michael Gelman, our executive producer who kept our ship afloat through the last quarter-century. And to our current staff and all the previous staffs over the years who have spent a good part of their lives trying to make me look good. You are all terrific.

At Worldwide Pants, Inc.: Dave himself, Jude Brennan, Eric Stangel, and Justin Stangel.

Special thanks, too, for various all but "lost" audio clips provided by Phil Gries, of the peerless Archival Television Audio, Inc., whose website (I'm told!) is a goldmine of great TV nostalgia (http://www .atvaudio.com/). Also invaluable were the terrific fact- and dialogue-finding editorial skills of Layton Ehmke; the additional transcribing efforts by Kelly Fehring; and my devoted longtime friend and previous coauthor, Bill Zehme, for suggesting that I attempt a book of resonant personal experience stories like this one and for his careful coaching along the way.

And finally, to those people who watched and watched over the years. From the gang in San Diego at the beginning of it all to the whole country in the last decades, I thank you for your loyalty and friendship. You've been great to me. I will always remember you.

Permissions

Steve Friedman: Insert 2, pages 1–3; Insert 2, page 7 top; Insert 2, page 15 bottom

William Pritchett Collection: Insert 1, page 5 top; Insert 1, page 6

Worldwide Pants, Inc.: Insert 2, page 8 bottom; Insert 2, page 9